STEELE

D0772524

THE INDIVIDUAL
IN PREHISTORY

Studies of Variability in Style
in Prehistoric Technologies

This is a volume in

Studies in Archeology

A complete list of titles in this series is available from the publisher.

THE INDIVIDUAL IN PREHISTORY

Studies of Variability in Style in Prehistoric Technologies

Edited by

JAMES N. HILL

Department of Anthropology
University of California, Los Angeles
Los Angeles, California

JOEL GUNN

Department of Anthropology
University of Texas at San Antonio
San Antonio, Texas

ACADEMIC PRESS   New York   San Francisco   London

A Subsidiary of Harcourt Brace Jovanovich, Publishers

ACADEMIC PRESS, INC.
111 Fifth Avenue, New York, New York 10003

United Kingdom Edition published by
ACADEMIC PRESS, INC. (LONDON) LTD.
24/28 Oval Road, London NW1

Library of Congress Cataloging in Publication Data

Main entry under title:

The Individual in prehistory.

    (Studies in archeology series)
    Based on papers presented at the 39th annual meeting
of the Society for American Archaeology, Washington,
May 2–4, 1974.
    Includes bibliographies.
    1.   Indians–Antiquities–Congresses.   2.   Industries,
Primitive–Congresses.   3.   Art, Prehistoric–Congresses.
4.   America–Antiquities–Congresses.   I.   Hill, James N.,
Date   II.   Gunn, Joel.
E61.I5   930'.1'072   77-11940
ISBN 0–12–348150–3

Contents

List of Contributors

Numbers in parentheses indicate the pages on which the authors' contributions begin.

J. M. ADOVASIO (137), Department of Anthropology, University of Pittsburgh, Pittsburgh, Pennsylvania

DALE R. CROES (155), Laboratory of Anthropology, Washington State University, Pullman, Washington

JONATHAN O. DAVIS (155), Laboratory of Anthropology, Washington State University, Pullman, Washington

JOEL GUNN (1, 137, 167), Department of Anthropology, University of Texas at San Antonio, San Antonio, Texas

MARGARET ANN HARDIN (109), Department of Anthropology, University of Maine, Orono, Maine

JAMES N. HILL (1, 55), Department of Anthropology, University of California, Los Angeles, Los Angeles, California

L. LEWIS JOHNSON (205), Department of Anthropology, Vassar College, Poughkeepsie, New York

MARVIN KAY (231), Quarternary Studies Center, Illinois State Museum, Springfield, Illinois

JON MULLER (23), Department of Anthropology, Southern Illinois University at Carbondale, Carbondale, Illinois

FRED PLOG (13), Department of Anthropology, Arizona State University, Tempe, Arizona

CHARLES L. REDMAN (41), Department of Anthropology, State University of New York, Binghamton, Binghamton, New York

ARNOLD RUBIN (247), Department of Art, University of California, Los Angeles, Los Angeles, California

Preface

This book examines the nature of style variability in ceramic, lithic, and basketry artifacts, with emphasis on the measurement and usefulness of those aspects of style peculiar to individuals. Our hope is that each chapter will contribute to the ultimate development of a theory of style and to the development of a more general theory of artifact "form." As an extension of this effort, the content of this book lays the groundwork for the development of an interesting new approach to describing variability and change in aspects of prehistoric social organization. The research results presented here represent the initial stage of a direction that should be taken in the interest of refining the archaeologist's capacity to understand past human behavior.

Archaeologists employ spatial distributions of artifacts and their attributes in studying the past. In order to assign behavioral meanings to these distributions, however, we must be able to relate the different kinds of attributes observed on artifacts to the appropriate behavioral contexts within which they were produced. At present, we are beginning to develop an understanding of many of the kinds of attributes produced within the contexts of manufacture and use, but remarkably little has been done toward distinguishing these from other kinds of attributes—especially those we call *stylistic*. Moreover, within the category of style attributes itself, there is a wide range of formal variability that can be assigned different behavioral meanings, depending on the contexts of *style production* involved. Some style attributes, for example, may be referable to the individual, whereas others are referable to social

groups, statuses, and so forth. We must be able to make all these kinds
of distinctions if our intent is to study the behavior represented by artifacts. Otherwise, we run the risk of associating attributes with inappropriate and misleading behavioral meanings.

Although this book deals to some extent with the nature of formal
variability in artifacts at all levels, it is focused on elucidating the nature
of attribute variability at the stylistic level. It focuses even more specifically on the nature of individual style variability and how it is distinguishable from other kinds of variation, both stylistic and otherwise.
Since archaeologists commonly make use of style distributions in testing
their hypotheses, we believe it is important to begin to learn more about
the various behavioral meanings that different attributes of style may
represent. Attributes referable to the individual are as important as any
other attributes in this regard. Indeed, we would argue that isolating the
nature of individual variation is a necessary basic step in beginning to
understand style variation at all levels.

Beyond contributing to our developing understanding of the nature
of style variability, this book also focuses on how individual variability
itself can be used with profit to answer a number of substantive questions of concern to archaeologists. As previously indicated, this research
has led to a novel approach to describing certain aspects of prehistoric
social organization. The basic idea is that one can employ individual
style variability to discover which artifacts in a prehistoric context were
made (or used) by which specific individuals. Then, by studying the
spatial distributions of these artifacts, one can elucidate the nature of
craft specialization, exchange, population movements, residence units,
and other things. Although the usefulness of this approach is as yet not
fully demonstrated, the results thus far suggest that it may become of
great importance.

The chapters in this book range from those concerned primarily with
theoretical or methodological aspects of studying style variability in
artifacts, to those emphasizing the analysis of specific archaeological,
ethnographic, or experimental data. Following the introduction and two
essentially theory–method chapters, there are three chapters on ceramics,
two on basketry, and three on lithics. The final chapter is an evaluation
of the entire undertaking.

We expect this book to be of interest to archaeologists, especially
those concerned with the nature and significance of style variability in
artifacts, and those who employ style distributions in their analyses.
It should also be of interest to those concerned with the nature of artifact variability in general, as well as those interested in methods and
techniques for describing prehistoric social organization. It may also

appeal to those interested in quantitative techniques useful for problems of typology (variable clustering).

Furthermore, we think the book should be of interest to art historians and classicists, since it is in a sense an outgrowth of their long-standing concern for identifying the works of individuals.

1

Introducing the Individual in Prehistory

JAMES N. HILL
JOEL GUNN

The focus of this book is on isolating, understanding, and using style variability in prehistoric technologies. More specifically, it is concerned with style variability that distinguishes the works of individuals. The primary goal in this research, however, is to contribute to the development of theory, method, and technique to be used in studying human groups, populations, and organizations, not individual behavior per se. The research efforts presented here represent the beginnings of a logical and important step that should be taken in the interest of increasing our ability to describe and explain variability and change in prehistoric societies. We think, in fact, that we are introducing the outlines of a new approach to the study of prehistoric social organization, as well as contributing to the ultimate development of a theory of style or form.

The 11 chapters that follow are derived from papers presented at a symposium entitled *The Individual in Prehistory: Style Variability in Technology* (Thirty-ninth Annual Meeting of the Society for American

Archaeology, Washington, D.C., May 2–4, 1974). Our hope is that these now greatly revised studies will stimulate others to further and more refined efforts in this area of research, and that they will serve as a guide that others may follow, or from which they may profitably depart. We are confident that they will provoke needed discussion, as they raise many fundamental issues that will take a great deal of future research to resolve.

Basic to this research is the development of methods and techniques by which we can isolate individual variability on artifacts and identify specific artifacts in an archaeological context as having been made (or used) by specific individuals. As indicated in several of the chapters, this effort is very similar to the long-standing concerns of art historians and police suspect-document examiners (Berenson 1962; Harrison 1958; Osborn 1910). In short, we are capitalizing on the well-known fact that individuals are always somewhat different from one another in their motor habits or motor performances; the artifacts they make or use will exhibit slight stylistic differences in execution or use-wear. We can use these differences to identify the works of different individuals.

Much of this interindividual variation is almost certainly subconscious and hence cannot easily be taught or transmitted from person to person. This fact makes it ideal for identifying the works of individuals as opposed to works associated with small groups of some kind. On the other hand, some interindividual stylistic differences are clearly conscious and teachable. It seems important to distinguish these two levels of variation, and it is in part the difficulty of doing this that leads to some of the differences of opinion expressed in this book.

We want to emphasize that this book does not represent the first recognition of the possibility of studying individual variation in archaeology. James C. Gifford, for example, considered it in his discussion of the type–variety method (1960); he proposed that "within the context of the type–variety concept, variation as a recognizable reality can be thought of as the product of the individual or relatively small social groups in human society [1960:341]." Such variation has also been examined by Deetz (1967:109–116), Donnan (1971), Hill (1972), Hill and Evans (1972:257–258), White and Thomas (1972:291–299, 304), and Johnson (1973:27–28, 90, 92, 107, 113), among others. But as far as we know, very little has actually been done in isolating individual variability, and most of what has been done has been intuitive and lacking in rigor. The reason for this state of affairs may be that archaeologists have thought the work to be too difficult or impossible to do; perhaps they have thought that it was simply not very useful.

Let us consider its usefulness first. Is this not a rather esoteric sideline to the rest of archaeology? Can we not study cultural systems without getting into such a specific and minute level of artifact variability? We think that, for many purposes at least, the answer is no. Fred Plog's excellent discussion (Chapter 2) supports this conclusion, as do the other chapters, either directly or by example. Our discussion here can thus be brief.

We begin by pointing out that the meat of archaeological study (as distinguished from its goals) lies in describing and explaining the spatial and temporal distributions of artifacts and their attributes. We cannot understand these distributions unless we can at the same time understand the *behavioral meanings* that can be associated with the artifacts and attributes in question. Any general class of artifacts possesses a wide range of attribute variability, and different kinds of attributes can take on different meanings for the archaeologist, depending on the behavioral contexts within which they were produced. Minimally, there are seven such basic contexts: (1) procurement, (2) manufacture, (3) use (and reuse), (4) maintenance, (5) storage, (6) transport, and (7) discard (Schiffer 1972:157–160). Attributes are always produced within one or more of these contexts (as well as by postdiscard environmental agents), and we attempt to assign meaning to them accordingly. Unfortunately, we know all too little about which kinds of attributes can be safely regarded as having been produced in which specific contexts.

The problem is further complicated by the fact that in each of these basic behavioral contexts some of the attributes produced are *stylistic* in nature—there are varying styles of procurement, manufacture, use, and so on, and all leave their marks on artifacts. These attributes, too, are subject to the assignment of differing behavioral meanings, depending on the contexts of style production in which they are produced. They may, for example, be associated with individuals, social groups, statuses, and so forth. Since archaeologists commonly employ style distributions in studying prehistoric behavior, it is essential to learn which kinds of style attributes are referable to which specific contexts of style production.

In sum, we are faced with a complex multivariate problem having at least three hierarchical levels: (1) distinguishing those kinds of attributes referable to each of the basic behavioral contexts just mentioned; (2) distinguishing *within* these the kinds of attributes referable to style variability; and (3) distinguishing *within* these style attributes those referable to individual behavior, group behavior, and so forth. Archaeologists must be able to make all these distinctions in order to develop increasing understanding of the behavioral meanings that can legitimately be assigned to the artifact distributions studied. For further discussions relevant to this contention, see Binford (1965) and Sackett (1966:376–390).

The specific point we are concerned with here is as follows: Since any given artifact (or class of artifacts) presumably possesses different kinds of variability that can be assigned meaning at each of these different levels, we must be able to distinguish and isolate the particular kind of variability that is of immediate relevance to us in answering a given research question or testing a given hypothesis. Even if we are not particularly interested in studying the behavior of individuals, we must be able to isolate and control for this variability in order to be certain that we are in fact studying that variability in which we are directly interested.

It may be, for example, that we are primarily interested in how a class of artifacts was used. Some of the variability in the so-called use-wear on the artifacts may actually be an artifact of how they were made or manipulated by different individuals, not of what tasks they performed. Or, we might be interested in tracing the spatial distributions of ceramic design styles in order to locate residence units. Some of the design variability may actually reflect not the residence units but the motor performances of the different individuals who made the ceramics. Many other examples could be adduced, but these should be sufficient to illustrate the importance of understanding the meanings of the variability we are examining in any given situation and to show the necessity for being able to "factor out" and control for individual variability. Failure to do so may sometimes seriously affect our interpretations of artifact distributions.

Thus far, there has been a great deal of effort devoted to distinguishing the kinds of variability (attributes) produced within two of the basic behavioral contexts—the contexts of *manufacture* and *use*—but remarkably little has been done toward learning to distinguish these from attributes of style. And even less has been accomplished with regard to distinguishing the different kinds of attributes within the style category.

This book contributes to the solution of the latter two problems. The primary emphasis in this regard, however, is on isolating those attributes of style referable to the individual and on distinguishing these from all other attributes (stylistic and otherwise). This appears to be a useful step in beginning to remedy the current confusion about the nature and significance of style variability; it is essential to the development of an adequate theory of style or form.

Another and perhaps equally important contribution made in this volume is that of showing how individual style variability can be used in elucidating a number of aspects of prehistoric social organization (in the broad sense). In fact, the approach developed here may sometimes be more useful than any other for this purpose.

We will not discuss this approach and its attendant applications in any detail in this chapter, because these concerns are elaborated in some of the individual chapters (see especially the chapter by Hill in this volume). However, a brief listing follows of some of the aspects of social organization that can presumably be measured and described, given that we are able to use individual variability in isolating artifacts made by different prehistoric individuals.

1. *Craft specialization.* Measurement of the degree of specialization in manufacturing, and its variability in space and time. (We may also be able to measure the degree of specialization in the *use* of artifact forms, but only if we can isolate variability reflecting individual usage.)
2. *Exchange.* Measurement of the nature and directions of the exchange of craft products and its variability in space and time.
3. *Residence units.* Discovering the locations, sizes, composition, and relationship of residence units, and variability in these in space and time.
4. *Sodality affiliation.* Discovering which residence units were participating in which localized sodality structures or areas (and hence also variability and change in degree or scope of social integration in space and time).
5. *Population movement.* Describing the directions and nature of population movements.

All these (and others) can potentially be measured using the approach developed in this book, although it is impossible to provide in this discussion the specific arguments that make the claim plausible. The approach may even lead to an ability to measure certain aspects of paleophysiology and paleopsychology if these become of interest (Chapter 5 in this volume).

We must point out, however, that the uses or objectives discussed have *not* been accomplished adequately in this volume; we are just beginning. Our focus is primarily on discovering the nature of individual variability, isolating it, and suggesting ways it can be used profitably in archaeological research.

Beyond the question of usefulness is the question of *feasibility.* Is it really feasible to isolate individual style variability and to associate prehistoric artifacts with specific individuals? We are confident that the answer is yes. Several of the chapters support this contention with archaeological, ethnographic, or experimental data, and the results are both convincing and exciting. This does not mean that all the contributors to this volume are equally enthusiastic about the results thus far—there are a number of issues that still need to be resolved. But these issues and arguments will become evident in the chapters themselves, and need not be detailed here. We must now turn to introducing the chapters themselves.

The book begins with those chapters most concerned with theory and method and proceeds to those more closely tied to empirical case material. Without severely compromising this arrangement, we have also ordered the chapters in terms of the general classes of materials studied. Thus, following the two predominantly theory–method chapters there are three dealing with ceramics, then two on basketry, and three on lithics. The final chapter is evaluative.

It is remarkable that the chapters are so tightly focused intellectually and yet so diverse in terms of the specific materials being studied, the geographic areas represented, the time periods considered, the complexities of the societies involved, and the specific techniques employed to isolate the works of individuals. This suggests to us the likelihood of widespread applicability for this kind of research.

Perhaps the most significant area of diversity is in the techniques employed—a fact that will undoubtedly stir discussion and controversy. But it is also notable that there is some diversity in the general kinds of research questions (and tentative answers) put forth; these differences, we feel, stem from differences in the theoretical or "paradigm" viewpoints of the authors. It certainly suggests that the applicability of this research is by no means restricted to any particular school of archaeology.

Fred Plog (Chapter 2) has provided an excellent introduction to the importance of the research efforts that follow. He points out that concern with individual variability in artifacts is both a logical and a necessary consequence of the trend toward increasing "sensitivity to the behavioral reality in which the artifacts that we find and excavate were produced [p. 13]." After critically reviewing the place of the individual in anthropology and other social sciences and relating this to archaeology, Plog addresses himself to the necessity for developing a "theory of form" (which includes style). Most important, he emphasizes the fact that in order to understand spatial distributions of artifact forms, we must understand the complex behavioral factors that generate style variability at different levels—regional, local, settlement, and individual. Variability that takes its meaning at the individual level is just as important as other kinds of variability—no more and no less. In closing, he discusses four major difficulties that must be overcome in developing a theory of form.

Jon Muller (Chapter 3) points out that anthropologists (including archaeologists) rarely study individual variation. He indicates, however, that it can be studied in the archaeological record, and discusses studies in art history that support this contention. Like Plog, he directs his efforts to the question of developing a theory of style, and he discusses a number of problems and variables that must be taken into account in so doing. He then introduces the concept of *microstyle*. This concept is similar to Redman's concept of *analytical individual* (Chapter 4), in that a microstyle may be equivalent to the style of either an individual or a group of some kind—the implication being that distinguishing the style of an individual from that of a small group may be difficult. Microstyles, he says, may be distinguished through analysis of both form and structure (rules), and they can be isolated statistically as attribute clusters, if adequate procedures are followed. He closes with two substantive examples illustrating the formal and structural analysis of style and pointing to some of the important difficulties that exist in understanding what particular clusters of style attributes may mean in terms of behavior.

Charles L. Redman (Chapter 4) emphasizes his belief that isolating the works of prehistoric individuals is difficult or even impossible, and probably an inefficient use of research effort. He outlines an alternative approach that permits the use of the entire range of style variability on artifacts. His approach involves isolating hierarchical groups of style similarity within any general class of artifact, such that the most general style groupings might represent large, even regional style sharing, whereas the smallest (most specific) style groups might represent individuals or small groups. The latter style groups refer to what he calls the *analytical individual* and are composed of clusters of style attributes on a very minute level similar to what Hill and Hardin (Chapters 5 and 6) call *motor-performance* attributes. He then discusses his procedures for hierarchical classification and analysis of the designs on painted ceramics from some 200 sites in the El Morro Valley, west–central New Mexico.

James N. Hill's chapter (Chapter 5) considers some of the specific uses to which research on individual variation can be put and then outlines a series of controlled experiments that clearly demonstrate that the works of individual artisans can be isolated quantitatively, using interval-scale measurements. He employs a combination of cluster analysis and discriminant analysis to show not only that the works of *known* artisans can be distinguished, but more important that one can discover the approximate number of artisans represented in a collection for which the number of artisans is *unknown:* He classifies sherds into clusters representing individual potpainters. The results also indicate the kinds of attributes that are most likely to vary among a group of potters and thus will be most useful in isolating the works of individuals (see also Hardin, Chapter 6). The analysis suggests that these motor-performance attributes are subconscious and unlikely to be taught or to be conveyed from one person to another, regardless of shared learning frameworks or kinship relations among artisans. The sherd clusters thus represent individuals, not groups or analytical individuals. Using handwriting data, Hill shows that long-term changes in an artisan's motor performance are probably minimal and do not interfere with distinguishing the individual involved. He concludes that despite certain difficulties, there is apparently no good reason to believe that the method will not work using prehistoric data.

Margaret Ann Hardin (Chapter 6) presents an ethnographic study of individual variation in ceramic painting, using data from 15 painters in a Tarascan village. She shows that individual variation is apparent at three levels—the organization of design configuration, the content or decorative alternatives used, and the execution of designs. The first two involve conscious choice to a great degree; the third, execution, is affected (although not always exclusively) by presumably subconscious patterns of motor performance peculiar to individuals. Execution can also be affected by conscious choice of paint or brushes used. She suggests, in fact, that the paint and brushes used can affect the motor performances of an artisan, and that a single individual can alter his execution simply by using different brushes. Furthermore, the purpose for which a vessel is made, as well as the speed of painting, can be important factors. There is also evidence that members of the same household can share techniques of execution. Nonetheless, Hardin concludes that although further ethnographic field investigation is needed, the archaeologist "should be encouraged by the fact that painters' execution . . . is sufficiently variable that one can select unique sets of features that mark the work of individuals [p. 135]."

Hardin's chapter is an important contribution in several respects: (1) It deals with individual variability on several levels and pinpoints the causes of this variability in a "living" situation; (2) it indicates the nature of the variability that is likely to be conscious, shared, and teachable, as opposed to that which probably is not; (3) it supports the idea that *unique* attributes of individual execution are most important in identifying the works of individuals; and (4) it points to major cautions we should heed.

J. M. Adovasio and Joel Gunn (Chapter 7) discuss the nature and importance of studying prehistoric basketry. They indicate that basketry possesses style variability that has meaning on several levels, including that of the individual. Using a collection of 29 Washo baskets made by three known individual weavers (whose baskets could easily be identified on a qualitative basis), Adovasio and Gunn subjected four interval-scale measures to principal-components and canonical discriminant function analysis with marked success. They then carried out similar analyses using a collection of 22 prehistoric basketry items from Antelope House, Canyon de Chelly, Arizona. They were able to discover style differences distinguishing the north, central, and south portions of the pueblo; but they conclude, primarily on the basis of nominal-scale data, that there were probably six or seven weavers in the community. These weavers tend to have been localized in particular sets of adjoining rooms. Adovasio and Gunn also carried out a combined analysis of the Washo and Antelope House basketry, which resulted in distinguishing variability at a broad "cultural" level that they relate to differences in adaptive requirements.

The contribution by Dale R. Croes and Jonathan O. Davis (Chapter 8) also deals with basketry material. The authors focus on a small collection of baskets, mats, and hats recovered from a large prehistoric house floor at the Ozette Site, on the coast of Washington. Because the site had been covered by a prehistoric mudslide, the basketry was well preserved and largely *in situ*. Croes and Davis propose and test the proposition that the house had been occupied by two or more families, with two or more individual weavers. It was expected that if this were the case, there should be a nonrandom distribution of those basketry attributes that could be argued to represent individual or small-group variation. This proved to be correct; the north and south portions of the house exhibited different basketry attributes. More important, however, is the authors' use of a sophisticated computer mapping technique for studying the distributions; it is flexible and suitable for use in studying other kinds of spatial distributions as well.

Joel Gunn (Chapter 9) quantitatively isolates individual variability in the knapping of stone tools—something we would have thought to be virtually impossible not long ago. He employs a laser diffraction technique (optical Fourier analysis) to examine variability in flake scar orientation on samples of bifaces made by six different *known* knappers. Using a combination of principal-components and discriminant-function analysis, he shows that even when the single variable of scar orientation is used, it is possible to isolate the works of individuals, although additional variables should improve the discrimination. The design of this controlled experiment is fortuitously similar to that used by Hill (Chapter 5), although the technique of measurement is quite different. Gunn's results are by no means ends in themselves; he provides a detailed design for the application of this kind of analysis to prehistoric demographic problems in the South Hills region of southeastern Idaho and northern Utah.

L. Lewis Johnson (Chapter 10) aims at discovering how stone tools were manufactured at a small Aguas Verdes quarry workshop in northern Chile. She points out that in order to do this, it is important to be able to distinguish individual "motor-skill" variation from variation resulting from techniques of manufacture. Thus, she attempts to factor out that variability resulting from motor-skill behavior so that the remaining variability can more likely be regarded as representing the basic attributes of manufacturing technique. She proposes tests to determine how many knappers worked at the site, and employs these tests to demonstrate the probability of only one knapper being represented. She then proposes replicative experiments to test further the reliability of her conclusions.

Johnson's chapter is similar in concept to Kay's (Chapter 11), in that the primary goal of her work is not isolating the works of individuals per se. She has found it necessary to do this, however, because failure to control for the effects of individual variability would make her proposed explication of the technological processes suspect, if not impossible.

Marvin Kay's study (Chapter 11) is an analysis of 69 beveled edge chert scraping tools from the Imhoff site (Middle Woodland, central Missouri). Recognizing the incorrectness of assuming that the so-called use-wear variability on these scrapers represents differences in the *tasks* for which they were employed, he proposes that individual variation in manipulating the tools might also account for it. A discriminant function analysis was used to discover whether or not the different types of wear correlated with the different types of tool morphology; since they did not, he suggested that the wear possibly was not task-specific. To test this suggestion, he conducted a series of experiments using beveled edge scrapers in a single task (hide scraping) to find out whether or not variations in tool manipulation would result in the expected edge-wear differences; they did not, and he concludes that the edge-wear variation at the Imhoff site is most likely a result of variation in the tasks for which the tools were employed.

The contribution here is not in the negative test results, but rather in the presentation of a research design that (with refinement) may permit archaeologists to understand better the meanings of the use-wear they observe on artifacts.

It should be emphasized that in both of the last-mentioned chapters (as well as in Hardin's and Redman's chapters on ceramics) the investigators are very much aware that the variability observed might be accounted for in different ways, only one of which is individual motor-performance. The mere fact that they recognize this and set up tests to distinguish these different "levels" of variability is a contribution in itself. These chapters are substantive examples of looking at variability in the manner proposed by Lewis Binford (1965).

The final brief chapter (by Arnold Rubin) is different in intent from any of the others. Rubin's task is to evaluate the entire enterprise. Since he is an art historian, he does this from an art-historical perspective, providing us with interesting insights into the nature and importance of similarities and differences between art history and anthropology. He sees the chapters as representing a challenge both to his field and to ours.

In closing, we must reemphasize the point that these chapters represent only a beginning; they may raise more lively issues than they resolve. Nonetheless, we think the accomplishment is substantial, and the advancement in knowledge the chapters portend is even greater.

ACKNOWLEDGMENTS

In the writing of this introductory chapter, valuable editorial assistance was provided by Patricia L. Garza (UCLA) and L. Lewis Johnson (Vassar College).

REFERENCES

Berenson, Bernhard
   1962   Rudiments of connoisseurship: Study and criticism of Italian art. New York: Schocken Books. (Published in 1902 as The study and criticism of Italian art. Second series. New York: Schocken Books.)
Binford, Lewis R.
   1965   Archaeological systematics and the study of cultural process. American Antiquity 31:203–210.
Deetz, James
   1967   Invitation to archaeology. Garden City, New York: Natural History Press.
Donnan, Christopher B.
   1971   Ancient Peruvian potters' marks and their interpretation through ethnographic analogy. American Antiquity 36:460–466.
Gifford, James C.
   1960   The type–variety method of ceramic classification as an indicator of cultural phenomena. American Antiquity 25:341–347.

Harrison, Wilson R.
    1958   *Suspect documents, their scientific examination.* London: Sweet and
              Maxwell.
Hill, James N.
    1972   Inferring prehistoric social organization through ceramic pattern
              recognition. In *Interdisciplinary Colloquium on Mathematics in the
              Behavioral Sciences, Colloquium Documents, 1971–1972.* Los Angeles:
              Western Management Science Institute, University of California, Los
              Angeles. Pp. 7.1—7.7.
Hill, James N., and Robert K. Evans
    1972   A model for classification and typology. In *Models in archaeology,*
              edited by David L. Clarke. London: Methuen. Pp. 231–273.
Johnson, Gregory A.
    1973   Local exchange and early state development in southwestern Iran.
              *Anthropological Papers, Museum of Anthropology, University of
              Michigan,* No. 51.
Osborn, Albert S.
    1910   *Questioned documents.* New York: Lawyers' Co-operative Publishing
              Company.
Sackett, James R.
    1966   Quantitative analysis of Upper Paleolithic stone tools. In Recent
              studies in paleoanthropology, edited by J. D. Clark and F. C. Howell.
              American Anthropologist **68**:356–394.
Schiffer, Michael B.
    1972   Archaeological context and systemic context. *American Antiquity*
              37:156–165.
White, J. P., and D. H. Thomas
    1972   Ethno-taxonomic models and archaeological interpretations in the
              New Guinea highlands: What mean these stones? In *Models in archae-
              ology,* edited by David L. Clarke. London: Methuen. Pp. 275–308.

2

Archaeology and the Individual

FRED PLOG

One can see in the history of archaeology a pattern of growth toward greater and greater sensitivity to the behavioral reality in which the artifacts that we find and excavate were produced. In the not so distant past, assigning a collection of artifacts to a culture or culture area was an intellectually satisfactory form of analysis. Later, definitions of phases and horizons or localities, aspects, and foci became both analytically feasible and intellectually necessary components of archaeological research. In the 1960s and 1970s, we have seen increasing concern with the particular activities and particular organizational contexts in which artifacts were made and used. Clearly, a concern with the individual, with individual behavioral variability, and with the extent to which these are manifest in the record of the prehistoric past is a logical next step in our efforts.

However, a concern with the individual is more than a logical consequence of a historical trend. It represents a necessary realization that the items of material culture with which we work were made and used by individuals. Consequently, the patterns in the distributions of artifacts we study are there because individuals in particular but variable circumstances made and used artifacts in particular but variable ways. Although this insight is an important one, it is also problematical. In this chapter, I shall examine a number of aspects of the problem: the individual in anthropology, the individual in other social sciences, and the individual, potentially, in archaeology. If some of the comments I make seem skeptical or critical of the enterprise, they are not so because I doubt its utility or its importance, but because I believe that there are many pitfalls to be avoided if the issue is to be successfully met.

THE INDIVIDUAL IN ANTHROPOLOGY

There is no doubt that most of the major theoretical traditions within anthropology embody some theory of the individual. But in only a few of these is the individual a focus of analytical as well as theoretical concern, and even where there is an analytical concern it is typically of limited scope.

The theoretical tradition with which archaeologists are typically most familiar, evolutionism, takes a rather clear stand on the relevance of the individual to anthropology and the topics it seeks to explain. This stand has been enshrined in the now famous observation that the history of Egypt would have been unaffected had Ikhnaton been a bag of sand (White 1959). Although such statements provide effective slogans for handling the often confusing relationship between individual behavior and major social events, they are ultimately irrational and unsatisfying. For they typically lead us to ignore not only Ikhnaton but also the interaction of behavioral variability and selective pressures. Variation at the organismic level is, after all, central to most evolutionary theories.

A majority of theories in anthropology incorporate the individual in a somewhat fuller fashion. Unfortunately, many if not most of these reduce individuals to virtual unibehavioral automatons. Thus, we are treated to theories in which individual behavior is the product of toilet training, Oedipus complexes, primitive sentiments, innate tendencies to aggress or to arrange the world categorically, norms, social rules, and so on. The failure of these theories is not that they do not incorporate the individual but that they do so in a fashion far too simplistic for adequately studying the more complex behavioral reality of the real world. Thus, when it proves to be the case that Ego not only calls his mother's brother Charlie but relates to him as Charlie, theoretical devastation can be avoided only to the extent that the investigator can ignore or conceal what he has seen.

Apart from specific theoretical formulations, one encounters many ethnographies that are rich in individual data. For many or each point the author makes, an illustration in the form of a description of an individual behaving is provided. Unfortunately, these efforts are rarely more than illustrative. Ideographically, the individual is tied to the analysis. But the material presented is rarely generalizable—there is no means by which the reader can know whether he is considering an isolated example or a legitimate and generalizable one.

In short, most of the literature of sociocultural anthropology is rather thin in cogent statements concerning individuals and individual behavioral variability. Discussions of individuals behaving are used to justify particular conclusions; assumptions about the whys and wherefores of individual behavior are similarly employed. But theories that systematically link the variable behavior of individuals to the patterned behavior of social aggregates are virtually nonexistent. In fact one finds in some recent literature the rather startling assertion that only what individuals say they do and not what they in fact do is the legitimate concern of anthropology. Rather than systematically elucidating the interaction of behavioral variability at different levels, much of the literature simply asserts the primacy of patterning at a given level of sociocultural reality and assumes out of existence the necessity of building upward or downward.

Quinn's (1975) recent summary of the emerging tradition of "decision theory" provides the best evidence that many of these difficulties are being addressed, perhaps resolved. But archaeology has already paid the price of the difficulties. If we once assumed that particular artifacts and artifact configurations could be equated with "cultures," it was because the stereotypic characterizations of large social aggregates in ethnology made this seem a reasonable course. If we assumed that lineal villages were operative organizational units, it was because ethnographic descriptions of villages generated such an image. And if we sought evidence of matrilocal residence patterns, it was because ethnographic accounts of postmarital residence failed to distinguish clearly between what the natives said they did and what they in fact did. Thus, the critical comments of authors such as Kushner (1970) and Allen and Richardson (1971), which chide archaeologists for their failure to notice the complex variability in almost any behavioral pattern one could choose to consider, are not so much wrong as they are incomplete. Archaeologists have been insensitive to variability. They have sometimes failed to distinguish symbolic and organizational behavior. But these problems have scarcely been resolved by our sociocultural colleagues.

THE INDIVIDUAL IN OTHER SOCIAL SCIENCES

A more satisfactory view of the individual and his behavior can be obtained from most introductory works in social psychology. Let me very briefly summarize major aspects of this viewpoint by focusing on two questions: Why is individual behavior varied? Why is individual behavior patterned?

Variation in Individual Behavior

Five factors are primary in the varying behavior of individuals:

1. Individuals find themselves in different situations. *Situation* in this context must be defined over a wide range of social and natural variables.
2. Individuals perceive the situations in which they find themselves differently. *Perception* here refers to both the differences in physiological equipment for perceiving and differences in the "symbolic screens" acquired in past interactions.
3. Individuals have learned and employ different decision-making processes for evaluating and selecting a response to their perceptions.
4. Individuals are differentially motivated to act on perceptions and carry out responses.
5. Individuals are variably capable of carrying out those responses in terms of both their own physiological equipment and the social and natural materials available to them.

All these factors act to produce variability in the behavior of individuals. But although that behavior is varied, it is not infinitely so.

Patterning in Individual Behavior

The patterning observed in the behavior of aggregates of individuals can be traced to a number of factors:

1. Individuals in similar situations have typically learned similar sets of responses to those situations.

2. Individuals act out roles they have come to play in both specific and general environmental contexts.
3. Such situations are not infinitely varied but tend to be repeated both within and between "cultures."
4. In any society some patterns of behavior are reinforced; others are not.
5. The effectiveness of socialization and reinforcement in different social groupings is itself a variable phenomenon that can result in more or less patterning at different levels of social organization.

It is perhaps worth emphasizing that this approach to the understanding of individual behavioral variability is not at all incongruent with some definitions of culture in the anthropological literature, specifically those definitions that emphasize culture as providing models of and for behavior, the transmission of those models by learning and reinforcement, the utility of the models in day-to-day problem solving, and the variable interpretation of the models by individuals.

I do not mean to suggest by these comments that if archaeologists are to study individuals they must study the relationship of artifacts to perception, motivation, motor skills, and the like. Nor do I mean to suggest that it is archaeologically feasible to become involved in testing social–psychological theories, although efforts in this direction have been made (Levey 1966; McClelland 1961; Wallace 1950). I take it as a given that any anthropologist interested in perception or motivation would choose to work with modern, living individuals rather than with prehistoric data. To attempt to infer different motivations or perceptions from artifacts and then to use variation in motivation and perception to explain artifactual variability is to become enmeshed in a hopelessly circular chain of argument. What I do want to suggest is that this time around archaeologists can be more sensitive to variability and to the complex factors that generate that variability than has been characteristic in many of the past efforts to work with sociocultural phenomena.

A THEORY OF FORM

Perhaps most important, I am arguing that sensitivity to the place of the individual within a social and natural milieu is a final step in an effort to generate a theory of style or form. In this sense, I do not see the study of individual variability in the archaeological record as an end in itself, but as a final and necessary step in generating a set of theories that will allow us to deal effectively with variability in the forms of artifacts we discover.

One can find evidence of the growth toward such a theory in a number of contexts. Let me focus on the one with which I am most familiar—the studies of variability in ceramic design elements by the Southwest Archaeological Expedition of the Field Museum of Natural History. The works of Longacre, Cronin, Hill, and Leone (Leone 1973; Martin *et al.* 1962, 1964, 1967) all identified particular patterns of variability in ceramic design elements within sites or regions of the Upper Little Colorado area of eastern Arizona. When the works of these authors are read individually, one finds emphases on specific patterns in the distribution of design elements and specific organizational inferences based on those patterns. When the works are taken as a whole, a quite different understanding emerges. Of the totality of design elements created by the prehistoric peoples who inhabited the Upper Little Colorado, some design elements are shared by the population of the region as a whole, some by the inhabitants of localities within that region, some by the inhabitants of individual sites, and some by one or more nested groupings within individual sites; others are unique to households, perhaps to individuals. The design of any particular vessel reflects the interaction of some or all of these factors. Thus, if one examines the design elements that Hill (1970) considers in his analysis of Broken K Pueblo, some elements are found throughout the pueblo, some are found in sets of rooms, and some are found basically in individual rooms.

I do not question that understanding individual variability is a necessary underpinning of such efforts. In the first place, variation at that level is every bit as real as variation at the local or regional level. Moreover, some of the intrasite groupings could represent a collection of vessels made by a single individual rather than the products of a group sharing a style of design. But the real effort must focus on understanding the manner in which regional, local, settlement, and intrasettlement design styles come to be expressed on a vessel; it must focus on a theory of form.

I use the term *theory of form* rather than the more usual *theory of style* to avoid senseless arguments about the relationship between style and function. Gorman's (1969) work with Paleo–Indian projectile points has shown the difficulty of trying to draw any clear boundary between the two. One suspects that style is first and foremost the name of as yet unidentified functions.

Although I see the interest in individual variability as important to the construction of a theory of form, I feel that a number of major barriers still stand in the way of generating such a theory. These barriers, which also stand in the way of an effective understanding of individual variability in the artifactual record, can be grouped as problems of categorization, synchrony, limited inference, and perseverance.

Categorization. Many of the efforts to understand the relationship between variation in artifact form and the organization of prehistoric populations have employed very simplistically conceived analytical units. I think particularly of studies of ceramic design elements. As the chapters that follow will show, specific design elements employed are far more similar to some alternative design elements than they are to others. Unless an analysis specifically recognizes variation in degree as well as in kind, the analysis is very unlikely to succeed. Since linguistics has often been cited as a justification for treating design data in discrete units, it is interesting and important to note the renewed interest in probabilism and continua as opposed to categories in this subfield of anthropology (cf. Sankoff 1974).

Synchrony. Perhaps the most debilitating weakness of some studies of design variability is their assumption that the vessels in question were made by individuals who lived at the same time. Such an assumption is never reasonable in archaeological contexts. The alternative, that the artifacts were made at different times, is far more appealing. Thus, it must be shown and not simply assumed that a particular set of artifacts represents a single point in time. Of equal importance to the study of individual variability is the need to control for variation over time in the style of individuals. Certainly, it is not reasonable to assume that individuals execute designs in exactly the same manner throughout their lives.

Limited inference. One of the most significant barriers to understanding individual variability or variability in form is the confusing of these topics with attempts to reconstruct past lifeways in a paleoethnographic context. Such concepts as matrilocality prove to refer to verbal and symbolic phenomena and only crudely to behavioral phenomena; they are ultimately an unnecessary appendage of studies of form or organization. *A style zone—whether within a pueblo or within a region —is, once identified, an important phenomenon in its own right.* It is an organizational entity in itself, as a style zone. One need not attempt to infer matriliny, matrilocality, or any other imputed pattern of organization in order to realize the analytical and empirical import of the existence of the style zone.

Perseverance. Perseverance may seem a strange subject to broach here. I do so because it seems to me that a lack of perseverance is a major reason efforts to understand the relationship between variation in artifact form and social organization are floundering. In his revision of *The*

Prehistory of North America, Jennings (1974) casually dismisses the recent efforts in "paleosociology" based on analyses of ceramic design style. And he cannot be blamed. The first studies in this tradition appeared in the early 1960s. Ten years later Jennings can refer to a string of critical articles, the point of several of which he appears to have missed, as evidence of the failure of the approach. A number of them are based on a comprehensive misunderstanding of the difference between verbal and nonverbal behavior, the statistical techniques employed in the analyses, and the nature of the patterning. But, to the best of my knowledge, a response has not as yet been heard to these criticisms. More important, the techniques used in the original analyses, like those in any pioneering effort, did have some flaws, some of which have not as yet been noticed and none of which have been corrected by subsequent analyses.

If the individual is to be discovered in artifactual variability, if 10 years from now archaeologists interested in the study of such variability are not to be casually dismissed as paleopsychologists, then the techniques and the models on which such studies are based must be tried and improved and retried until they are satisfactory for the task at hand.

REFERENCES

Allen, W., and J. Richardson
   1971   The reconstruction of kinship from archaeological data: The concepts, methods, and the feasibility. *American Antiquity* **36**:41–53.
Gorman, F.
   1969   The Clovis hunters: An alternate view of their environment and ecology. *Kiva* **35**:91–102.
Hill, J.
   1970   Broken K Pueblo: Prehistoric social organization in the American Southwest. *Anthropological Papers of the University of Arizona*, No. 18.
Jennings, J.
   1974   *The Prehistory of North America.* New York: McGraw-Hill.
Kushner, G.
   1970   A consideration of some processual designs for archaeology as anthropology. *American Antiquity* **35**:125–132.
Leone, M.
   1973   Archaeology as the science of technology: Mormon town plans and fences. In *Research and theory in current archaeology,* edited by Charles L. Redman. New York: Wiley. Pp. 125–150.
Levey, W. T.
   1966   Early Teotihuacan: An achieving society. *Meso American Notes* **7–8**:25–68.

Martin, P. *et al.*
    1962   Chapters in the prehistory of eastern Arizona, I. *Fieldiana: Anthropology* **53**.
    1964   Chapters in the prehistory of eastern Arizona, II. *Fieldiana: Anthropology* **55**.
Martin, P., W. Longacre, and J. Hill
    1967   Chapters in the prehistory of eastern Arizona, III. *Fieldiana: Anthropology* **57**.
McClelland, D.
    1961   *The achieving society*. Princeton, New Jersey: Van Nostrand-Reinhold.
Quinn, N.
    1975   Decision models of social structure. *American Ethnologist* **2**:19–46.
Sankoff, G.
    1974   A quantitative paradigm for the study of communicative competence. In *Explorations in the ethnography of speaking*, edited by R. Bauman and J. Sherzer. New York: Cambridge University Press. Pp. 18–49.
Wallace, A. F. C.
    1950   A possible technique for recognizing psychological characteristics of the ancient Maya from an analysis of their art. *American Imago* **7**: 239–258.
White, Leslie
    1959   *The evolution of culture*. New York: McGraw-Hill.

3

Individual Variation
in Art Styles

JON MULLER

The study of individual variation has been relatively neglected by anthropologists, perhaps because of a feeling that such studies are more properly the area of the psychologist. In anthropological studies of language, for example, relatively little attention has been paid to idiolect, and not one article in Hymes's reader on linguistics and anthropology (1964) deals directly with the individual. In archaeology, for the most part, the individual has been studiously avoided. Some have even said that it is impossible to study the individual in archaeology. Yet, the great body of research that has been done in the fields of art history and classical archaeology leads to the conclusion that the identification of individuals from "archaeological" records is indeed possible.

Anthropologists who work with living peoples do not need to be reminded that the behavior they study is that of individual human beings, on one level at least. Archaeologists, on the other hand, deal not with behavior, but with the *results* of behavior—artifacts, remains of houses, and the like. From such scattered and incomplete traces, they construct models for past behavior. These models, in turn, form part of the data used by archaeologists who seek to do anthropology.

Not the least of the reasons archaeologists have ignored the individual is the predominant view of culture as "normative." This view as encouraged models of behavior that are predominantly typological in character—a development that finds relatively little support in studies of human psychology (cf. Muller 1974).

Lack of attention to the nature of social groups has been a source of error in archaeological interpretation. No matter how closely a work group may be organized for one particular function, the same individuals are not necessarily organized into the same groups for other functions. Similarity in artifacts usually does result from high degrees of social interaction, but we cannot assume that the social groups defined in this way are characteristic of the society as a whole. We may demonstrate the existence of a group of potters, for example, but we cannot assume that the group also constitutes a residence unit or any other kind of social unit.

The dimensions of variability in art styles make the usefulness of individual studies all the more relevant. If art styles do result from social interaction in groups, then the identification of individual artisans can greatly clarify the nature of interaction in such groups.

It is perhaps ironic that a man commonly thought of as extremely subjective—the critic Bernhard Berenson—has provided us with the most detailed discussion of the methodology of stylistic identification of individuals (Berenson 1962). Berenson deals specifically with the question of attribution—the recognition of schools and individual artists. Using Italian Renaissance painting as an example, he points out that certain attributes—types of faces, compositions, groupings, and general tone—distinguish particular schools of painting. Within each school, "followings" can be pinpointed, and the spirit and quality of a work will tell us whether we are dealing with a master or a third-rate painter. Because there are historical records for the Renaissance, the field of possible authors of a work can be narrowed. But to proceed to single out the actual author of a work, a new frame of reference is needed. It becomes necessary to reexamine the known paintings for differences, rather than similarities. The next step, according to Berenson, is to look to morphology (1962:125). He suggests that the artist tends to fall back into habitual or conventional patterns when painting items he considers to be unimportant—in Italian painting, the ears (1962:129), for example. Berenson gives us, therefore, the following principle: Features of a work of art are useful for identification of the artist to the extent that they

1. are not vehicles of expression;
2. do not attract attention;
3. are not controlled by fashion;
4. allow the formation of habit in their execution;
5. escape imitation and copying, either because of the minuteness of the peculiarity, or of the obscurity of the artist (Berenson 1962: 132–133).

Berenson adds that such mechanical tests diminish in value in relation to the "greatness" of the artist (1962:147). To the extent that quality is measured by creativity, this may well be so. There are many other discussions of ways individual artists in various media may be identified. Nonetheless, Berenson's discussion is the apotheosis of these attempts as far as theory is involved.

The applications and usefulness of skill in identifying individuals are obvious in the art market and in museum studies. Other applications include such topics as forgery detection (Jeppson 1970) and technological studies (Burroughs 1971). Data similar in character to those of the archaeologist are used to identify individuals in criminal investigations and in espionage. (In espionage, the identity of a radio operator is checked by reference to his individual style on the "key.") In most of these applications, though, the procedures still depend to a great degree on the expertise of the analyst; they remain extremely subjective.

Dependence upon the connoisseurship of the analyst is somehow dissatisfying, however; and although Berenson's discussion is helpful, substantial problems remain. How, for example, can an individual be distinguished from a group of artisans who are working closely together? Part of the answer is that in such a case, the significance of conclusions is not seriously compromised, because of the closeness of interactions. In such cases, individuals *may* be identified by very minor differences along lines similar to those discussed by Berenson. Even so, in an archaeological context the recognition of differences between one artist and another on this level may not be as important as the recognition of the high intensity of social interactions. It would be well to remember in archaeological and historical instances that the "individuals" we recognize may sometimes be *analytical individuals*—our "individuals" may sometimes be more or less than one actual person.

Here it is necessary to introduce some terms that can be used in discussing this problem. The underlying patterning of an artistic system can be thought of as a *style*. Styles are usually, but not always, restricted to either one medium or to a few closely related media. On this level, styles are representative of co-participation in an artistic system by a number of artists. Although it is possible to speak of an individual style, greater preciseness would require individual and small-group variations to be distinguished as *microstyles*. *Stylistic tradition* refers to the persistence of a style through time. Art historians have distinguished a number of different levels of similarity and differences within styles and have referred to these as *schools* and *workshops*. Although there is much to be said for making these distinctions, it may not be useful to try to establish too many such units *a priori*. The fine level of distinctions attempted (sometimes successfully) by art historians may be seen in Beazley's statement, "I make a distinction between a vase by a painter and a vase in his manner; and . . . manner, imitation, following, workshop, school, circle, group, influence, kinship are not, in my vocabulary, synonyms [1963:xlvi–xlvii]."

What has actually been done in the definition of individual styles or microstyles? In classical studies, archaeologists sometimes have signatures of potters and artists. There can be little doubt that individual attribution is justified in these cases. In the more common situation where such evidence is lacking, workers such as Beazley have identified great numbers of individual artists as well as numerous works "in the manner of" a particular artist or school. Beazley has, for example, identified over 500 potters in the Attic red-figure vase style (Beazley 1963). The character of these identifications, however, is largely subjective, though there is no reason to doubt Beazley's skill and expertise. The following excerpt gives some ideas of the difficulties:

> In past discussions . . . I put together a number of black-figure vases and called the painter . . . the Lysippides Painter. . . . I said that he might be the same as the Andokides Painter—the painter of the red-figure portions of these vases—but I would not decide. Later, . . . I made up my mind that these two were the same; but [later] I came to the conclusion they were not, and I revived the name of "Lysippides Painter" [Beazley 1963:2].

The scientific, not to say scientistic, bent of most anthropological archaeologists will cause them to cringe at this sort of statement, but their own formulations of "types" have been no less subjective. In any event, characterizations of artists in art history have been like those given by Richter in her classic study of Attic red-figured vases where, for instance, an artist is described in terms of "the quiet amplitude of his style" and the style is described as "fleshier, more plastic" (Richter 1958:143).

The record for anthropological archaeology is scarcely more formal. One of the outstanding attempts to deal with individual styles is Lothrop's study of Coclé (1942). In this work Lothrop defined a number of temporal phases, but he indicated that assessment of style in the end depends on "imponderable qualities incapable of exact measurement or analysis [1942:183]." He went on, however, to point out that certain aspects of styles could be expressed with exactitude. Lothrop discussed the nature of transmission of styles, but his discussion is naive. For example, he simply assumed the existence of virilocal residence as a factor in transmission of styles (1942:184). He has pointed out the possibility of a potter having more than one style, however. But there is not much discussion of the procedures used to distinguish individual styles (i.e., microstyles), and Lothrop closes with a statement that reminds us again of how much we have lost because of the chronological preoccupations of the 1940s: "At the same time, the identification of the products of individual potters is so intriguing that at one time this appeared to be an end in itself. Somewhat reluctantly, however, we have confined our discussion, for the present, largely to chronological phases [1942:187]."

How can individual artisans and groups of artisans be recognized? Perhaps there will always be some subjective judgment involved, but one goal must be to reduce subjectivity as much as is possible. One way out of the morass of difficulties is to distinguish dimensions of variability in technique, form, and structure. *Technique* is simply the actual behavior in the execution of the artifact. The major source of variation useful for identification of individuals on this level is difference in motor habit on the level used by handwriting experts to identify a person's "hand." Technical or motor-habit differences are probably the quickest way to identify the individual. Other chapters in this volume treat this problem in more detail, so I will not discuss it at any length here. Because of the close relationship of such differences to biological and organismic responses, they are relatively secure ways of identifying individuals, but are limited in their ability to tell us about the relationships of the individuals to one another. Since these kinds of relationships are one of the reasons for seeking to identify individuals in the first place, it is often necessary to go beyond technical distinctions to distinctions relating to form and structure.

Form is closely related to technique in that it is relatively objective and observable. Form is simply the shape and morphology of the artifact. Most of the criteria suggested by Berenson are of this type—the shape of ears, for example. A good example of the distinction between form and technique may be drawn from painting—technique is the level exemplified by the handling of the brush as seen in brushstrokes, whereas form is exemplified by the shapes of the objects represented.

Structure, on the other hand, is not directly observable save in its very real effects on the organization of the final work. Structure means the relationship of the forms to one another and to the work as a whole. There are many ways of formally (in a different sense of *formal!*) presenting such relationships as I have discussed elsewhere (Muller in press). One example of structural aspects of art and artifacts is the "composition" of a work, but structural relationships may go considerably deeper than mere composition.

Unfortunately, to be useful as models of individual or group behavior, such structural and morphological treatments must take into account the psychological nature of human beings. This only means that a general theory of human behavior should not violate the limitations required by our knowledge of human capabilities; it does not imply that our models must be ideational, cognitive, behavioral, or any other brand of psychological model. An example of the kinds of problems involved may be found in theories of style concerned with transmission from one person to another. In such a case, the substantial differences between childhood and mature learning processes may be significant. Furthermore, there must be some effort to distinguish human universals from the particular characteristics of a given style. [See, for example, Berlin and Kay's study of color perception (1969).]

In practical and immediate terms, however, many studies of individual variation will not require such detailed analysis of style. At the same time, the appreciation of the role of form and morphology in the operation of a more complete behavioral system does suggest the need for much more careful and detailed studies of form. The better the initial analysis of morphology is, the better the conclusions based on this analysis will be. Although the specific character of the morphological "traits" to be identified must depend to a great degree on the problem, the identification of individuals and social groups *is* concerned with matters of styles, and naive classifications of "design elements" are probably the major source of error in published attempts along these lines. Given the special purposes for which traditional typologies in archaeology were created (chronology, for the most part), we can expect that such units would usually be useless in distinguishing social groups, much less individuals.

As useful as classifications of form and technique may be for many purposes, there are many styles in which the variation in structure may be as significant, or even more significant. For example, certain geometric art styles leave very little room for variation in either form or technique in the execution of a work. In such cases, the best procedure for the identification of an individual artisan will require attention to structural as well as technical and morphological variation. Example 1, to be discussed in detail in the next section, is concerned with some examples of probable individual (or, at least, microstyle) differences in the conditions under which certain treatments are used.

In this example, individual or microstyle differences are shown in the application of a rule that has the effect of quadrupling particular elements. On this level, the differences between one microstyle and another lie in the restrictions placed on the use of the rule. One artisan, in effect, quadrupled only certain elements on one portion of the design; other microstyles exhibited a much more general quadrupling of elements in many locations. It may not seem that a very rigorous kind of structural analysis would be necessary to see such differences, but this is only a simple example and much more subtle relationships exist. In addition, in the absence of rigorous structural analysis, neither these simple structural differences nor adequate morphological definitions have been forthcoming. In the latter case, it can be argued that the only really adequate (for descriptive purposes, that is) definition of morphological elements is one that is developed in relation to the structure. It is clear that in the Broken K Pueblo report by Hill (1970), for example, many of the design elements are structurally related to one another, so that great care should be taken in interpreting the correlations.

Structural analyses can be presented in a large number of different formats ranging from flow charts to "grammars," although not all formats are equally useful or adequate. Linguistically inspired formats include the program-like statements of Watt (1967) and the grammars for prehistoric art styles that I have developed (Muller 1966a, in press). I have presented arguments supporting this kind of analytical procedure at some length in the latter paper (in press).

Another area of individual difference in representation is in the semantic area. This is obviously a difficult problem for archaeological analyses, but it may be that certain kinds of structural analysis can approach this problem to some degree (see, e.g., Gardin 1967). The general relationship between structure and meaning is a matter for considerable discussion in fields such as linguistics, so for the present it may be best simply to note that differences do exist between individuals on this level.

It is also important not to confuse statistical and metric studies of differences in art styles with structural and formal treatments. The differences detected through statistical techniques *may* be caused by stylistic variation in structure and form—but only if the data fed into the statistical procedure are properly defined. As the computer experts say, "Garbage in, garbage out." If the metric data processed through statistical techniques are poorly defined, then it is doubtful that the correlations, clusters, and other output will be meaningful. Statistical procedures can reduce the time and energy required to carry out an adequate analysis, but the statistical material is not the final product; statistics are simply devices for reducing complexity in a set of data without regard to the quality of the data.

The following example is concerned with the use of minor differences in the structure of rules and the restriction upon the use of rules in the definition of microstyles. Note that these rules are part of models of an artistic system and are *not* to be taken as reflecting "what was in the minds of the makers." For a much more detailed account of the definition of styles and their structure, see my "Structural Studies of Art Styles" (in press).

EXAMPLE 1

Material.   Shell gorgets in the Lick Creek style (Muller 1966a, b, in press), fifteenth to sixteenth century, from eastern Tennessee and the surrounding area (Figure 3.1).

General discussion.   Almost all the gorgets in the Lick Creek style are of the so-called rattlesnake theme. There is relatively little variation in the basic structure or in the elements employed, and internal varia-

Figure 3.1.   Lick Creek shell gorget.

tion is best defined in the utilization of certain kinds of morphological rules governing the forms of sections of the design. Few archaeological data exist on the identity or status of gorget makers in their societies. Many illustrations of historic Indians from the general area show males wearing gorgets (though of different designs), but known specimens are from burial contexts where at least as many females and children as adult males are represented. It is possible to identify a number of microstyles within the Lick Creek style. Most are not clearly associated with a single site or locality but are found over much of the total range of the style. The data suggest either considerable mobility on the part of gorget makers, or considerable dispersal of gorget makers and exchange of finished items, or both.

Definition of microstyle. One of the largest of the microstyles is characterized by a shell disk rather wider than it is tall, often tending to be squarish in shape. The neck area of the head is constricted, and the head is generally close to perpendicular. The last feature, however, is common to many gorgets of what appear to be the later temporal phases of the style. Decoration of the neck area is relatively simple. The shape of the mouth is triangular with a curved upper border, and there is usually an excised triangular area at the lower left side of the mouth. Execution of the gorget is competent and the engraving of lines is "confident" with little indication of "hesitation" marks around the lines. All these features occur in areas of the gorget that appear to have the greatest degree of variation in execution and it seems unlikely that these are zones that are significant to the "meaning" of the gorget.

The characteristics discussed so far are primarily formal rather than structural differences of this microstyle from others. In terms of composition (actually something closer to "surface structure" in the linguistic sense), the body area of the so-called rattlesnake figure in many variants of the style is usually divided into segments. In this particular microstyle, however, part of the body area is divided longitudinally into two narrower zones of decoration. In other microstyles, the segmental division of the body area is done in such a fashion that the segments correspond to a cross-like division of the whole design field. In this microstyle, some four-part (cross-like) organization remains, but is subordinated to other organization of the design field. The net effect is to create a new design field division so that rules that in other microstyles apply to the whole field now are applied to only a portion of that field. In the informal statement of this that follows, *TN* is simply an arbitrary symbol, the specific referent of which would be determined at a lower level of the grammar as a whole. The important point here is the relationship of the symbol to others—i.e., the structure.

In other microstyles (in general),

> *Context:* *Body*
>
> *Rule:* $TN \Rightarrow TN + TN + TN + TN$

This means that when the symbol *TN* occurs in a context where it is derived by the rules from the symbol *Body*, it will be quadrupled.

In the microstyle under discussion, however,

> *Context:* *Bodypart 1*
>
> *Rule:* $TN \Rightarrow TN + TN + TN + TN$

The structural rule itself is not changed, but the application of the rule has been restricted to that part of the structure derived through the rules from a new symbol, *Bodypart 1*. As it happens, this structural analysis of the difference in the design field shows how a relatively minor change in the context limiting the application of a rule can have far-reaching consequences on the level of composition and morphology. Furthermore, the actual character of the difference is specified precisely rather than in intuitive terms.

In the rules just given, the symbol *TN* ends up in its final "realization" on most gorgets as either a chevron or a straight line unit. Just as there is a structure to the layout of the whole design field, there is a structure to the morphology itself, as in the following morphological rule:

$$Context: l_1 + l_2 + l_3 + l_4$$

where each l is a line unit whose subscript number indicates its position relative to other such line units. In this case, the position of the line unit l determines which of a number of features the line unit will possess. Thus, in most of the microstyles of the Lick Creek style,

$l_3 = $ '−' bend	and all other	$l = $ '+' bend
'−' open		'−' open
'−' shape		'−' shape
'−' circle		'−' circle
•		•
•		•
•		•

This simply means that the line in most locations will be "realized" as a chevron, but that in the location l_3 the line will be a straight line. In the particular microstyle being discussed here, this general rule is usually applied, but in approximately 40% of the cases an additional "doubling" rule is introduced so that l_3 position is filled by two line units rather than one. So,

$$l_3 \implies l_{3a} + l_{3b}$$

In this case, only unit location l_{3b} would show the feature $'-'$ *bend*.[1]

Example 1 shows how variation in structural characteristics can be presented in explicit form. In its complete form, such a statement is a mathematical statement of relationships (Boolean algebra, in fact). The choice between one algebraic statement of relationships and another is neither simple nor trivial, and judgment of the "correctness" of a grammar is actually a judgment of its adequacy and its mathematical elegance. Such decisions are, for better or for worse, little more difficult in archaeological material than in the study of extant cultural systems.

So far, this discussion has been concerned mainly with the identification and description of individual variation—but what are the sources and dimensions of individual variation? First, as already suggested, the sources of variation in an artistic system may or may not be the same events that cause variation in other areas of a culture (as Binford has indicated in a discussion of mortuary practices, 1971). This makes it extremely dangerous to go directly from a statement of differences between individuals and groups in one medium to statements about relationships of people in the society as a whole.

Views of prehistoric groupings have been based on such assumptions to a disproportionate degree. Whole "societies" have been "identified" on the basis of single-medium stylistic groupings, most often those in pottery. The important point is not that some other medium may be as useful as pottery, but rather that for the definition of prehistoric social groups no study of any single tradition will suffice. This principle is an extension of comments made by Hill (1970) and Deetz (1968:45 and elsewhere) that determination of residence patterns had to deal with traditions of both sexes. The same general principle is true

---

[1] There are several alternative ways of achieving the same result through different kinds of rules. Here the same result could be achieved somewhat more simply by applying a doubling rule to l_2 rather than to l_3. This would not require a restatement of the feature rule. Unfortunately, in this case, difficult problems with still other rules not discussed here are created. In actuality, the change in the microstyle from other microstyles is probably even more pronounced than suggested by the rules as given here. In any case, the example is somewhat clearer as given than it would be if stated more correctly (i.e., more elegantly in terms of the total grammar).

for all social groupings. Any society, even the most technologically simple, has many kinds of social settings and situations. Co-participation in one of these settings cannot necessarily be linked to common participation in other situations. Any hypothesis that stylistic differences show the existence of different social units requires testing of the auxiliary hypothesis that the stylistic variation is significant in social situations beyond those of the technological tradition per se. For example, if social boundaries among potters are to be used to distinguish "tribes," then the connection between social units in general and those of potters must be shown.

In these terms there are certain general issues that require much more attention in our discussion of individual and group variation.

First, as Binford has pointed out, there is a danger in assuming that explanations of culture change, as such, must involve "flow of information" kinds of models. The idea of information as knowledge applied in planning is discussed by Binford:

> The comparative study of forms of cultural content as a measure of variability in flow of information among and within cultural systems is misleading; structural variability alone among cultural systems strongly conditions the degree that information and knowledge will be translated into culturally organized behavior [1971:25].

Even if we disagree with Binford's culturological viewpoint, it is necessary to recognize that differences on this issue have not been resolved.

Second, the postulate that similarity and difference are reflections of the *degree* of social interaction in and between groups is reasonable as long as it is recognized, as repeatedly emphasized earlier, that this kind of interaction is specific to the group in question. To take one well-known example, modern English working-class interaction relationships in the work situation may be quite different from the interactions of the leisure setting and may involve quite different groups of people.

Third, because styles are so complex, it is generally true that stylistic continuity results from face-to-face contact between artisans. However, there are examples that show that this is not always true (see, e.g., Holm 1965). Furthermore, continuity or discontinuity cannot always be demonstrated solely by morphological or formal comparisons. Structural analysis is vital to understanding the operation of a style (Muller in press).

Fourth, to the extent that how a style is learned is important to some hypotheses about the location of the individual in some social group, it is also necessary to note that learning is a complex process. For example, learning may take place in an adult rather than a childhood setting. Psychological research suggests that the mechanisms of learning in these two settings may be very different (see, e.g., Lenneberg 1967). If this is so, in some cases we may need to show just what kind of learning was involved before we can speak of kin-based or residential learning situations. Given the presence of nonkin and nonresidential associations in adult life, it is naive to assume that learning per se implies descent or even residential propinquity.

Fifth, it follows from the foregoing that styles are not necessarily contiguous with whole societies, and examination of living societies suggests that they rarely are. Participation of an individual in a style, however, does imply membership in some kind of social group, but these groups may be based on one of many kinds of social status. The individual may simply have taken the trouble to learn the style, for example, or he may belong to groups based on status in terms of sex, age, residence, kinship, and so on.

Sixth, and finally, stylistic analysis generally does not directly explain *why* differences have occurred. Rather it provides a direct and explicit statement of *what* the differences actually are. Although change in time is not a primary concern of this chapter, stylistic analysis may also show *how* changes have come about between one time and another by specifying the potentialities for change. Thus, for both temporal change and for microstylistic variation on the same time level, variation may occur on morphological levels without involving alteration of the structural principles controlling combination of elements. An example of change (and in some cases the lack of expected change) toward structural and formal consistency may be found in the historic changes in the alphabet as discussed by William Watt (1973:22–23 especially). As Watt points out, in the alphabet some kinds of changes appear more likely than others when structural considerations are taken into account. In such cases, synchronic microstylistic variation may also be more understandable when examined structurally. If structural analysis, then, is not usually *explanation* in the commonly used sense, it may still be a necessary part of such explanation.

A second example may provide some reason for caution in the study of individual variation, however. The point is not that we should be pessimistic about the utility or possibility of archaeological studies of individual variation, but rather that great caution and care is necessary here as in all other archaeological work. The study of individual (or supposedly individual) variation on morphological and structural lines cannot be a panacea for our problems, however useful it may be.

EXAMPLE 2

Material. Pressed-iron wheel covers in the Detroit stylistic tradition, late twentieth century, Nacirema culture (Figure 3.2).

General discussion. Decorative wheel covers were developed in the 1940s as a part of Nacirema vehicle design. No formal–logical description has been completed, but preliminary analysis suggests considerable complexity of design. Although many external factors, such as overall vehicle design, influence the character of the wheel covers, examination of the designs suggests that this influence is not as great as generally supposed. A number of style horizons exist, many of which appear to result from copying the appearance of wheel designs in other media (e.g., wire wheels and magnesium alloy wheels). Little has been published on the designers, but they are separate from the artisans who actually fabricate the objects. Furthermore, by extension from published data on other aspects of the Detroit tradition, it seems unlikely that finished designs represent the work of a single designer. Instead, work

Figure 3.2. Detroit wheel cover.

seems to be carried out by teams who often must design within limits set by other experts. (I began a pilot study of wheel cover design with Ann Schlosser in 1969, but the project was terminated when it became obvious that the stylistic system was extremely complex and did not present the simplified character suitable for a "quick and dirty" analysis problem for use as a classroom example.)

Definition of microstyle. One of the interesting aspects of the Detroit stylistic tradition in wheel cover design is that it shows considerable cyclicity. Although there may be some debate about the definition of styles (is there a Ford style, or is this simply a microstyle?), examination of the production of a single company through time shows some elements that repeat in a cycle ranging from 1 to 3 years in duration. One example is found in Chevrolet wheel covers of 1955–1967. A narrow, repeated slot-like motif close to the circumference of the wheel cover appeared in 1955. This motif was enlarged slightly in 1956. For the next 2 years, the motif was not used. Then in 1959, the motif in its 1956 form reappeared. The same form was used in 1960. In 1961, the slot was replaced by a repeating square unit. In 1962, the 1956 motif was used again. In 1963, both the slot and the square unit were used, but the following year only the square unit (like that of 1961) was used. In 1966 and 1967, the slot form was used alone. Similar forms do occur on the wheel covers of other manufacturers, but the alternation of forms is often different both in duration and the elements employed.

Aside from being a seriationist's nightmare, this situation presents some interesting lessons. First, the kind of formal variation used to define individual styles is present here, but differences actually represent alternate states of the same cyclical system. If there were no controls on date or manufacturer, it would be easy to postulate the existence of two separate artists, whereas the truth is that each year's product has to have maximum differentiation from the previous year's product while still maintaining the "marque" identification. Although it is clear that special conditions prevail in the industrial Nacirema society, the problems posed here should not simply be shrugged off and should serve as a caution to glib interpretations of what microstyles represent. It is likely that careful analysis of the total style would provide internal checks upon this cyclical phenomenon since the period of different elements is often different and many elements and motifs do not show this cyclical feature at all.

Even if the Detroit tradition is taken as a single style, the situation is little different. It may even prove difficult to identify different groups of designers, since a company's wheel covers are sometimes more similar to those of a competitor than to its own products of a few years earlier.

Several conclusions can be drawn from this case. One is that work situations exist in which variation from one artifact to another may not be solely the result of individual difference in artisans. It also shows that there are some situations in which interaction between one group of artisans and another may be very far from face to face and still produce results similar to those of face-to-face situations, i.e., *interaction is not synonymous with face-to-face interaction.*

Although this closing example shows the need for caution, it is nonetheless true that the explicitness and rigor of formal–logical treatments of styles and of individual variation make the testing and assessment of such presentations much easier than is the case with the present, nonrigorous descriptions of variation. A proposal that one individual "used" rules of combination in a slightly different (but explicitly stated) way, whether ultimately right or wrong, is still preferable to the state of affairs in which we concern ourselves with "the quiet amplitude" of one person's style, however right such an attribution may be in empirical terms. In the latter case, we are simply obliged to trust in the connoisseurship of the expert. In the former case, the explicitness of the statement allows it to be judged not only in empirical terms, but also in terms of its elegance and adequacy.

REFERENCES

Beazley, John D.
  1963 *Attic red-figure vase-painters.* 2nd ed. New York: Oxford University Press (Clarendon).
Berenson, Bernhard
  1962 *Rudiments of connoisseurship: Study and criticism of Italian art.* New York: Schocken Books. (Published in 1902 as *The study and criticism of Italian art.* Second series. New York: Schocken Books.)
Berlin, Brent, and Paul Kay
  1969 *Basic color terms: Their universality and evolution.* Berkeley: University of California Press.
Binford, Lewis R.
  1971 Mortuary practices: Their study and potential. *Society for American Archaeology, Memoir* **25**:6–29.
Burroughs, Alan
  1971 *Art criticism from a laboratory.* Westpoint, Connecticut: Greenwood Press.

Deetz, James
    1968   The inference of residence and descent rules from archaeological data. In *New perspectives in archaeology*, edited by S. R. Binford and L. R. Binford. Chicago: Aldine. Pp. 41–78.

Gardin, J. C.
    1967   Methods for the descriptive analysis of archaeological materials. *American Antiquity* **32**:13–30.

Hill, James N.
    1970   Broken K Pueblo: Prehistoric social organization in the American Southwest. *Anthropological Papers of the University of Arizona*, No. 18.

Holm, Bill
    1965   *Northwest Coast Indian art: An analysis of form.* Seattle: University of Washington Press.

Hymes, Dell (Ed.)
    1964   *Language in culture and society.* New York: Harper.

Jeppson, Lawrence
    1970   *The fabulous frauds, fascinating tales of great art forgeries.* New York: Waybright and Talley.

Lenneberg, Eric H.
    1967   *Biological foundations of language.* New York: Wiley.

Lothrop, Samuel K.
    1942   Coclé: An archaeological study in central Panama, Part II. *Memoirs of the Peabody Museum of Archaeology and Ethnology, Harvard University*, Vol. VIII.

Muller, Jon
    1966a   An experimental theory of stylistic analysis. Unpublished Ph.D. dissertation, Department of Anthropology, Harvard University.
    1966b   Archaeological analysis of art styles. *Tennessee Archaeologist* **23**:25–39.
    1974   Out of site, out of mind: Psychological implications in archaeology. Paper prepared for a seminar on "Beyond a Study of Archaeology," at Southern Illinois University, Carbondale, April 1974.
    in press   Structural studies of art styles. In *The visual arts: Plastic and graphic*, edited by Justine Cordwell. The Hague: Mouton.

Richter, G. M. A.
    1958   *Attic red-figured vases, a survey.* Rev. ed. New Haven, Connecticut: Yale University Press.

Watt, William C.
    1967   *Morphology of the Nevada cattlebrands and their blazons*, Part two. Department of Computer Science, Carnegie–Mellon University.
    1973   Some observations on the study of design elements. *Social Sciences Working Papers*, No. 30. School of Social Science, University of California, Irvine.

4

The "Analytical Individual" and Prehistoric Style Variability

CHARLES L. REDMAN

The investigations discussed in this volume stem from the renewal of interest in discovering the individual craftsmen who created specific archaeological objects. It is not a new pursuit; our colleagues in classical archaeology and art history have long sought the identity of artists responsible for specific works. Because their purpose is to understand developments and changes in art styles, they have focused on individual pieces of art as important in themselves; only secondarily do they see the objects as reflections of the society in which they were produced. Clearly, the motivations behind the research reported in this volume are of a different sort. Here, identifying individuals responsible for particular archaeological objects is seen as a step toward a more thorough understanding of prehistoric craft specialization and distributive networks (Hill and Evans 1972:257).

Archaeologists have begun to formulate models that could be more effectively tested if it were possible to identify the products of individual craftsmen. This type of insight would allow a great leap forward in organizational studies both within communities and over entire regions. Although I accept the position that the idiosyncratic behavior of most craftsmen makes their work potentially identifiable, I do not consider such identification the most effective way to gather information on organizational interaction. My working assumption is this: Although it is possible to identify objects that were made by the same person, it is extremely difficult to demonstrate conclusively that they *were* made by the same person. If we are to use variations in certain habits, tools, or patterns of learned behavior as criteria of delineation, we must know the range of variation in each of these variables and have a sufficient sample size to demonstrate that the mode, or cluster of attributes, is produced by one person. The identification is even more difficult because, in pottery making for example, a single potter will vary her techniques from pot to pot, and over a period of time. My skepticism may be excessive, but I believe that a preoccupation with identifying individuals will lead to debates over the validity of identification displacing our primary concern—for the processes to be explicated with this information. All too often it seems as though scholars who study the behavior of particular individuals do so at the cost of more general investigations.

Although I consider the identification of individual craftsmen an inefficient use of the prehistorian's research effort, I do think that the questions pursued and many of the techniques suggested by the contributors to this volume are important. Even more to the point, I think that there are alternative strategies that would circumvent much of the unnecessary controversy over whether one has succeeded in isolating the works of a single person. These alternative strategies are related to what I consider to be two equally viable chains of logic employed by archaeologists (Figure 4.1). The most frequently used procedure for formulating and testing general models of behavioral changes involves organizing research to discover specific patterns of cultural manifestations. These data can then be used to reconstruct patterns of prehistoric behavior that in turn can be generalized into nonspecific behavioral models (logical chain A–B–C–D–E in Figure 4.1). This procedure uses archaeological data to reconstruct the details of specific situations, and uses these specific instances to test general models. As an alternative, I propose formulating an investigation and analysis to discern general patterning in material objects that is directly usable in testing general models of cultural behavior (logical chain A–B–E in Figure 4.1). By sidestepping the stage of reconstruction of specific lifeways the archaeologist neither relies on difficult-to-demonstrate interpretations nor requires the additional difficult step in the chain of reasoning. General variables with relative values, such as degree of interaction, heterogeneity of assemblage, or specializa-

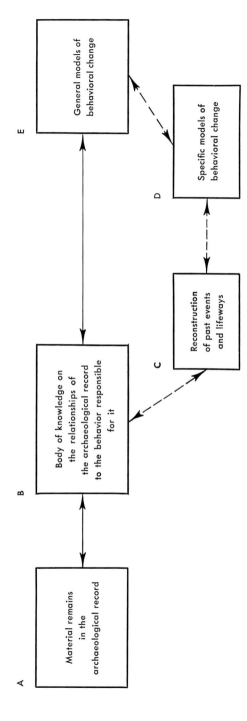

Figure 4.1. Two alternative chains of reasoning (A to B to E, or A to B to C to D to E) for using the archaeological record to formulate and test general models of behavioral changes. Note that reasoning can proceed from left to right or right to left and usually does both.

tion of activities, can be directly measured in the archaeological record. These variables are then immediately usable in testing the models of general behavioral changes constructed with them.

I suggest that using hypothetical hierarchical groups of varying sizes would be just as effective as determining the products of specific individuals. The groups could be defined on the basis of the relative intensity of interaction between group members as reflected in the similarity in the style of objects they produced. Techniques similar to those suggested for identifying individuals could be used to measure interaction or shared learning experience. For example, I have classified pairs of painted pots as different or similar according to numerous empirical criteria; the pots that are most different have been assigned to the largest interaction group (little contact), whereas objects displaying great similarity along several axes of variation have been identified as from one of the "smallest interaction groups" (intense contact). A smallest interaction group might in fact be single craftspersons, sisters, or mother–daughter teams. To trace distributive networks or craft specialization within a community it is sufficient to know that these pieces are from a particular smallest interaction group. Because this is the smallest size group the analysis differentiates, I refer to this unit as an *analytical individual*. The question of whether one or more persons are included is only interesting in a limited sense, and not for a general understanding of prehistoric organizational processes. Using a number of different observations to measure interaction, each of which is sensitive to minor variations in learning patterns, it is possible to differentiate equivalent groups of varying sizes, and overlapping sets of groups that are determined on differing bases. This is particularly useful in situations where solidarity groups crosscut kinship ties.

The position I advocate is now an ongoing research strategy; only preliminary results are available. The materials being utilized are painted ceramics recovered by the Cibola Archaeological Research Project in the El Morro Valley, west–central New Mexico. This expedition, directed by Patty Jo Watson, Steven A. LeBlanc, and myself, located over 200 sites by intensive surface survey. We have conducted excavations at 12 of these sites. The initial goals of this project are to describe the lifeways and to explain the cultural changes that occurred within the region. The El Morro Valley area has great potential as an archaeological laboratory for testing hypotheses on certain types of prehistoric behavioral processes. During a relatively short period of time there was a great increase in the valley's population followed within 50 or 75 years by almost total abandonment. Hence, within the bounds of this single valley, we can examine processes of rapid growth, integration, complex organization, and decline. An accurate and detailed chronology is made possible by previous descriptions of pottery similar to that found in the El Morro Valley (Carlson 1970), preliminary ceramic seriation analyses carried out by members of the project (LeBlanc 1975; Marquardt 1974), and the relative abundance of dendrochronological dates from the excavations. The combination of good chronological control, a dense prehistoric population, and a sophisticated material assemblage offers a unique opportunity for investigating processes involving complex societies in the American Southwest.

SYSTEM OF POTTERY CLASSIFICATION

The analysis of the artifacts and other information recovered by the Cibola Archaeological Research Project reflects a conjunctive, multivariate view of cultural processes. Diverse sets of data are being analyzed to produce information on temporal order, subsistence pursuits, technological know-how, and trading networks of the prehistoric inhabitants. One of the major research interests is the relative amount of interaction between and within settlements, especially with respect to the processes of rapid growth, integration of large populations, and rapid decline. Interest focuses on which settlements traded or communicated regularly with which others, which settlements were involved in social relations leading to intermarriage, and the actual movements of groups of people within the valley. The delineation of human groups of varying sizes, including the identification of the works of analytical individuals, is essential to the problems being pursued. Our primary source of information has been an analysis of the painted pottery found during excavations and surface survey. Techniques have been adopted and modified from several different systems of classification used on Southwestern pottery.

Painted designs were applied to ceramic bowls and jars by prehistoric potters for a variety of reasons. Traditionally, pottery manufacture in the American Southwest was almost exclusively the province of women, so that young girls learned the skill from their mothers, grandmothers, or other close female relatives or friends. We know from ethnographic studies that the learning and practice of pottery manufacture vary considerably from community to community, and often between groups within a single community. This type of intracommunity variability is characteristic of home industry products. The variation in painted design is usually sufficiently distinctive so that individual vessels can be assigned a general location and approximate time of manufacture.

Tularosa, St. John's, or Heshota pottery are the classical types of Southwestern painted pottery used throughout the major occupation of the El Morro Valley. Although these "type" designations were useful at first, we quickly discovered that only a fraction of the pottery excavated conformed completely to the type definitions, and that a tremendous amount of information encoded on this pottery was obscured by the type classification system.

In order to obtain the kind and variety of information desired, Patty Jo Watson and I devised a hierarchical multivariate design analysis for the painted pottery (Figures 4.2–4.6). Our first goal using this system is to record numerous categories of objectively defined stylistic variations that are at least indirectly a reflection of diverse cultural phenomena. Our second goal is to make the system flexible enough to record both fragmented sherds and entire pots. Whole pots have more sets of information and are more distinct than small potsherds, but they do not occur in sufficient numbers nor in every excavated room. Potsherds contain fewer sets of information but are far more numerous and widely distributed. In this way data on the type of paint and basic design motif are available from every sherd recovered, and data preserved only on large sherds and complete pots, such as the number of partitions in the design field or the symmetry of the total design, can be studied on a limited number of pieces, providing insights not reflected on small sherds. Hence, this analytical system uses the information available from the whole range of ceramics recovered. To concentrate on one set of data to the exclusion of the other would be to limit unnecessarily the potential of the conjunctive approach.

Another advantage of this system of recording over past techniques is its hierarchical structure. The importance of the hierarchical structure is twofold: First, the differences between pairs of painted design motifs are not equal, nor can they be assumed to reflect equivalent types of information. Several different operations (i.e., decisions) are required during the painting of even a single design element. Some of these decisions are paralleled by different elements, but some are not. The present system attempts to allow for these differences by arranging the hierarchy into levels of reasonably equivalent decisions, within which specific variations can be compared, and new examples can be added. The second advantage of this hierarchical system is that even if the sherd is so fragmented that a design element is only partially preserved it is still possible to record the remaining recognizable information (e.g., to record a design as "hatching"). Thus, at a very basic level of comparing designs, such as hatched versus solid designs, large numbers of sherds that otherwise would be ignored can contribute to the statistical results.

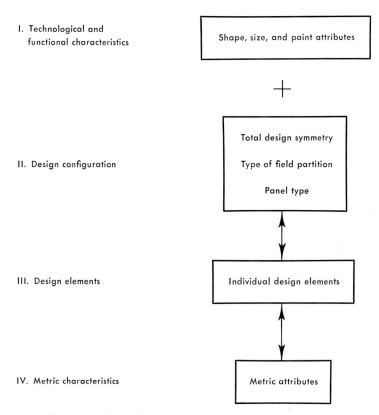

I. Technological and
    functional characteristics

Shape, size, and paint attributes

+

II. Design configuration

Total design symmetry

Type of field partition

Panel type

III. Design elements

Individual design elements

IV. Metric characteristics

Metric attributes

Figure 4.2. Categories of attributes recorded in the four-step painted pottery design analysis procedure.

Recording design attributes for both complete vessels and sherds is done in four steps, each of which considers a different category of attributes (Figure 4.2). As a first step, certain formal characteristics of each sherd are recorded. These include vessel form, size, paint, and slip color. They are related to technological and functional decisions made by the prehistoric potters. It has been suggested that some of these attributes have changed in a regular fashion over time during the period of occupation of the El Morro Valley (Carlson 1970; LeBlance 1975; Marquardt 1974).

The second step is to record the total configuration of the designs on larger sherds and complete pots (Figure 4.3). Included in this stage is the number of partitions in the field, the shape of each partition, and the basic symmetry of the design. The symmetry of both total designs and panel designs may be related to different social groupings and may con-

Figure 4.3. An example of the recording of the total configuration of the designs on larger sherds and complete pots.

tain as much or more information than the content (elements) of the designs. To record these patterns in a systematic fashion, symmetry categories developed by D. Washburn are being used on the Cibola pottery (Washburn n.d.).

The third step involves coding individual design elements or portions of elements (Figure 4.4). This is done according to a master chart of 203 possible elements developed by detailed examination of the pottery being analyzed, and is defined in terms of geometric possibilities (Figure 4.5). Different levels of the hierarchy represent certain decisions the potter made. Each level of the hierarchy can be examined separately to determine what level of the hierarchy represents certain decisions that the potter made. Each level of the hierarchy can be examined separately to determine at what level of design certain cultural patterning is reflected most clearly. It could be the level of basic elements (hatching, lines, solids, and so on), bounded shape (bands, triangles, steps, and so on), or even orientation of the hatching within the shapes that encodes the most interesting data. Patterning of different details of execution comprising generally similar overall designs should be a reflection of spe-

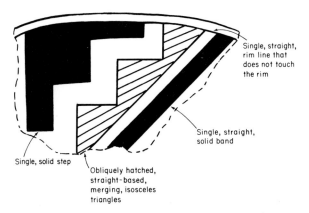

Single, straight, rim line that does not touch the rim

Single, straight, solid band

Single, solid step

Obliquely hatched, straight-based, merging, isosceles triangles

Figure 4.4.   An example of the classification of individual design elements on a rim sherd.

cific learning groups, and as such may be a key to understanding the interactional networks of the prehistoric occupants.

The fourth step in the recording procedure is to code, for each painted design element, the metric attributes that reflect the tools and motor habits of the potter (Hill and Evans 1972). These attributes include the width of the painted lines, the frequency of lines in hatched designs, and the width of individual elements (Figure 4.6), and are related to learning patterns, tools used, agility, and patience of the individual painter.

By combining these four steps of recording it is possible to investigate the patterning of several different levels of design attributes for any set of archaeological units. It may be the symmetry of the entire design field of complete pots that reflects a particular cultural variable; the actual elements selected may be representative of other phenomena, and the width or frequency of painted lines may be related to a third set of cultural factors. We have assumed that much of the variation in each of these four categories of information is related to the learning patterns and individual decisions of the potters. Modes of attribute patterning in each category delineate groups of varying sizes, and the covariation of attributes in all classes of data identify minimal units of interaction, or what I have called analytical individuals. Preliminary results indicate that analysis of symmetry yields a single major grouping for all the material, whereas patterns of technology delineate the material according to a chronological continuum. The categories of design and metric attributes provide complex patterns that vary in scope from uniformity over the entire collection to certain attributes differentiating room clusters.

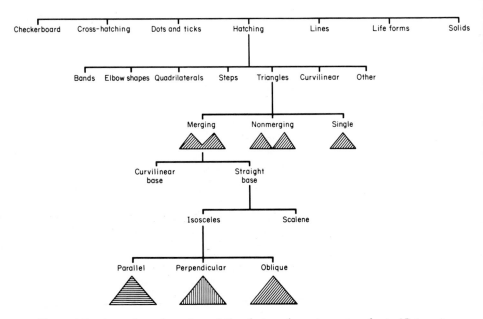

Checkerboard   Cross-hatching   Dots and ticks   Hatching   Lines   Life forms   Solids

Bands   Elbow shapes   Quadrilaterals   Steps   Triangles   Curvilinear   Other

Merging   Nonmerging   Single

Curvilinear   Straight
base   base

Isosceles   Scalene

Parallel   Perpendicular   Oblique

Figure 4.5. A condensed version of the design element master chart. (Categories leading to obliquely hatched, straight-based, merging, isosceles triangle are fully represented.)

THE PROGRAM OF ANALYSIS

We are conducting four relatively independent sets of analyses with the data collected. One analysis involves the accurate and detailed description of ceramics from the El Morro Valley and their appearance in closely dated archaeological contexts. We are using information on the

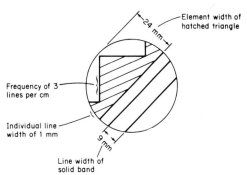

Element width of
hatched triangle

24 mm

Frequency of 3
lines per cm

Individual line
width of 1 mm

9 mm

Line width of
solid band

Figure 4.6. An example of the recording of metric attributes of individual design elements.

covariation of attributes that have hitherto been crucial to type definitions, also microvariations in design and technology that covary with independent sources of information on relative and absolute chronology. This analysis is aiding in the dating of sites that are only known from surface collections, and will eventually help refine the pottery chronology of the entire region.

The second analysis involves producing data to test hypotheses about the organizational and interactional changes occurring in the El Morro Valley. We are assuming that the similarity in learned repertoires of the prehistoric potters is related to the relative interaction of the potters or the groups with which they were associated. This interaction could take the form of actual teaching, contact for other reasons, intermarriage, or trade. The more interaction, the more similar will be details of pottery design. We expect that during periods of population growth and decline the range and amount of interaction will vary as an integral element in the process. An understanding of these interactional patterns and the different size of interaction units is a major step in explaining the organizational structures that existed in thirteenth-century El Morro Valley. Identifying products of minimal interaction units (analytical individuals) is fundamental to the formulation of refined models of distributive networks and movement of specific groups of people.

The third analysis is aimed at eliciting a better understanding of the way cultural behavior is reflected in material remains (cultural transformations). If we can hold constant the transformations of the archaeological remains caused by natural factors, then we can hypothesize that patterns of behavior that covary with observed patterns in the artifactual debris are related. As a first approximation, it is fair to assume that natural transformations are not skewing the results, because all the material for analysis comes from similar contexts (abandoned rooms) that have been subjected to generally the same postdepositional factors. The discovery of specific ways that painted pottery designs reflect specific behavioral patterning is accomplished by a two-step procedure. First, we define archaeologically observable behavioral patterns on the basis of information other than the design analysis. Such information would include room function (functional), subsistence success (functional and organizational), site location (geographic), community size (organizational), and relative chronology (temporal). Second, we define the diverse patterns of the material remains, including the painted pottery. It should be possible to correlate patterns of culturally related variation with patterns of variation observed in the artifactual remains. The discovery of patterns of design variation and their association with cultural variables is accomplished partially on the basis of logically derived relationships based on knowledge of human behavior in relation to material remains. In addition, we are using a method of computer analysis that systematically searches the data bank of pottery design information for examples of patterns that satisfy a predetermined set of criteria and rules (Kintigh n.d.). The development and testing of this type of computer technique is important for solving a variety of archaeological problems. It accomplishes the integration of available archaeological expertise about the material at hand and assumptions about their empirical relations with an inductive search for the suspected patterns through all available evidence. We hope it will be possible to discover, at least for the societies being studied, what ways important cultural changes are reflected in painted designs. For example, are different levels of the design hierarchy representative of changes in specific categories of behavior? Do different types of communities (e.g., large versus small, habitation versus special activity) produce recognizable variants of superficially the same pottery style? A goal of this aspect of the analytical program is to suggest these types of relationships on the basis of Cibola pottery and test them with subsequent fieldwork and analysis, in both the El Morro Valley and other areas.

The fourth analysis is concerned with the system of classification itself. By storing the information recorded in a computer in a form that reflects the structure of the recording system, we can investigate the effect on analytical results of altering the structure of the design system. Trial runs will be made on the basis of results ordered according to different possible variations of the hierarchy. The order in the design hierarchy was determined by our understanding, but might have been ordered differently by another researcher (i.e., in the hierarchy in Figure 4.5 the bounded shapes could have been on top, instead of techniques such as hatching). In this manner, we can learn how the formulation of the categories and classification system directly affects the nature of the results.

The majority of the questions being investigated and the patterns discovered by this system of pottery analysis bear on the specific processes and cultural manifestations of the El Morro Valley. Attempts to associate different levels of stylistic variation with different types of cultural behavioral patterning help us to formulate hypotheses about the relationship between patterns of representation and human behavior. We can then test these hypotheses by using material from other projects. In addition, the conjunctive intercorrelation of the diverse sets of information collected by the design analysis and other categories of data contribute to the creation and testing of general models of settlement growth, interaction, and abandonment. We believe that the methods of recording and analysis used in the Cibola Project will make possible the efficient formulation and examination of hypotheses that rely on a knowledge of the products of "individuals" in the prehistoric record.

REFERENCES

Carlson, Roy L.
    1970   White Mountain Redware. *Anthropological Papers of the University of Arizona*, No. 19.
Hill, James N., and R. K. Evans
    1972   A model for classification and typology. In *Models in archaeology*, edited by David L. Clarke. London: Methuen. Pp. 231–273.
Kintigh, Keith W.
    n.d.   A seriation rule synthesizer. Unpublished manuscript, Department of Anthropology, Stanford University.
LeBlanc, Steven A.
    1975   Micro-seriation: A method for fine chronologic differentiation. *American Antiquity* **40**:22–38.
Marquardt, William
    1974   Late prehistoric societies in the eastern Cibola area: A chronological perspective. Unpublished Ph.D. dissertation, Department of Anthropology, Washington University, St. Louis.
Washburn, Dorothy
    n.d.   Symmetry analysis of Pueblo III ceramic designs from the Upper Gila, New Mexico. Unpublished manuscript, Department of Anthropology, University of California, Berkeley.

5

Individual Variability in Ceramics and the Study of Prehistoric Social Organization[1]

JAMES N. HILL

Anthropological archaeologists are becoming increasingly interested in explaining aspects of prehistoric social organization. Before testable explanations can be attained, however, we must be able to describe accurately and quantitatively those aspects of variability or change we want to explain. My goal here is to present a methodological approach that should be useful as a supplement to other approaches in this regard.

Fundamental to this effort is the development of methods and techniques by which we can discover and identify which artifacts in prehistoric contexts were made (or used) by which specific prehistoric individuals. I shall consider the relevance of doing this later in the chapter.

Most of my experiments employ ceramic data, primarily the individual motor-habit—or motor-performance variability—that occurs in the

[1] I gratefully acknowledge the following organizations for their financial support: the Academic Senate at UCLA, the UCLA Archaeological Survey, and the UCLA Health Sciences Computing Facility (NIH Grant RR–3).

painting of ceramics. However, the methods used are clearly applicable to other aspects of ceramic manufacture and use, and to other kinds of artifacts. I have restricted the effort to examining individual differences in the execution of painting on ceramics.

I emphasize that although identifying the works of individual artisans is new to archaeology, at least in terms of concerted and rigorous application, it is by no means new to other disciplines—and this is one reason I am so certain it can be done in archaeology. Police suspect-document examiners do it with handwriting (FBI Laboratory 1973; Harrison 1958; Osborn 1910), and art historians do it with works of art (Berenson 1962). Moreover, individuality in motor performance has also been studied and documented by kinesiologists (Cratty 1973; Grenzeback 1958), by psychologists (Allport and Vernon 1933; Modlin 1969; Sonnemann 1950), by educators (Harris and Rarick 1955; Myers 1963), and by graphologists (Bunker 1963; Malespine 1951). It has also been recognized by physicians, especially in relation to trauma and aging (Kanfer and Casten 1958; Welford 1958). Ethnologists have been aware of it (Bunzel 1929/1972:62–68; see Chapter 6 by Hardin in this volume), as indeed have some archaeologists (Deetz 1967:109–116; Donnan 1976: 34–41; Gunn 1975; Hill 1972, 1974; Hill and Evans 1972:257–258; Huse 1976; Johnson 1973; Lothrop 1942; White and Thomas 1972).

Individuality in motor performance and artistic expression has been so well confirmed that no one would doubt it. But equally significant is the fact that much of this individuality is subconscious (Harrison 1958: 367; Lewinson and Zubin 1942:3; Singer 1968:45). If we can be confident that we are measuring subconscious individual variability on prehistoric artifacts, we can be confident that the clusters of artifacts we isolate with this kind of variability represent real prehistoric individuals, and not small groups of people, statuses, and so on. This is so because the subconscious attributes of artifact manufacture are presumably rarely, if ever, things that can be shared to an appreciable degree by members of a community; they are almost impossible to teach or even copy (Harrison 1958:361–365).

These are the kinds of attributes I am considering here. They are attributes below the level of the design "element," yet they are usually not so minute as to represent intraindividual variability. Still, they represent a portion of the wide range of variability we call *style*; and I hope this chapter will contribute to the development of a theory of style.

I intend to demonstrate not only that the works of *known* individuals can be identified, but also that individual works can be identified in a collection of ceramics for which the number of individuals involved is *unknown*; equally important, I shall indicate the kinds of variability that have so far proven most useful in doing this, as well as the techniques that were found useful. I shall also provide a brief research design for using this approach with data from an archaeological site, together with some of the difficulties involved in this and other aspects of the research.

My results also suggest the following:

1. Most of the motor-performance attributes employed are indeed subconscious, such that they can not easily be shared or taught.
2. The context of learning is relatively unimportant, in that neither siblings nor those taught by the same teacher share the same motor-performance characteristics.
3. Interindividual variability is much more conspicuous using these attributes than is intraindividual variability.
4. Individual motor performances change little through time, indicating that temporal variability in individuals' motor performances should not interfere with identifying the works of individuals.

There are other findings as well, although these are the most significant. This chapter summarizes a great deal of research, and it is impossible to include all the detail, documentation, and technical information that I might wish.

USEFULNESS

Some of the uses for this research have been outlined in Chapter 1, which included a discussion of the need to control for individual variation in artifacts so that we can more easily distinguish the remaining variability as representing other things we are interested in (e.g., manufacturing techniques and task performance). In this section I shall deal in more detail with how studying individual variability *itself* may contribute to describing aspects of prehistoric social organization.

Craft specialization. If we can discover, within any class of artifacts, the approximate number of people who were making the artifacts, we have a direct interval-scale measure of the *degree* of craft specialization relative to that class of artifact. If, for example, we find that in one time period there were approximately 30 people per 100 making a class of artifact, and the number later shifts to only about 10 people per 100, the magnitude of change in specialization is evident. We should be able to study both diachronic and synchronic variability in this regard, and do it in both intracommunity and intercommunity contexts. If we do this with several classes of artifacts simultaneously, we should be able to derive an overall measure of variability and change in craft specialization. Further, if we study individual variability in the ways artifacts were used (as distinguished from their manufacture), we will have a measure of *task* specialization. These measures are, of course, relevant to studying the evolution of organizational complexity.

Exchange. Knowing which artifacts were made by specific individuals in a community should facilitate measuring the nature and directions of the exchange of craft products in space and time, both within and between communities. If, for example, we find that the craft products of a single individual are in more than one location within or among sites, we might infer that exchange had taken place. Conversely, if we hypothesize that exchange was occurring between two or more units of population, we would expect the products of specific individuals to be found in these locations. We might then be able to study not only the directions and distances involved in exchange systems, but also the volume of exchange and the sizes of the units participating in it. This method should be especially promising for studying intrasite exchange, since there may be no other good way to do it. (The matter of distinguishing exchange from the movement of individuals themselves is addressed briefly at the end of this section.)

Residence units. It should also be possible to identify the locations, sizes, and compositions of residence units, and maybe even describe residence patterns (see especially Hill 1970; Longacre 1970). If we can discover which artifacts were made by specific individuals, the locations of these artifacts within and among sites may permit us to pinpoint the locations of these individual manufacturers, and thus (in many cases) their residence units. If, for example, we find a cluster of artifacts made by a specific individual in a localized area or group of rooms within a community, we might infer that this unit constitutes the location and size of the person's residence. And if we can discover the *number* of individuals manufacturing artifacts within a residence unit, we may be able to make statements about the composition of the unit with regard to craft manufacturing—and maybe even say something about the division of labor represented. Such localized clusters of the artifacts of individuals might, of course, represent craft guilds or something other than residence units, and the ability to make such distinctions depends upon testing with independent archaeological data.

This approach should give us much greater confidence than we had previously that we are actually describing the locations and interresidence unit movement of male and female individuals, rather than measuring style sharing among different groups of individuals. This is certainly the case if the variability measured is subconscious and unlikely to be communicated or taught.

Burial relationships. If we can identify the artifacts made by specific individuals within a community, we can discover which grave goods in the community cemetery were made by each of these individuals—ceramics should be especially useful in this regard. This might permit us to discover a great deal about the organization of the community. If, for example, each of the residence units was highly autonomous economically and socially, we might expect to find localized or nonrandom clusters of burials in the cemetery, each of which containing grave goods made primarily by individuals from a specific residence unit. If, on the other hand, there was a high degree of socioeconomic integration, we might expect to find many of the burials accompanied by grave goods made by members of several different residence units. And if there had been a high degree of political centralization, we might expect to find a special group of burials, perhaps centrally located, associated with especially large quantities (and special types) of items made by the several residence units—and so on. Moreover, we might learn something about residence patterns from the differential grave good contributions made to male versus female burials by the different residence units.

Sodality affiliation. If localized sodality structures are present in a village or larger area, we may be able to discover which residence units were participating in the sodalities by finding artifacts in the structures that had been made by individuals belonging to the different residence units.

Endogamy–exogamy. If a given prehistoric village was largely endogamous, we might expect to find the artifacts made by both males and females of the village primarily within the village, and not in other nearby villages. If, on the hand, it was largely exogamous, we should find the artifacts made by either males or females (or both) in the surrounding villages as well. (This assumes, of course, that we are able to study the artifacts of several contemporaneous sites in an area.) If this can be done, interesting inferences regarding the degree of socioeconomic autonomy of the villages, as well as certain inferences about demographic processes, become possible.

Population movement. It should also be possible to describe the directions and nature of population movement, within or between sites. The evidence for this, in terms of the spatial distributions, is the same as that suggested earlier for exchange—that is, we would expect to find artifacts made by specific individuals in at least two locations.

Thus, in distinguishing a case of population movement from one of exchange, we must employ additional archaeological data (test implications). Although I cannot outline many of the test implications here, I will give two illustrations involving ceramic artifacts. First, if pottery were exchanged, I would expect that only certain vessel forms would be exchanged (presumably those in demand), so that the variety of vessel forms would probably not be the same in the two locations; if people had moved, however, I would expect them to continue making the entire range of vessel forms in their new location. Second, if exchange were involved I would expect primarily the "finer" vessels to be traded; for population movement the entire range of quality would be expected in both locations.

I am aware that some of these examples of usefulness for identifying the works of individuals may seem beyond current practicality, especially as it is not feasible to provide detailed arguments and test implications here for demonstrating and distinguishing each of these things. Further, I recognize that the research investment involved, especially where data from multiple sites are required, would be great indeed. Nonetheless, I think most of these areas of research are feasible right now, assuming only that it is in fact possible to identify the works of individuals in archaeological contexts—and I am confident that it is.

I emphasize my belief that although this approach is relevant to both intra- and intersite analyses, it may be most immediately important with regard to the former. Intrasite microsocial organizational analyses are notoriously complex and difficult, and this approach may offer the best way to avoid many of the problems involved.

In the long run, however, it may be equally useful in locality and regional analyses. Perhaps most important, it offers a way to measure aspects of social organizational variability and change on an *interval* scale and thereby overcome some of the pitfalls of the "culture area" and "phase" systems currently still in use. For example, instead of having to measure craft specialization (and other things) as present or absent in certain areas or time periods, we may be able to derive quantitative measures of the *degrees* to which such things were present. We may then be able to discover where and when major variations in these things actually occurred, rather than employing the somewhat arbitrary culture area and phase divisions; such divisions imply marked or rapid variation and change only at their boundaries, which may be a false representation of reality (Plog 1977). The development of an ability to measure quantitatively both amounts and rates of change is crucial for archaeology (see also Binford's discussion in Hill 1977, "Discussion" section).

THE PILOT EXPERIMENTS

There were two pilot experiments, which I will discuss only briefly. The first one was designed not only to test the idea that the works of individuals can be distinguished, but also to discover something about the nature of the attributes that would be best for doing so. I began by painting a single design element on a 3 × 5 inch card (similar to those in Figure 5.1). I then asked each of five adult individuals to paint 20 exact copies of this element on similar cards using the same brush. It took two students only an hour to sort 99 of the 100 cards correctly in terms of the individuals who had painted them—the differences in motor performance were obvious.

The next step was to quantify this observation. I selected 21 discrete (presence–absence) attributes that I felt might differentiate the works of the five individuals. Chi-square tests (Siegel 1956:104–111, 175–179) showed that each attribute was associated with one or another of the individuals at the .001 level of significance. (Although I will not list these attributes here, three are shown in Figure 5.1.) The result was that the works of all five individuals were easily distinguished.

Figure 5.1. Design element cards painted by three of five different individuals for the 3 × 5 card experiment. Note three of the presence–absence attributes that differentiated the works of these individuals: *Top:* Borderlines over twice as wide in some places as in others. *Middle:* Left-hand hatch lines over twice as close together as other hatch lines. *Bottom:* Left-hand borderline extends below baseline in fuzzy streaks.

Following this, five interval-scale attributes were measured:

1. Area of the box—the area enclosed by the four borderlines
2. Length–width ratio of the box
3. Acute borderline angles—the acute angles formed by the intersection of the left and right borderlines with the top and bottom baselines
4. Widths of the hatch lines—mean width per card
5. Widths of the spaces between lines—mean width per card

One-way analysis of variance tests (BMD05V, Dixon 1970:543–557; Dunn and Clark 1974: Chap. 5) showed that for each variable there were significant differences among the means of the individuals. The F values were as follows:

F Value	Variable
141.42	Area of box
60.79	Borderline angle
50.50	Length–width ratio of box
22.38	Width of hatch lines
18.95	Width of spaces

Using Scheffe's multiple comparison technique (Brownlee 1965:317), it was possible to compare the mean for each individual with the mean for each other individual (for each variable), and thereby discover that the works of all five individuals could be easily distinguished using these five variables. This can in fact be done using only two of the variables: borderline angle and width of spaces.

Further conclusions resulting from this pilot experiment are as follows:

1. The works of individuals can be distinguished using either interval- or nominal-scale measurements, or both.
2. The kinds of attributes employed are suited to the task—e.g., line and space widths, angles, and the use of space in general.
3. Individual variation in motor performance is unavoidable and probably subconscious (since each individual's performances departed from the template in different and regular ways, even though the subjects were asked to copy it exactly).

It is also significant that four of the individuals were husband and wife (i.e., two married couples). Both couples had been married over 10 years, yet there is no indication that this kind of close association leads to increased similarity in motor performance. All five individuals were distinctively different in this regard.

Realizing that the results of this experiment might be criticized because unskilled artisans were used, and because the materials employed were not prehistoric, I carried out a second pilot study. For this, I used 11 whole ceramic vessels from the prehistoric Rainbow Bridge collection (Beals, Brainerd, and Smith 1945), housed at UCLA. The sample included all the Rainbow Bridge vessels that had hatching designs—that is, designs similar to the one used in the previous experiment. Figure 5.2 shows a drawing of one of these pots. I made the assumption that each pot had been painted by a different individual, which is reasonable given that each had come from a different site.

The surface of each pot was divided into segments the size of a "sherd" (3 cm radius), each segment containing hatched lines. There were 80 such sherds distributed roughly evenly among the 11 pots, and the following attributes were measured on each sherd:

1. Width of hatched lines
2. Ratio of the width of one hatched line to the width of one line and one space, combined
3. Acute angle of the hatched lines with the borderlines
4. Width of the borderlines

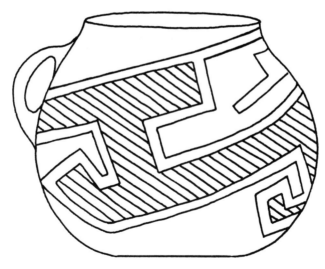

Figure 5.2. Drawing of ceramic vessel from the prehistoric Rainbow Bridge collection.

5. Thickness of the sherd (This has nothing to do with painting, but was thought to be of interest.)

The object, of course, was to see whether or not these attributes would distinguish the pots from one another. As in the previous experiment, the mean for each attribute on each sherd was used in analysis.

The first analysis employed the same analysis of variance test used previously, and the results were similar; the F values were all significant:

F Value	Variable
48.71	Width of borderline
29.69	Width of hatch line
17.59	Thickness of sherd
9.13	Angle of hatch lines
7.43	Ratio of line to line plus space

Thus there were significant differences among the 11 pots in the means for each of the variables.

One problem with this analysis, however, is that it is not multivariate; that is, it does not take account of the interactions among all the variables simultaneously in distinguishing the pots (or potters). A stepwise discriminant function analysis is a technique suited to do this (Afifi and Azen 1972:246–250). This method defines a discriminant function that is a linear combination of all the variables. A sherd is classified as belonging to a particular group (in this case a pot) if its discriminant score for that group is larger than it is for any other group. The analysis requires, of course, that we know ahead of time which sherds belong to which groups; and it also assumes that the data are distributed normally, and that the groups have nearly equal sample sizes.

Simply stated, the discriminant program (BMD07M, Dixon 1970: 214a–214t) required that the computer be told how many pots there were, and which sherds belonged to each pot. The output then showed how the program had classified the sherds with respect to the pots. From this I could see what percentage of the sherds had been misclassified by the computer, or in other words, how well the program was able to discriminate the pots. In the Rainbow Bridge case, 88.8% of the 80 sherds were classified correctly, indicating a high degree of discrimination, and indicating that all five variables were useful. It would have been sufficient to use only two or three of the variables.

Beyond this, the analysis showed the relative importance of the variables in making the discrimination. The program first identifies the variable for which the means among the pots are most different; this is the variable with the highest one-way analysis of variance F value. Then in the following steps additional variables are chosen, in order of decreasing F values (decreasing usefulness for discrimination). The results were as follows:

Step	F Value	Variable
1	48.71	Width of borderline
2	29.34	Width of hatch lines
3	14.42	Thickness of sherd
4	9.35	Ratio of line to line plus space
5	7.88	Angle of hatch lines

These results are almost identical to those derived by the first analysis; this was expected, of course, since the computations involved are essentially the same. It is noteworthy that most of the measurements used were similar to those employed in the earlier 3 × 5 inch card study. Such measurements as line widths, space widths, ratios of these, and angles seem to be useful.

Two important difficulties were raised by this study, however. First, I could not be certain that each pot was painted by a different potter, or that the pots were representative of each potter's work. And second, it is evident that in using prehistoric sherds we generally cannot know ahead of time which sherds were painted by which potter; we will not have "prior groupings" to feed neatly into a discriminant analysis. To resolve these problems, I analyzed a collection of ceramic vessels that had been painted for me in Tijuana, Mexico.

THE TIJUANA POT EXPERIMENT

In Tijuana, two interpreters and I bought 75 unpainted pots. We then selected four design patterns that were already in evidence in the shop, and we had a painter paint these designs on one of the pots (as in Figure 5.3). Using this pot as a template, we asked each of four different painters to copy it exactly on 15 of the pots, and the template painter to copy it on the 14 remaining pots. We wanted the men to think they were all painting exactly the same thing. The template pot was placed in front of the five men so that it could be seen by all, and so that each man could see the pots the others were painting. We observed the event to ensure that each man painted his own pots. Since the men were all using the same types of paint and brushes, and were trying to copy the

Figure 5.3. Tijuana ceramic vessels painted by two different individuals. Note the minute differences in execution. Three of the four design elements were used in the analysis: Element A, vertical hatching on the rim; Element B, "S with staircase" above the flower design; and Element C, "wavy line with dots" below the hatched rim. The flower-and-leaf design was not used in the analysis. Vessel height, 18.6 cm; diameter, 27 cm.

template, I feel that the differences in execution among them were largely subconscious. These differences are exemplified by the two vessels shown in Figure 5.3.

Of the 75 pots painted, 65 of them were large (18.6 cm in height, and 27 cm in diameter), and 10 of them were small (12.5 cm in height, and 21 cm in diameter). Each painter painted 13 large pots and 2 small ones. The importance of this will be considered later.

The pots were taken to UCLA, photographed, and then broken into sherds. Each sherd was marked on the back with its painter, pot, and sherd numbers. Only sherds exhibiting large portions of three of the four design elements were selected for study. Element A was the hatched element around the rim; Element B, the "S with staircase" element above the flower design; and Element C, the "wavy line with dots" element below the hatched rim. The fourth element (flower design) was not used in the analysis.

The sample consisted of 166 sherds, containing a total of 469 elements (cases). Table 5.1 shows the number of design elements of each type, by potter, for both large and small pots. Fewer cases were used in many of the analyses, however, because it was necessary to have roughly equal sample sizes for each of the potters—and it is obvious from Table 5.1 that Potters 2 and 4 had extremely large numbers of cases from the large pots. The actual number of cases used in most of the analyses is shown in Table 5.2.

TABLE 5.1

Number of Design Elements (Cases) of Each Type, by Potter, for Both Large and Small Vessels

Design element	Pot size	Potter					Totals
		1	2	3	4	5	
Element A	Large	22	45	23	30	19	139
(hatching)	Small	3	5	6	6	4	24
Element B	Large	18	41	21	24	19	123
(S/staircase)	Small	2	5	6	4	4	21
Element C	Large	23	44	22	30	19	138
(wave/dot)	Small	3	5	6	6	4	24
Totals	Large	63	130	66	84	57	400
	Small	8	15	18	16	12	69

TABLE 5.2

Actual Number of Design Elements (Cases) of Each Type, by Potter, Used in Most of the Analyses

| Design element | Pot size | Potter | | | | | Totals |
		1	2	3	4	5	
Element A	Large	22	23	23	23	19	110
(hatching)	Small	3	5	6	6	4	24
Element B	Large	15	18	21	19	19	92
(S/staircase)	Small	2	5	6	4	4	21
Element C	Large	23	22	22	22	19	108
(wave/dot)	Small	3	5	6	6	4	24
Totals	Large	60	63	66	64	57	310
	Small	8	15	18	16	12	69

Using calipers and protractor, I measured 14 different variables on the three design elements; these are variable numbers 1, 3, 5, 7, 9–15, 16, 18, and 20 (Table 5.3). Seven additional variables were calculated from these, giving a total of 21 variables; most of these were standard deviations of the original measurements (numbers 1–21, Table 5.3). Fourteen more variables were then derived through transformations, giving a total of 35 variables (numbers 22–35, Table 5.3). Although this was a far larger number of variables than would be needed in working with prehistoric potsherds, my aim was to find out what *kinds* of variables would be best for distinguishing the works of individuals.

The next step was to execute a series of data screening and cleanup procedures, including testing the data for normality using the Shapiro and Wilk W statistic (Shapiro and Wilk 1965). Most of the variables were reasonably normally distributed, though the untransformed and log transformed ones were most normal.

In order to discriminate analytically among the potters, the next procedure was to examine each of the 35 variables with a one-way analysis of variance, as had been done in the pilot studies (Dunn and Clark 1974: Chap. 5). The results for each of the three elements are seen in Table 5.4, where N is the total number of cases used for each test, and n is the number of cases for each of the five potters. For those variables listed above the dashed line, there is less than a 5% chance that the means for the five potters could have come from the same population. For those lines, and the ratios between them. And of the 18 best variables, 13 are

TABLE 5.3

Variables Used in Tijuana Pot Experiment

Number	Name	Description
		Element A (hatching)
1	xbar 1	Mean distance between hatching lines
2	s1	Standard deviation of distance between lines
3	xbar 2	Mean width of line
4	s2	Standard deviation of width of line
5	xbar 3	Shape of line; mean ratio of distance from maximum width of line to bottom, to the total length of the line
6	s3	Standard deviation of xbar 3
7	xbar 4	Mean angle of hatch line with rim
8	s4	Standard deviation of xbar 4
		Element B (S with staircase)
9	xbar 5	Mean height of top part of S
10	xbar 7[a]	Mean width of black vertical line in S
11	xbar 8	Mean width of black horizontal line in S
12	xbar 9	Mean width of white horizontal line in S
13	xbar 10	Mean frequency in black stair-step
14	xbar 11	Mean amplitude in black stair-step
15	overlap	Mean amount lines are overlapped
		Element C (wave with dot)
16	xbar 12	Mean width of black line in wave
17	s12	Standard deviation of xbar 12
18	xbar 13	Mean width of all three lines in wave
19	s13	Standard deviation of xbar 13
20	area	Mean area of dots on sherd
21	ratio	Shape of dot; mean ratio of minimum width to maximum width of dot
		Element A (hatching)
22	log s1	
23	log s2	
24	log s3	
25	log s4	
26	L/L+S	Ratio of width of line to width of line plus distance between lines
27	L/S	Ratio of width of line to distance between lines
28	s1/xbar 1	Coefficient of variation for width of line
29	s2/xbar 2	Coefficient of variation for distance between lines

(continued)

[a] xbar signifies a mean. xbar 6 was omitted, as it was found to be missing on many of the sherds.

TABLE 5.3 (Cont.)

Number	Name	Description
		Element B (S with staircase)
30	x11/x10	Ratio of amplitude to frequency in stair-step
31	x8/x8+x5	Ratio of width of line to width of line plus height of the top part of S
32	x8/x5	Ratio of width of line to height of top part of S
		Element C (wave with dot)
33	s12/x12	Coefficient of variation for black line in wave
34	12/12+13	Ratio of width of black line to width of black line plus height of wave
35	x12/x13	Ratio of width of black line to height of wave

without an asterisk (most of them), the chance is less than 1%. In short, all but two of the variables served to distinguish the potters.

An examination of the F values clearly suggests that the best variables

TABLE 5.4

Analysis of Variance Tests for the Tijuana Pot Experiment, All Five Potters Compared[a]

	Element A		Element B		Element C	
N	110		92		108	
n	22, 23, 23, 23, 19		15, 18, 21, 19, 19		23, 22, 22, 22, 19	
$F.95$	$F (4, 105) = 2.47$		$F (4, 87) = 2.49$		$F (4, 103) = 2.48$	
	F Value	Variable	F Value	Variable	F Value	Variable
	235.65	xbar 4	92.92	xbar 9	46.89	area
	108.02	xbar 1	75.25	11/10	28.34	xbar 13
	84.60	L/L+S	55.04	xbar 10	22.14	ratio
	32.13	xbar 2	50.33	xbar 11	19.72	xbar 12
	31.00	xbar 3	49.95	xbar 7	*4.85	s12
	24.06	L/S	42.48	8/5	*3.95	12/13
$p < .05$	11.54	log s2	38.36	8/(8+5)	*3.86	12/12+13
	11.37	s2	31.45	xbar 5		
	10.89	log s1	19.48	overlap		
	10.73	s1	10.18	xbar 8		
	7.35	s1/xbar 1				
	7.00	log s3				
	6.99	s3				
	*4.31	s2/xbar 2				
	*4.05	s4				
	*3.15	log s4				
$p > .05$					2.05	s13
					.78	s12/x12

[a] Asterisks indicate value of the F statistic is not significant at the .001 level ($p > .001$).

are the angles and distance measures, such as thicknesses and lengths of the originally measured nonderived or transformed variables (Table 5.3). Notice that the less useful variables are the standard deviations of the distance measures and angles, and the coefficients of variation. Log transformations apparently make little difference in the F values, as these values are similar for both the transformed and untransformed variables.

Analysis of variance tests were also used to discover whether or not the variables would distinguish several pots of a given potter from one another. In these analyses a few of the variables did exhibit differences among the pots; but there were few such cases, and the F values were much lower than they were when distinguishing the works of different potters. Most of these F values were not significant at the .05 level. Furthermore, 82% of the variables were not significant at the .001 level; only 23% were not significant at this level when the potters were compared with one another. Thus it is clear that the variables used are much more likely to distinguish the works of potters than to distinguish the individual pots of any single potter.

As in the pilot experiments, however, the analysis of variance does not indicate that the means of the artisans are all different from one another, nor does it handle interactions among the variables. So, as before, a stepwise discriminant analysis was employed (Afifi and Azen 1972: 246–250), to see how the potters would be distinguished using multiple variables (BMD07M, Dixon 1970:214a–214t). Table 5.5 gives information from the BMD07M summary table, showing which variables discriminated the potters best. Elements A, B, and C were analyzed separately, as shown in the upper, middle, and lower sections of the table. For each element, three or four separate analyses were done using somewhat different sets of variables in each; these are shown in the *columns* of the table. The steps in the analyses at which each variable entered, together with the "F to enter" statistic and the variable name, are given in each column. The variables listed in the steps above the horizontal line (step 6, in the first analysis) had significant F values, and were thus most useful in distinguishing among the potters.

A comparison of Tables 5.4 and 5.5 reveals that both the one-way analysis of variance and the discriminant analysis show essentially the same variables to be most important. And again, the best ones tend to be the original angle and distance measures rather than the derived variables.

In addition, an examination of the BMD07M classification tables showed that most of the cases were classified correctly by potter. For example, in the first set of variables for Element A (after step 5 in Table 5.5), only 5 out of 110 cases (4.5%) were misclassified. Similar results obtained for the three other sets of variables used. For Element B, only 3 out of 92 sherds were misclassified, regardless of which of the three

TABLE 5.5

Determining Best Sets of Variables with Stepwise Discriminant Analysis

ELEMENT A

POTTERS 1, 2, 3, 4, & 5 — N = 110; n = 22, 23, 23, 23, 19

Step	F Value	Variable	F Value	Variable	F Value	Variable	F Value	Variable
1.	235.65	xbar 4	235.65	xbar 4	235.65	xbar 4	235.65	xbar 4
2.	102.91	xbar 1	102.91	xbar 1	102.91	xbar 1	102.91	xbar 1
3.	14.61	xbar 2	14.61	xbar 2	27.31	L/L+S	14.61	xbar 2
4.	4.15	s2	4.28	log s2	6.31	xbar 3	4.15	s2
5.	2.92	xbar 3	2.92	xbar 3	4.20	s2	2.92	xbar 3
6.	1.94	s1	1.87	log s3	2.90	xbar 2	1.94	s1
7.	1.92	s3	1.77	log s1	2.16	s1/xbar1	1.92	s3
8.	1.74	s4	1.30	log s4	1.76	s2/xbar2	1.57	L/S

Steps 1–5: $.05 > p$ Steps 6–8: $.05 < p$

POP by Potter ($.05 > p$)

POTS BY POTTER 2 — (1, 2, 3); N = 24; n = 5, 6, 7

Step	F Value	Variable
1.	6.75	xbar 2
2.	7.81	xbar 3

POTS BY POTTER 3 — (4, 7, 8, 12); N = 20; n = 8, 6, 6

Step	F Value	Variable
1.	17.78	L/L+S
2.	4.47	L/S
3.	4.01	xbar 3

POTS BY POTTER 4 — (7, 10, 13); N = 16; n = 5, 5, 6

Step	F Value	Variable
1.	34.74	xbar 4
2.	8.67	xbar 2

POTS BY POTTERS 2, 3 & 4 — N = 60; n = 5, 6, 7, 8, 6, 6, 5, 5, 6

ELEMENT B (continued)

p > .05

Group 1

Step	F Value	Variable
3.	2.67	L/S
4.	2.09	s2
5.	1.48	L/L+S
6.	1.34	s3
7.	1.27	xbar 4
8.	.83	s4
9.	.27	s1/xbar1
10.	.42	s1
11.	.22	xbar 1

Group 2

Step	F Value	Variable
4.	.70	s2
5.	1.12	xbar 2
6.	.48	s3
7.	.30	s4
8.	.14	xbar 1
9.	.59	xbar 4
10.	.02	s1
11.	.42	s1/xbar 1

Group 3

Step	F Value	Variable
3.	3.47	s1/xbar 1
4.	2.74	xbar 3
5.	1.28	s1
6.	1.16	L/S
7.	3.26	s4
8.	.34	L/L+S
9.	4.18	s3
10.	.57	xbar 1
11.	.17	s2

Group 4

Step	F Value	Variable
7.	1.23	s2

POP

POTTERS

1, 2, 3, 4, & 5

N   92

n   15, 18, 21, 19, 19

p < .05

POP

Step	F Value	Variable
1.	92.92	xbar 9
2.	49.89	xbar 11
3.	54.25	xbar 10
4.	31.83	xbar 7
5.	10.09	xbar 5
6.	7.29	overlap
7.	5.43	xbar 8

POTTERS

Step	F Value	Variable
1.	92.92	xbar 9
2.	58.33	11/10
3.	42.33	xbar 7
4.	22.54	xbar 11
5.	14.13	xbar 10
6.	10.86	8/8+5
7.	13.41	xbar 8
8.	7.15	overlap
9.	4.45	xbar 5

POTTERS

Step	F Value	Variable
1.	92.92	xbar 9
2.	58.33	11/10
3.	44.08	8/5
4.	23.58	xbar 11
5.	15.63	xbar 8
6.	16.46	xbar 10
7.	7.45	overlap
8.	6.70	xbar 7
9.	2.61	xbar 5

(continued)

TABLE 5.5 (Cont.)

ELEMENT B (cont.)

POP	POTS BY POTTER 2 (4, 9, 12)			POTS BY POTTER 3 (1, 2, 3)			POTS BY POTTERS 2 & 3		
N	17			20			37		
n	5, 5, 7			8, 6, 6			5, 5, 7, 8, 6, 6		
	Step	F Value	Variable	Step	F Value	Variable	Step	F Value	Variable
$p > .05$	1.	20.24	xbar 7	1.	55.41	xbar 5	1.	79.55	xbar 9
	2.	8.73	xbar 10	2.	32.07	xbar 7	2.	42.28	xbar 5
				3.	8.06	xbar 10	3.	23.36	xbar 7
				4.	6.62	11/10	4.	7.34	xbar 10
				5.	9.57	xbar 11	5.	5.38	11/10
							6.	2.58	8/5
$p < .05$	3.	3.20	xbar 11	6.	.97	xbar 8	7.	1.80	xbar 8
	4.	3.08	xbar 8	7.	1.02	8/5	8.	1.29	xbar 11
	5.	1.36	11/10	8.	.38	xbar 9	9.	1.07	overlap
	6.	.91	xbar 9	9.	.12	overlap			
	7.	.34	overlap						
	8.	.15	xbar 5						
	9.	.01	8/5						

ELEMENT C

POP	POTTERS 1, 2, 3, 4, & 5					
N	108					
n	23, 22, 22, 22, 19					
	Step	F Value	Variable	Step	F Value	Variable
$p > .05$	1.	46.89	area	1.	46.89	area
	2.	12.67	ratio	2.	12.67	ratio
	3.	12.04	xbar 13	3.	12.70	1/13 (mistake)
	4.	3.78	12/12+13	4.	3.11	xbar 12

$p > .05$	5.	1.96	s13	5.	1.95	s13	5.	1.98	s13			
	6.	.48	s12	6.	1.20	xbar 12	6.	1.08	12/13			
				7.	.57	s12/x12	7.	5.64	12/12+13			
				8.	.76	s12	8.	2.10	xbar 13			
POP	POTS BY POTTER 2 (4, 7, 8, 12)			POTS BY POTTER 3 (1, 2, 3)			POTS BY POTTER 4 (7, 10, 13)			POTS BY POTTERS 2, 3 & 4		
N	24			20			16			60		
n	5, 6, 6, 7			8, 6, 6			5, 5, 6			5, 6, 6, 7, 8, 6, 6, 5, 5, 6		
	Step	*F* Value	Variable	Step	*F* Value	Variable	Step	*F* Value	Variable	Step	*F* Value	Variable
$p < .05$	1.	31.22	ratio	1.	26.82	ratio	1.	4.89	ratio	1.	25.93	area
	2.	18.84	xbar 13	2.	4.11	xbar 13				2.	14.54	xbar 13
	3.	5.86	12/12+13							3.	12.70	ratio
	4.	4.67	s13							4.	7.98	xbar 12
										5.	2.32	s13
$p > .05$	5.	1.77	xbar 12	3.	1.22	s12	2.	3.10	s13	6.	2.08	12/13
	6.	1.38	12/13	4.	1.89	12/13	3.	.49	s12	7.	1.41	12/12+13
	7.	.63	area	5.	1.76	xbar 12	4.	2.04	s12/x12	8.	1.59	s12
	8.	.64	s12	6.	.55	area	5.	1.12	xbar 12			
	9.	.34	s12/x12	7.	.44	s13	6.	.64	12/13			
				8.	.06	s12/x12	7.	1.65	12/12+13			
							8.	3.25	xbar 13			
							9.	1.23	area			

sets of variables was used; thus more than 96.7% were correctly classified. For Element C, the results were not as good; the F values were smaller than for Elements A and B; and 40 out of 108 sherds were misclassified after step 4 (37%) for two of the three sets of variables. This was expected, however, since the usefulness of Element C was greatly diminished by the fact that the attributes of the wavy lines in it were often influenced by incised designs that had been placed on the pots prior to firing; the painters tended to be influenced by these lines. Ignoring Element C, then, 96% of the cases were classified correctly with respect to the potter who had painted them!

In discriminant analysis, a good way of determining the success of the discrimination (besides checking the percentage misclassified) is to submit some new cases not used in the discriminant function calculation to see how they are classified. There were 21 sherds from Potter 2 and 7 from Potter 4 that had not been included in the computations. When these were added to the analysis for Element A, 95% of Potter 2's sherds and 100% of Potter 4's sherds were correctly classified. For Element B, *all* the sherds were classified correctly. As expected, the results were not as good for Element C. Overall, there can be no doubt that the variables served to distinguish the works of the different potters.

Moreover, as in the previous study, a series of analyses was carried out to see whether or not it was possible to discriminate individual pots made by single potters. The results showed that this could not be done very well (see Table 5.5); and it must be concluded that the variables used serve to distinguish the works of the different potters rather than individual pots.

As previously suggested, however, there is still a fundamental problem that must be considered. It is the question of how one can discover the numbers of artisans represented in a collection for which this is not known ahead of time. Discriminant function analysis is not, by itself, suited to this task.

The solution was to submit the sample of Tijuana sherds to a cluster analysis technique called Neighborhood Limited Classification or NLC (Oxnard and Neely 1969). This is a cluster analysis on cases, programmed for use by Dwight W. Read of the Department of Anthropology, UCLA. It is especially useful because one need not know the groupings or clusters in the data ahead of time; the analysis discovers them. Furthermore, the data need not be normally distributed, or the intergroup sample sizes equal. NLC treats each case with its n measurements as a point in n-dimensional space, finding associations among cases, then grouping the cases that are most highly associated, step by step. In short, it discovers clusters of sherds that are grouped because they are similar with regard to their several measurements—and the hope is that each cluster represents the sherds of a different potter. In the Tijuana pot study, this could of course be verified.

An example of the NLC output for Element B is shown in Figure 5.4. Each column represents the joining of two sherds. The obvious clusters appear as peaks; the sherds for each are boxed and labeled as to their respective potters. The joining process begins at the top of the sheet and ends at the bottom, where all the sherds are ultimately grouped as a single cluster. Although more should be said about the output, as well as about the mathematics involved, this will suffice for present purposes. I will note, however, that 0,1 transformations of the data worked best as input to the program. Similar results were obtained when using the BMD program P2M (Dixon 1975:323–337), although the mathematics used in the clustering process are different.

The clusters in Figure 5.4 are clear, and each is generally composed of sherds belonging to a specific potter, as expected. But there are 10 clusters instead of the expected 5, and the sherds of a given potter are often separated into two or more of the clusters (see numbers in cluster peaks). Notice, for example, that potter 5's sherds occur in three different clusters. Furthermore, notice that some sherds are not clearly associated with a specific cluster. In some of the analyses, there were even sherds placed in wrong clusters.

A procedure was needed to determine whether or not any of the obvious clusters on the NLC output should be combined, and also to see how the as yet unclassified sherds should be added to the various clusters. The stepwise discriminant analysis program (BMD07M) was useful in these regards, as is described later. Although this analysis requires roughly normally distributed data and nearly equal sample sizes, various studies had already shown that the data met these requirements adequately.

The procedure was to submit the obvious NLC clusters (those boxed in Figure 5.4) to the discriminant analysis program as the required prior groupings. Then, using several passes of the program, it was possible to combine clusters and add the unclustered sherds to them. Only six variables were used for this, since it was important to see how well the clustering procedure would work with fewer variables. For Element B, the variables were xbar 7, 8/5, xbar 9, xbar 10, xbar 11, and 11/10. I cannot give all the details here for how the combining and adding is done, but the combining is made possible by the fact that BMD07M gives an F matrix for Hotelling's T^2 test of $H: \mu_l = \mu_j$. This is done for each pair of clusters.

This is shown in Table 5.6. The obvious NLC clusters are the 10

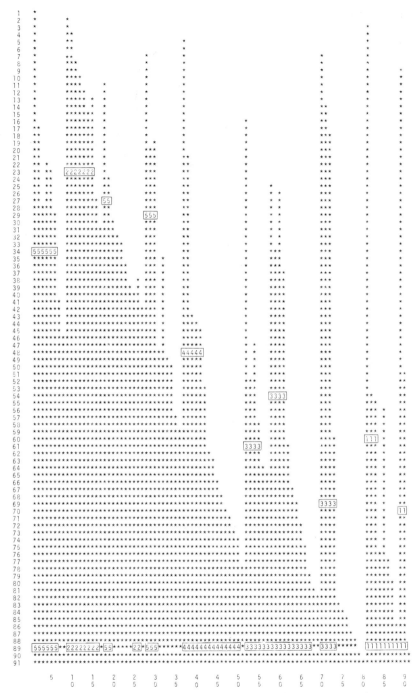

Figure 5.4. Neighborhood Limited Classification output for Element B. The clusters appear as peaks. Each column of stars represents a sherd (case) that is clustered with another case at the steps indicated by the numbers to the left. Case numbers are shown at the bottom. The boxed numbers in the peaks are the cases belonging to specific pot-painters (Potters 1–5); these are the "prior groups" used in later discriminant analysis. The boxed numbers near the bottom indicate the groups as shown by this analysis.

TABLE 5.6

Establishing Sherd Clusters for Each Potter (Element B)[a]

Step 1

Clusters defined by NLC and submitted as groups in BMD07M

1potr1	2potr1	1potr2	1potr3	2potr3	3potr3	1potr4	1potr5	2potr5	3potr5
1 2 3	1 617	2 4 1	3 3 1	3 1 1	3 2 2	4 1 1	5 1 2	5 3 2	5 718
11024	112 7	2 4 3	3 3 2	3 1 2	3 2 3	4 1 2	5 1 3	5 813	5 8 5
111 5	11218	2 411	3 3 3	3 1 3	3 2 4	4 2 1	5 3 1	51130	51126
11122		2 6 6	3 3 5	3 1 5	3 2 5	4 420	5 3 3		513 4
		2 723	3 3 6	3 421	3 2 6	411 3	5 722		
		2 818				41119	5 724		
		21213					510 5		
		21219							

BMD07M pairwise F tests on the above groups

	1potr1	2potr1	1potr2	1potr3	2potr3	3potr3	1potr4	1potr5	2potr5
2potr1	11.71								
1potr2	112.05	84.35							
1potr3	138.90	97.00	65.46						
2potr3	78.48	57.29	51.40	12.49					
3potr3	143.15	99.27	35.15	29.89	29.81				
1potr4	101.95	117.35	148.14	122.04	78.59	153.41			
1potr5	46.57	51.63	49.03	62.71	26.55	77.34	50.87		
2potr5	45.24	41.71	11.32	28.52	14.42	32.05	49.61	4.73	
3potr5	47.91	47.07	22.46	35.94	16.76	45.77	53.46	2.74	.77

Step 2

Groups for BMD07M after step 1

Potr 1	Potr 2	Apotr3	Bpotr3	Apotr4	Bpotr4	Potr 5
*1 2 1	2 4 1	3 1 1	3 2 2	4 1 1	*4 421	*5 1 1
*1 2 2	2 4 3	3 1 2	3 2 3	4 1 2	*4 7 7	5 1 2
1 2 3	2 411	3 1 3	3 2 4	4 2 1	*4 7 9	5 1 3
*1 421	*2 5 2	*3 1 4	3 2 5	4 420	*4 716	5 3 1
1 617	*2 512	3 1 5	3 2 6	411 3	*4 9 2	5 3 2
11024	2 6 6	*3 1 6		41119	*410 2	5 3 2
1 115	2 723	*3 1 7			*411 7	*5 7 1

(continued)

[a] Asterisks indicate sherds not included in the groups used for the discriminant analysis computations in the preceding step, but added at this step because of their high posterior probability and low distance function for being in the group.

TABLE 5.6 (Cont.)

Potr 1	Potr 2	Apotr3	Bpotr3	Apotr4	Bpotr4	Potr 5
11122	2 818	*3 1 8			*41311	5 718
112 7	*212 6	3 3 1				5 722
11218	21213	3 3 2				5 724
	21219	3 3 3				5 8 5
	*21315	3 3 5				5 813
		3 3 6				510 5
		3 421				51126
						51130
						513 4

BMD07M pairwise F tests on the above groups

	Potr 1	Potr 2	Apotr3	Bpotr3	Apotr4	Bpotr4
Potr 2	96.22					
Apotr3	88.75	75.31				
Bpotr3	102.29	43.40	26.31			
Apotr4	50.32	58.01	55.64	76.99		
Bpotr4	86.57	70.57	72.34	85.60	6.74	
Potr 5	56.06	34.04	47.65	64.14	19.51	38.27

groups of sherds represented by their identification numbers at the top of step 1. The first digit of the identification number identifies the potter. The second part of step 1 shows the F matrix from the first run of BMD07M for testing $H: \mu_i = \mu_j$. The boxed numbers are very low, indicating that the groups involved are not very distinct and should be combined. Three of them are lower than the tabled value F .999 (6, 35) = 4.93; the others are simply the smallest values for the pairs of groups involved.

Step 2 shows the number of groups, now reduced from 10 to 6, and shows how the groups were combined. It also shows the previously unclassified sherds that were added to the groups on the basis of the first run of the program. Sherds were added on the basis of having a combination of high posterior probabilities for belonging to a particular group, and low Mahalanobis distance functions (Afifi and Azen 1972); these values are part of the discriminant analysis output. The groups shown in step 2 were used as input for the second run of the program, and the same procedures were carried out again and again, further combining groups and adding more sherds to the groups.

Although I have not illustrated them here, four runs of the program were made in this manner for Element B. It would have been possible to continue until all the groups were combined into a single large cluster containing all the sherds. It was found, however, that the third run pro-

TABLE 5.7

Results of Step Three of the Analysis (Element B)[a]

Clusters defined

1potr	2potr	3potr	4potr	5potr
1 2 1	2 4 1	3 1 1	4 1 1	5 1 1
1 2 2	2 4 3	3 1 2	4 1 2	5 1 2
1 2 3	2 411	3 1 3	4 2 1	5 1 3
1 421	2 5 2	3 1 4	*4 2 2	5 3 1
1 617	*2 5 8	3 1 5	4 418	5 3 2
11024	2 512	3 1 6	4 420	5 3 3
111 5	2 6 6	3 1 7	4 421	*5 3 4
111 6	2 723	3 1 8	4 7 7	5 7 1
11122	2 818	3 2 1	4 7 9	*5 7 8
112 6	*2 918	3 2 2	4 716	5 718
112 7	*212 2	3 2 3	4 9 2	5 722
11218	212 6	3 2 4	410 2	5 724
	21213	3 2 5	411 3	5 8 5
	21219	3 2 6	411 7	5 813
	*21226	3 3 1	411 8	*5 9 6
	21315	3 3 2	41119	510 5
	21331	3 3 3	41311	51126
		3 3 4		51130
		3 3 5		513 4
		3 3 6		*1 5 6
		3 421		*1 6 4
				11219

BMD07M pairwise F tests on the above groups

	1potr	2potr	3potr	4potr
2potr	76.58			
3potr	84.07	68.55		
4potr	91.37	69.88	98.91	
5potr	55.67	21.14	50.31	37.63

[a] Asterisks indicate sherds not included in the groups used for the discriminant analysis computations in the preceding step, but added at this step because of their high posterior probability and low distance function for being in the group.

duced the optimal solution. It is shown in Table 5.7, where we see that there are now five clusters, each representing one of the five potters. And of the 89 sherds now included in groups, only 3 (those by Potter 1 in Potter 5's cluster) are not correct. Eighty-nine of the 92 sherds from the NLC analysis are now clustered into the correct number of potters, with only 3.37% of them in the wrong cluster!

The same kind of combined cluster and discriminant analysis procedure was carried out for Element A. After three runs of the discriminant analysis, 96 of the 110 sherds used were assigned to one of five clusters, and 93.8% of these were clustered correctly. In fact, upon examining the results of the analysis of Elements A and B, it was found that the same sherds classified as belonging to a given potter for Element A were also assigned to the same potter in the Element B analysis. Element C was ignored, for the reason previously given.

It is notable that although six variables were used in these analyses, an examination of the F statistics (Tables 5.4 and 5.5) suggests that good results could have been obtained using as few as three variables.

It was here that an important problem arose. Just how far should one go in continuing to combine clusters by means of the discriminant analysis? Using prehistoric potsherds we cannot simply assume that stopping after the third run will be optimal, yielding the correct number of potters. There are several solutions to this problem that should be used in combination; I shall discuss them only briefly here.

The first solution is to look at the optional canonical plots BMD07M (not illustrated here). The plots give a two-dimensional visualization of how well the clusters are separated from one another at each step. Based on the data used here, one might stop the combining procedure on the particular run of the program that yields the most clear-cut separations of the groups. This may be insufficient in itself, however; the next thing to do is to compare the plots with the NLC clusters to see how well they agree. Experience shows that the best stage to stop the cluster combining is when the two outputs agree most closely with regard to their separation of the clusters. We would not, for example, want to stop the combining at a stage when two or more widely separated and distinct NLC clusters are shown on the canonical plots to be combined as a single cluster (or overlap heavily); this would be carrying the combining procedure too far.

Furthermore, if a study is done on sherds containing two design elements (as this was), one can check where the clusters in both elements are most alike. Simply compare the identification numbers found grouped together for both elements at each step of the discriminant analysis, then pick as the "correct" stage the one where the greatest number of identification numbers for a cluster are grouped together for both elements.

A further method, not relying on having two or more design elements per sherd, was discovered through simulation studies. One can simply observe, as the clustering stages of the discriminant analysis proceed, the relation between the last significant "F to enter" in the BMD07M summary table and the smallest F value found in the F matrix of the corresponding step in the output. When the ratio is less than .90 or .95, the combining of groups should continue; when it is close to 1.0 and then jumps up rapidly, the combining has probably gone too far. This will occur when the final F to enter is no longer significant.

But the final, and currently necessary, test to employ is to examine at each stage the spatial distributions of the clusters in the archaeological site or context being studied to see if they make sense! At the combining stage where the clusters distribute nonrandomly and make sense in terms of their spatial associations with independent archaeological data (such as rooms, room blocks, or other style distributions), the combining procedure should stop. If, for example, a stage in the analysis is reached where each cluster is found in a different area of a site (or in some other intelligible patterned distribution), the combining procedure has probably gone far enough.

I emphasize that the solution to the question of when to terminate cluster collapsing is not easy, and there is as yet no good one-step solution. If one follows as many of the designated procedures as possible, however, and looks for the cluster-combining stage at which there is most agreement among them, the results should be reasonably correct.

The Tijuana pot study, as a whole, has demonstrated not only that the painting of different potters can be distinguished, whether the number of painters is known or unknown, but also that there is a reasonably good set of quantitative techniques for doing it. Furthermore, the kinds of attributes that seem most useful in measuring individual variability have been noted. But there are other interesting results as well.

Perhaps most interesting was the discovery that in all likelihood artisans who are siblings and are taught to paint by the same teacher will share no more similarities in their motor performances than will artisans who are unrelated and taught separately. Three of the Tijuana painters were brothers (Potters 2, 3, and 5). Two of them had been taught to paint by their father (Potters 2 and 5); and they in turn taught their other brother (Potter 3). To test for similarities and differences among all the potters we used Hotelling's T^2 to test $H: \mu_i = \mu_j$ for each pair of potters. (This is a multivariate version of the two-sample t test; see Afifi and Azen 1972:234–235.) The results are shown in Table 5.8, where each pair of potters compared is given, together with the F value for each. The asterisks indicate pairs of potters who are siblings. The smaller the F value for a pair, the more similar the potters are in terms of our measures of motor performance; the larger the F value, the more different the potters.

Even a cursory examination of Table 5.8 reveals that sibling relation-

TABLE 5.8
Pairs of Potters Compared (Hotelling's T² Test)[a][b]

Element A		Element B	
F Value	Potters paired	F Value	Potters paired
22.52	4 5	26.22	4 5
33.96	*2 3	26.65	1 5
35.98	1 2	31.38	*2 5
56.30	1 4	34.10	*3 5
56.79	*2 5	42.71	1 2
79.46	2 4	45.34	1 4
87.89	1 5	49.29	*2 3
90.01	1 3	52.42	2 4
109.92	3 4	54.22	1 3
152.07	*3 5	68.74	3 4

[a] Given in the order of most similar to least similar.
[b] Asterisks indicate siblings.

ship had no influence on motor performance. For Element A, two unrelated potters are most alike (4 and 5), and two brothers (3 and 5) are least alike. And for Element B, both those most and least alike are unrelated.

Notice also that if the context of learning affects similarity in design execution, Potters 2 and 5 should be more alike than pairs of either potter with 1 or 4 or the pair Potter 1–Potter 4. Looking at the F values for all possible pairs, however, there are four pairs that have a smaller F value than that for the Potter 2–Potter 5 pair in Element A, and two pairs having a smaller F value for Element B. It can also be seen that Potter 3, who should be most similar to Potters 2 and 5, is not.

Clearly there is no evidence here to support the hypothesis that either inherited similarities in coordination or shared contexts of learning (or both) account for the similarities and differences among artisans. The finding is not surprising when one considers how formalized and detailed the instruction of handwriting is in schools, and what the resulting differences inevitably are.

I also wanted to find out whether the potters executed their designs differently on the small pots as opposed to the large ones used in the preceding analyses. If so, there might be problems when prehistoric sherds from varying sized pots are used in the cluster and discriminant analysis procedure. To check this, discriminant analysis was used on sherds from both the large and small Tijuana pots, calculating the discriminant functions with sherds from the large pots only; the sherds from the small pots were then entered to see if they would be classified correctly by potter. Many of them were not! For Element A, for example, 12 out of 24 small sherds were misclassified, although Potter 3's sherds were all correctly classified. For Element B, however, only 2 out of 23 sherds were misclassified.

Although additional analyses of a similar nature indicated that pot size might not be as important as suggested, I wanted to see whether sherds from small pots would affect the sherd clusters in the NLC analysis. Using sherds from both large and small pots in the NLC, it was found that the presence of the small sherds had very little effect on the clusters. This suggests that differences in pot size may not be important enough to worry about when examining prehistoric data—but I am not sure. More experiments of this nature should be done; and when using prehistoric data, gross extremes in pot size should certainly be recorded and their behavior examined in the cluster and discriminant analyses.

Finally, it was also possible to demonstrate that greatly unequal sample sizes (i.e., numbers of sherds from each potter) do not affect the NLC clustering results. (This was expected, since NLC does not assume equal sample sizes.)

THE HANDWRITING EXPERIMENT

After completing the aforementioned studies, another major problem became apparent. The experiments had not taken account of the fact that there is some change in a person's motor performances through time. It was suggested to me, in fact, that an artisan's style of painting will change so much during his lifetime that I might easily classify his later sherds as being painted by someone else—particularly if he should paint pots for 20 or 30 years. Although I knew that changes in motor performance do occur, I did not believe the changes are ordinarily anywhere near this drastic; if they are it could virtually destroy any reasonable chance of discovering the numbers of potters in an archaeological context, or of associating sherds (or other artifacts) with individuals. We would almost always err on the side of discovering more artisans than had actually existed. I thus devised an experiment that sheds light on this question; a search of the literature corroborates the results.

Ideally, perhaps the best test would be a detailed study of change in motor performance evidenced in a large collection of pots painted by several different individuals over a span of 30 years or so. This could have been done, as such large collections either exist or can be assembled; but the task of doing so did not seem easy, especially when one bears in mind that the ideal collection should have the *same* design element painted on all pots. I therefore decided to study handwriting instead, on the reasonable assumption that the variability and change exhibited by it is similar to that found in painting on ceramics. In other words, if the motor performances exhibited by individuals in handwriting change significantly through time, we can also be confident that such changes will occur in painting pottery—in fact, they would occur in any medium. Conversely, if there is little change in the handwriting of individuals, we can be sure of the same for pottery painting; the minute details of execution in both represent the motor-performance reflections of deeply ingrained habit. I have found nothing in the literature to contradict this premise, and much in support of it.

The data for the experiment were drawn from collections of personal and business letters written by four late-nineteenth- to mid-twentieth-century British novelists. I selected a total of 21 letters, written (at intervals of about 8 to 10 years) over periods ranging from 20 to 60 years per person. There were between 3 and 7 letters per person (Table 5.9). All the letters were written in longhand, with fountain or dip pen, and all exhibited grossly similar writing styles. The data were obtained from the Special Collections Section, University Research Library, UCLA.

TABLE 5.9

Personal Letters by British Novelists, Divided into Early and Late Periods

	Date of letter	
Author	Early period	Late period
1. Sir Henry Rider Haggard	Feb. 11, 1880 (1) Feb. 11, 1880 (2) Apr. 21, 1894 Jan. 4, 1902 June 2, 1902	Oct. 22, 1915 Apr. 14, 1923
2. Eden Philpotts	Jan. 13, 1891 Dec. 27, 1900 Feb. 11, 1912	Mar. 20, 1921 Mar. 12, 1930 May 9, 1942 Nov. 10, 1951
3. Stanley John Weyman	Sept. 30, 1891 Jan. 5, 1902	Dec. 15, 1912 Nov. 28, 1922
4. George MacDonald	Dec. 15, 1870 Sept. 23, 1878	July 23, 1890

The idea was to test the hypothesis that there would be more similarity in the motor-performance characteristics of each individual through time than there would be between individuals. In other words, I hoped to find that no matter when the individuals had written their letters I would be able to assign the letters to their authors correctly using quantitative methods. If this could be done, it would indicate that we can do the same with potsherds.

Interval-scale measurements were taken on only one design element, which occurred frequently in each of the letters. This was the *th* combination as it begins words written in lowercase. The measurements are indicated in Figure 5.5. Seven of these eight measurements were used as variables in the analysis; measurement number 3 was excluded in order to avoid using nonindependent variables (i.e., number 7 would not have been independent of numbers 3 and 4).

All *th* cases in all the letters were measured, yielding a total of 208 cases—41 for Author 1, 89 for Author 2, 43 for Author 3, and 35 for Author 4. Fewer cases were used in the initial analyses, however, since outliers and many cases having missing values were excluded. I also excluded 49 of Author 2's cases, simply because the statistical analysis employed requires approximately equal sample sizes for each group

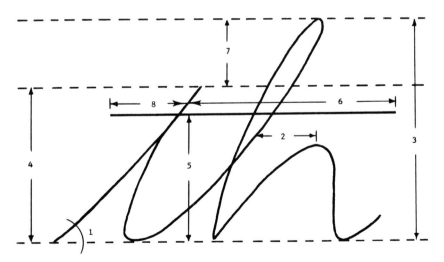

Figure 5.5. Measurements on *th* cases of British novelists: 1, angle of *t*-vertical with the horizontal; 2, distance from *h*-vertical to top of *h*-hump; 3, height of *h*-vertical above horizontal; 4, height of *t*-vertical above horizontal; 5, height of *t*-crossing above horizontal; 6, length of *t*-crossing to *right* of *t*-vertical; 7, difference in heights of *t*- and *h*-verticals (plus or minus); 8, distance from *left* end of *t*-crossing to left or right of *t*-vertical (plus or minus).

(author). This left me with 140 cases—35 for Author 1, 40 for Author 2, 34 for Author 3, and 31 for Author 4.

This sample was used for the first three analyses; I then carried out the same three analyses again using the larger 208-case sample. The stepwise discriminant analysis (BMDP7M, Dixon 1975:411–451) was employed throughout.

In the first set of analyses, the initial analysis involved giving the computer four "prior groupings" of cases corresponding to the four individual writers. This was done simply to see how well the measurements would discriminate the writing styles of these people, using all the data from the entire time span over which the letters had been written. The results were excellent. Using all seven variables the program classified 100% of the *th* cases correctly, by author, for two of the four authors (2 and 3); it classified 86% correctly for Author 1, and 87% for Author 4.

Both the classification table and the *F* statistics from the summary table are given in Table 5.10. All the variables were significant discriminators at the .001 level, although the first five variables to enter were sufficient to classify most of the cases correctly (Table 5.10). Notice that Variable 1 (angle of the *t*) has by far the largest *F* value; this should

TABLE 5.10

Results of Stepwise Discriminant Analysis of the Handwriting of Four British Authors[a][b]

Group	Number of cases classified into group				Percentage correctly classified
	Author 1	Author 2	Author 3	Author 4	
Author 1	30	1*	0	4*	86
Author 2	0	40	0	0	100
Author 3	0	0	34	0	100
Author 4	3*	0	1*	27	87

Step number	Variable entered	F Value (to enter or remove)
1	1	112.05
2	6	76.79
3	4	38.52
4	7	41.72
5	5	15.45
6	8	9.86
7	2	10.09

[a] *Top,* classification table; *bottom,* order of variable entry and *F* statistics.
[b] Asterisks indicate misclassifications.

be expected, since angle measurements were among the best discriminators in all analyses reported in this chapter.

The purpose of the second analysis was to examine intraindividual
change through time. Each author's *th* cases were divided into two
groups, early and late (see Table 5.9). This gave me two groups of samples for each person, or a total of eight groups. These eight groups were
fed into the discriminant analysis to find out whether or not it would
discriminate each author's early and late samples as belonging to the
correct author, and to see whether or not it would discriminate the early
and late groups for each author as being so different from one another
that they might be classified as two different people instead of one.
The same seven variables were used; the number of cases for each group
can be derived from the classification table (Table 5.11).

The results were as expected, and can be seen in Table 5.11. Similar
to the results of the previous analysis, 100% of the cases were classified
correctly with regard to author for Authors 2 and 3; 86% for Author 1,
and 90% for Author 4. An examination of the classification table reveals,
however, that many of the cases were *misclassified* as belonging to an
individual's early period when they actually belonged to the late period,
and vice versa. If we look at only those cases for each author that were

TABLE 5.11

Classification of Cases for Stepwise Discriminant Analysis of Early and Late Period Handwriting[a]

| | Number of cases classified into group | | | | | | | |
| | Author 1 | | Author 2 | | Author 3 | | Author 4 | |
Group	Early	Late	Early	Late	Early	Late	Early	Late
Author 1								
Early	14	1*	1*	1*	0	0	2*	1*
Late	3*	12	0	0	0	0	0	0
Author 2								
Early	0	0	16	4*	0	0	0	0
Late	0	0	5*	15	0	0	0	0
Author 3								
Early	0	0	0	0	15	0	0	0
Late	0	0	0	0	3*	16	0	0
Author 4								
Early	2*	0	0	0	0	0	15	0
Late	0	1*	0	0	0	0	3*	10

[a] Asterisks indicate misclassifications.

classified correctly as belonging to that author (Table 5.11), it is evident that 7% of Author 1's early cases were classified as being late, whereas 20% of his late cases were classified as early. For Author 2 the discrepancies are 20% and 25%; for Author 3 they are 0% and 16%; and for Author 4 they are 0% and 23%. These are telling figures, given that only 5.7% were misclassified as to *author*. They indicate that even though the early and late samples could be discriminated, the discrimination was not as good as it was for the individuals themselves. This suggests that if these *th* samples had been design elements on prehistoric sherds, the cluster and discriminant analysis technique would group them by individual rather than by time period.

Another way to test this further, using the same output, is to examine the Mahalanobis distance (*D*-square) measures for each *th* case. This measure is the square of the distance of a particular case from the centroid of all the cases in a given group, in *n*-dimensional space. In essence, the lower the *D*-square (*D*) for a case, the closer it is to the centroid of the group, and vice versa. This tells us how strongly a given case is associated with a particular group, and how close it is to being classified as belonging to a different group than the one to which it belongs.

In brief, I hoped to discover in this information that for any given case *known* to belong to a particular group (author and time period), the two lowest *D*s for the case would be for its association with *both* the early and late periods for the individual involved—whereas the other *D*s for the case would be higher (thus showing the case to be a long distance away in terms of similarity from the centroids of any of the other groups). This is largely what happened. Out of 140 cases, 113 met this expectation (80%); 27 cases did not.

When these statistics are broken down, however, a somewhat different picture emerges. Although 100% of the cases for Authors 2 and 3 met the expectation, only 57% of Author 1's cases and 61% of Author 4's cases met it. This suggests that in a cluster analysis, as would be performed with prehistoric sherds, many of the cases belonging to Authors 1 and 4 might be clustered with the wrong person.

I doubt that this would happen, however, because the discriminant analysis classified 86% of Author 1's cases as belonging to Author 1; it classified 90% of Author 4's cases as belonging to Author 4. This was because the *D*-squares for all these cases were smallest for belonging to these persons. It is clear that the program discriminated the works by individual much more strongly than it discriminated the works from different time periods within each individual's total period of writing.

In the third analysis in the initial set of discriminant analyses, I used a somewaht different approach. Only the individuals' *early* cases were used in calculating the discriminant functions (i.e., four prior group-ings); the idea was to see to what degree the program would classify the late cases as belonging to these groups. If most of each individual's late cases were classified with his early cases (rather than with those of another individual), we would have strong support indeed for my "little change" hypothesis. The result was that 100% of the late cases for Authors 1, 2, and 3 were classified correctly! For Author 4, unfortu-nately, only 43% were so classified; the other 57% were classified as belonging to Author 1.

I take these results as strong support for the hypothesis, however, since weak results for Author 4 were not unexpected. This individual complicated matters by having two different ways of crossing his t's, in addition to often not crossing them at all (thus necessitating missing-value replacements in the data). I doubt that there is a very high per-centage of mature individuals having motor performances as erratic as Author 4's. Given this problem, it is remarkable that so many of his cases were classified correctly in the other analyses (87–90%). The over-all results suggest that even when there is a great deal of normal varia-tion in an individual's performances, his works are probably still gen-erally identifiable.

These results may be criticized, however, because in the initial data screening and cleanup procedures I deleted outlying cases *by individual*, and reduced the sample size for Author 2. In using prehistoric potsherds one obviously would not be able to delete cases in this manner, since case groupings by individual would be unknown. Having made such nonrandom deletions in the present analyses, I recognized the possibility that this might result in improving the interindividual discriminations beyond what might be possible with prehistoric material. Though it may be true that one can make these kinds of deletions after performing a cluster analysis on prehistoric data (and deriving clusters regarded ten-tatively as belonging to different individuals), I could not be sure of how well such a procedure would work. Therefore, to be conservative, I wanted to find out what would happen in the handwriting analysis if no outliers were removed, and nothing was done to equalize sample sizes. I thus carried out a second set of three discriminant analyses, the same as before, but using all 208 cases.

Surprisingly, the results were virtually unchanged. In the first run of the program I used four prior groups corresponding to the four authors, and found that it classified 82% of the cases correctly for Author 1, 98% for Author 2, 100% for Author 3, and 89% for Author 4.

In the second analysis, using eight groups corresponding to the authors' early and late periods, the percentages classified correctly by writer were 85, 98, 100, and 91. Moreover, although most of the cases were classified correctly by *author*, many were misclassified with regard to each author's early and late periods. Of Author 1's early cases, 5% were classified as being late; 20% of his late cases were classified as early. For Author 2 the discrepancies were 16% and 12%; for Author 3 they were 11% and 25%; and for Author 4 they were 0% and 23%. At the same time, only 5% were misclassified as to author. Furthermore, an examination of the Mahalanobis distances revealed that in 165 out of 208 cases, the two lowest Ds for the cases indicated that these cases would necessarily be classified correctly as to author, regardless of the time periods in which they had been written (79% of the cases).

In the third analysis, using only the four early groups in calculating the discriminant functions, the results were equally good. All the late cases for Authors 1 and 3 were classified as early cases for these authors; the figures for Authors 2 and 4 were 98% and 43% respectively. Again this provides a strong positive test for my hypothesis, though again the results are slightly flawed by the erraticism of Author 4.

One final test was supplied by examining the F matrices of all four of the eight-group discriminant analyses discussed here. It is evident from this that if one begins with eight groups and tries to collapse them into fewer groups, the first groups to be combined would be the early and late groups for each individual—*not* groups representing different individuals. This is indicated by the fact that the smallest F values occur for the group-pairs that represent each individual's early and late cases (see the earlier discussion of cluster collapsing). This means, of course, that one would not confuse these individuals' early or late cases as belonging to the wrong person.

I conclude, therefore, that even though individual motor performances do change somewhat through time, the amount of change involved is unlikely to be enough to prevent identifying the works of individuals. This is supported in two different sets of analyses—one using a small refined sample, the other using a large unrefined sample with greatly unequal sample sizes. The two sets of results are nearly identical. If my conclusion holds true for prehistoric pots, as it should, we should have little difficulty distinguishing the pots or sherds of given individuals regardless of the span of time over which they were manufactured.

In talking with two police suspect-document examiners, this conclusion was corroborated. Both Sergeant George Hahn and Sergeant Frankie E. Franck (Los Angeles Police Department) informed me that for most persons handwriting becomes quite stable after adolescence and does not change significantly until the individual is beset by the infirmities of old age. There is usually some change, but ordinarily not enough to interfere with the correct identification of handwriting. This is also repeatedly confirmed by what is perhaps the leading published guide for suspect-document examiners (Harrison 1958). Harrison says that some change often occurs during periods of illness, stress, fatigue, and so on, but such change is usually more in the general appearance of the writing (or printing) than in the fundamentals ("master pattern") of the manner in which it is executed. Such change is called "natural variation," and does not usually interfere with handwriting identification unless the person is extremely or terminally ill and has lost most of his muscle control (Harrison 1958:297–307, 407–412). (This stability in motor performance is by no means restricted to handwriting; see Cratty 1973; Jones 1949.)

I have, moreover, been led to believe by the sources just mentioned, that relative stability in writing can occur prior to adolescence. The primary reason it usually does not do so is that people in our Western world today do not begin to use their handwriting as a consistent and necessary tool in the serious business of living until after adolescence, so it is then that they begin to settle into a characteristic master pattern (see Harrison 1958:296). It would appear that in societies where certain tasks (such as pottery making) are learned and necessarily regularly practiced at an earlier age, we can expect stability in motor performance to occur much earlier.

Beyond the fact that every individual is in many respects unique in the execution of his handwriting (1958:305–308, 341–342), Harrison points to several other things relevant to my research. First, handwriting is largely subconscious (1958:290–291, 367), such that the essential motor-performance characteristics of a person cannot be taught to others (1958: 295, 305–307). In fact, a person's handwriting cannot even be copied accurately, regardless of whether or not tracings or other techniques are used (1958:361–365). What is more, a person usually cannot even consciously alter or disguise his *own* handwriting to the degree that it would not be recognized as his (1958:290–291, 334, 371–372), even if he uses the other hand (1958:376). And all this is generally true regardless of the types of writing tools and inks used (1958:332; see also Hofsommer *et al.* 1965:14–24), regardless of the speed or carelessness of the writing, and regardless of just about any other condition (1958:301–303). I believe these things are equally true of the motor performances exhibited in pottery painting, or anything else for that matter.

A further interesting finding is that the more expert a writer is, the less variability is exhibited in his motor performances, and thus the easier it is to distinguish his work from that of others (Harrison 1958:357, 360, 374–375, 414). This was certainly true in the Tijuana pot study, where the most expert painter not only had a very narrow range of variability, but also executed his work more quickly than the others. Therefore, since I presume that most prehistoric artisans were experts at their crafts (if they made and left behind many artifacts), it follows that it should be reasonably easy to distinguish their work.

Finally, it is worth noting that the attributes I have used to distinguish the products of individuals throughout this research are identical to the most important attributes used by suspect-document examiners, even though the examiners ordinarily employ more intuitive procedures than used here. These attributes are such things as angles (including slope), line widths and lengths, spacing (and use of space), and ratios of various kinds—although the police measure these as discrete or unique characteristics, much as I did in the pilot 3 × 5 card experiment (Harrison 1958:293–341). I thus conclude that the attributes I am measuring are of the right order.

THE COYOTE CREEK SITE

The next logical step in this research is to employ data from an archaeological site, in an effort to distinguish the works of potters and use the results in an analysis of various aspects of social organization. I have decided to use data from a site in Arizona. Unfortunately this research is not yet completed, but it is important to make some statements about it here, so that the reader may understand how it is being done, as well as some of the difficulties involved in using prehistoric data in any such effort.

I must emphasize my belief that this discussion is applicable to doing this kind of analysis in sites virtually anywhere in the world, so long as the sites contain commonly occurring artifacts that exhibit style variability. I am using Southwest data here only in an effort to provide a concrete example of wrestling with the kinds of problems that will be involved using prehistoric data anywhere. Thus, although my discussion is cast in terms of sherds, pueblo rooms, and so forth, the reader should be able to translate the discussion into terms suitable to his own data. One does not need sites with architecture and pottery; the research can be done using grid areas in nonarchitectural sites, and employing many kinds of nonceramic artifacts (possibly even lithics; see Chapter 9 by Gunn in this volume). By the same token, it should be easy to see that this discussion applies to intersite analyses, where one might be comparing entire sites instead of rooms or grid squares. I have chosen to cast the discussion in concrete terms, rather than making it more obviously general, simply because abstract discussions seem less convincing to me.

In this way, it will be clear that my ideas stem from real experience in the world of archaeological data.

The site is Coyote Creek Pueblo, a thirteenth-century pueblo in eastern Arizona (DeGarmo 1975). It is a rectangular block of 29 rooms, the major portion of which was probably not occupied more than 40 years. DeGarmo has excellent evidence showing that these rooms belonged to two major residence units (in the north and south halves of the site), with a separate task area between them. I hope to isolate the works of individual pot-painters, plot their distributions in the site, and discover that these distributions make sense in terms of the residence units—or at least that they occur in nonrandom spatial patterns, thus supporting my contention of having isolated the works of individuals.

I decided to study the most common and widely distributed design element in the site (Figure 5.6). There are 145 cases of it, and it occurs in all the rooms. Interval-scale measurements have been taken on all the cases (Table 5.12). I will submit these cases to factor-analytic techniques (following Christenson and Read 1977), in an effort to reduce redundancy among the variables and create new variables, or factors, which can then be input into cluster and discriminant analyses as was done with the Tijuana pot data. I will also use the same procedures, but without the factor analysis, in order to compare the results.

There is already some indication that the results will be successful. A discriminant analysis has shown that DeGarmo's two residence units can be discriminated as distinct clusters of motor-performance characteristics. This not only supports the existence of the proposed units, but also suggests that each unit had its own potters. These results are insufficient for my purposes, however, since my goal is to discover how *many* potters there were.

After discovering sherd clusters that purportedly represent each of these potters, it will be necessary to carry out independent analyses to

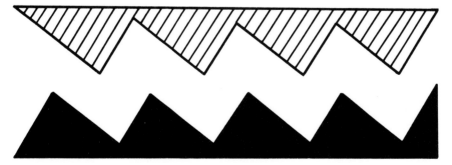

Figure 5.6.   Design element 35, Coyote Creek Pueblo.

TABLE 5.12

Variables Measured on Coyote Creek Site Design Element[a]

Number	Name	Description
1	LINEW	Width of hatching lines
2	SPACEW	Width of spaces between hatching lines
3	HEIGHTB	Distance from base to apex of black triangles
4	HEIGHTH	Distance from base to apex of hatched triangles
5	V-POINTB	Distance from convergence point of black triangles to base of triangles
6	V-POINTH	Distance from convergence point of hatched triangles to base of triangles
7	WIDTHLF	Width of left-hand borderlines of hatched triangles
8	WIDTHRT	Width of right-hand borderlines of hatched triangles
9	EXT-HB	Distance of extension of left borderlines of hatched triangles to contact with black triangles
10	EXT-BH	Distance of extension of left borderlines of black triangles to contact with hatched triangles
11	WIDTHBAS	Width of baselines of hatched triangles (top horizontal line in Figure 5.6)
12	H-APEX	Angle of apex of hatched triangles
13	H-LARGE	Angle of the largest of the two angles of the hatched triangles (other than the apex angle)
14	H-SMALL	Angle of the smallest of the two angles of the hatched triangles (other than the apex angle)
15	H-RATIO	Ratio of smallest to largest angle in hatched triangles (other than the apex angle)
16	H-VANGL	Angle formed by convergence of two hatched triangles
17	B-APEX	Angle of apex of black triangles
18	B-LARGE	Angle of largest of the two angles of the black triangles (other than the apex angle)
19	B-SMALL	Angle of the smallest of the two angles of the black triangles (other than the apex angle)
20	B-RATIO	Ratio of smallest to largest angle in black triangles (other than the apex angle)
21	B-VANGL	Angle formed by convergence of two black triangles
22	RAT-LLS	Ratio of width of hatched line to width of line plus space

[a] Means to be used in analysis.

test the idea that these clusters do in fact represent the works of different individuals. There are several ways to do this. One way is to redo the analysis using only the large sherds that have at least two design elements on them. If each of these elements is analyzed separately, and I find that both elements on the same sherd fall into the same clusters, I will have good evidence for real individuals.

A second method is simply to analyze two or more different elements, not necessarily on the same sherds, to see if the resulting clusters for each distribute in congruent spatial patterns in the site.

A third approach, using only the element already chosen, is to look for discrete or nominal-scale attributes of painting technique that are so peculiar that they can be argued as being unique to specific individuals. These could be such things as blobs on lines only in specific locations, lines that consistently overlap, lines that curve on one end, and so on. If even one such idiosyncratic characteristic occurs solely on sherds belonging to a single one of the clusters previously discovered using interval-scale measurements, it will strongly support the idea that all the clusters so derived represent the works of different individuals.

A fourth method is to measure some attributes on the sherds other than those involving painting technique—such things as sherd thickness, type of paste or temper, or attributes of firing. If such attributes as these take on different ranges of values each of which is associated with one or another of the previously derived clusters, it would provide good corroborative evidence that the previous clusters are meaningful in terms of individual variability.

A fifth way is to examine the motor-performance characteristics exhibited by artifacts other than ceramics, in the hope of finding that each of the style clusters derived from analyzing them will distribute spatially within the site in nonrandom patterns congruent with the distributions of the different ceramic clusters.

I also hope to find that each sherd cluster purporting to represent the works of an individual is distributed only in rooms or areas that can be shown to have been occupied nearly contemporaneously. Individual potters ordinarily do not make pottery for more than 20 or 30 years. Thus if one of the ceramic clusters was found distributed in rooms of greatly different ages, it would suggest that the cluster does not represent the work of a single individual (unless one can demonstrate that statistically significant numbers of vessels were kept for many years as heirlooms). The existence of significant numbers of heirlooms seems unlikely in practice, since pots usually do not have life spans of more than 5 or 6 years (Bunzel 1972:63). This test cannot be carried out at the Coyote Creek site, of course, since its entire length of occupation was very short.

A final test, though a very time-consuming one, would be to lump together collections of a single design element from two or more different contemporaneous villages that are more than a day's walk distant from one another. The idea would be to treat this as a single collection, isolating the motor-performance clusters purporting to represent potters, and then examining their intra- and intersite distributions. One would ordinarily expect any given cluster to be found in only one of the villages. If even one or two clusters were found in more than one village, one would strongly suspect that perhaps none of the clusters represented individuals—especially if the villages used were unlikely to have been involved in intervillage trade or population movement.

There are almost certainly other means for ensuring that we are isolating the works of individuals. These examples should show that it is not necessary to rely on guesswork, personal opinion, or ethnographic analogy to test for the correctness of results using prehistoric data.

There are some difficulties that can be encountered in using prehistoric data in this kind of analysis, however. They are as follows:

1. Sample sizes may be small. One probably needs at least 50 sherds of each design element (preferably 80 or more) simply to use the analytical procedures I have described. These figures are based on my experience with the other analyses reported here; it would be useful to experiment further in this regard.
2. One must hope that each potter painted at least 8 or 10 of the sherds used in analysis. Also each sherd must have precisely the same design element on it (see Harrison 1958:301, 356, 434, 445).
3. A given design element may occur in a localized area of a site or locality. One must use only an element that is widely distributed throughout the site or locality, in the hope that it is common enough to have been painted by all the potters present. If some of the potters never painted the design, one cannot expect to discover the number of prehistoric potters that existed. Still, if one selects an element that is extremely common, errors resulting should probably be minimal. My feeling is that, in pueblo sites at least, there are some elements painted by all the potters—hatching and triangles, for example, are ubiquitous at Coyote Creek and in the surrounding area. I suspect that in most areas of the world one can find design elements (whether on painted ceramics or not) that are equally common. Even if one can only identify the works of some or most of the artisans in a site, however, it is still feasible to use the results in a number of analyses of prehistoric social organization (see under Usefulness, earlier in this chapter). Studies of craft specialization would be most seriously affected by this problem.
4. Sherds are often so fragmentary or deteriorated that many of the desired measurements cannot be taken; this can force a further reduction in sample size and/or the use of regression replacements

or averages for the missing values. These solutions should be employed sparingly.

5. Sherd curvatures can make measurement difficult, especially for angle measurements. One solution is to make slide photographs of the sherds so that they can be projected on a flat surface for measuring. This also facilitates measurement by blowing up the size of the design.

6. Measurement is time consuming, even though, as previously suggested, fewer attributes need be measured than I have measured for the analyses reported here. It is important to explore optical Fourier analysis and other photometric means to simplify the measuring procedure. One of the most individually distinctive attributes is probably wavyness or "messiness" of painted lines, and I have found no easy way to measure this.

A final difficulty that might be encountered is that all or most of the pots in a site may on occasion have been imported from elsewhere. Although this may be rare, it could confound the analysis. The derived clusters might indeed represent the works of individual potters, but not the potters who had occupied the site. If this could be demonstrated, of course, it would provide an interesting measure of the numbers of individuals who had been trade sources; this would be useful in describing the complexity of the exchange network.

CONCLUSIONS

The experiments reported here are contributions to the development of a novel methodological approach to describing aspects of prehistoric social organization. The results should also be useful in the development of a theory of style. The basic idea is that by identifying the artifacts made by specific individuals in prehistoric contexts, one can plot the spatial and temporal distributions of the artifacts, and thereby derive accurate descriptions of variability and change in various aspects of social organization (see under Usefulness, earlier in this chapter).

My primary task has been to demonstrate, using experimental data, that it is indeed possible to isolate the works of individuals, and that it is feasible to do so using collections in which the numbers of artisans represented are either known or unknown ahead of time. There is no doubt that the variables used measure real individual variation; the clusters derived thus represent the works of individuals rather than analytical individuals or small groups of some kind (see Chapter 4 by Redman in this volume).

The results were equally good using four diverse data sets—3 × 5 cards painted by contemporary residents of Los Angeles, prehistoric ceramics from northern Arizona, ceramic vessels from Tijuana, Mexico, and personal letters written by nineteenth-century British novelists. I thus conclude that the approach is applicable cross-culturally and is not limited by space–time boundaries. It should work with any data exhibiting style variability, so long as these data meet the requirements set forth.

One of the most important contributions of this research is the elucidation of the kinds of attributes likely to be most sensitive to measuring individual variation in ceramic painting styles. The results indicate that the most sensitive variables are similar to those used by police suspect-document examiners (Harrison 1958:293–341). They include (1) the *angles* at which parts of a design come together; (2) various *distance* measures, including line thickness (width), distances between lines (and ratios of these), the *relative* heights or lengths of portions of a design, and the frequency and amplitude of repeated portions of a design; and (3) the *areas* and *shapes* of portions of a design, including lines as well as other figures; length–width ratios are significant as measures of shape. In general, variability in the use of space is significant.

The least sensitive variables were absolute lengths of portions of a design.

I must add here my belief that attributes of the same general nature as used in these experiments will also be useful in isolating individual motor-performance variability in *all* materials, not just ceramics. They are evidently among the primary or fundamental attributes of motor-performance variation, regardless of the nature of the motor performance involved. The attributes of angle, distance, and use of space in general vary among individuals in all tasks performed, from tying shoelaces to driving an automobile. Although kinesiologists are aware of additional motor-performance characteristics, those mentioned may be the most easily measurable when dealing with artifacts.

It is also notable that the variables found to be most useful probably do *not* represent either intra- or extraindividual variation. Intraindividual variation was ruled out in the Tijuana pot experiment, where it was demonstrated that pots painted by single individuals could not be easily distinguished from one another using these variables—whereas the pots of the different painters could be easily discriminated. Extraindividual variation was ruled out in the same experiment, since it was shown to be unlikely that either shared heredity or environment (including learning environment) can lead to significant interindividual similarity in the execution of the variables measured. This last conclusion is further supported by the results of the 3 × 5 card experiment. It thus seems evident that the kinds of variation I have measured are subconscious and largely unsharable and unteachable among individuals. Most aspects of subconscious motor-performance are peculiar to individuals, even when several individuals are trying to produce exact copies of a template—and the literature supports this conclusion (Bunzel 1972:64–66; Harrison 1958:290–295, 305–307, 334, 361–367).

A further conclusion, based on the handwriting study, is that individual motor performances change so little over time that one is unlikely to confuse a person's early and late performances as representing two or more different people. This is significant since any other finding in this regard would cast serious doubt on the likelihood of ever discovering in archaeological contexts groups of artifacts manufactured by single individuals. The literature supports my finding here as well (Cratty 1973; Harrison 1958:296–307, 407–412; Jones 1949).

There are, of course, several things that can cause short-term modifications in an individual's motor performances, but these things are probably too minor to interfere with distinguishing the individual's work from those of others. It is probably true, for example, that an artisan's motor performances will be affected to some degree by differences in the kinds of materials and tools he uses (see Chapter 6 by Hardin in this volume); but there is strong evidence that these effects are minor (Harrison 1958:332; Hofsommer *et al.* 1965:14–24). Even changes in the *sizes* of executed designs seem to have no great effect on motor-performance characteristics.

The effects of alterations in speed or of carelessness of execution are also minimal, and would not confound this kind of analysis (Harrison 1958:301–303). Bunzel (1972:65–66) points out that even when a potter makes mistakes in painting, her works are nonetheless readily distinguishable.

Even during periods of fatigue, illness, or stress, the fundamentals (or master pattern) of motor performance are usually not greatly affected. Although the general appearance of the product may change somewhat, the kinds of motor-performance characteristics I am measuring do not, because they are too deeply ingrained (Harrison 1958:297–307, 407–412). This is, in fact, why it is relatively easy to discover and measure individual variability. None of the kinds of natural variation considered here can affect a person's master pattern appreciably (Harrison 1958:301–303).

This means, of course, that attributes of individual variation are probably the easiest aspects of style to which to assign meaning. They are referable only to individual peculiarity, since they are rooted in the physiology and psychology of the individual. Others aspects of style—the conscious ones—are more difficult to assign meaning to because there are so many different meanings that humans can assign to them arbitrarily; they are aspects of human symboling, much as are linguistic symbols. If this study can contribute anything to a theory of style, it is in showing what individual variability looks like, and in distinguishing it from other aspects of style.

Beyond the substantive contributions, there are some contributions that can be classified as technical in nature. The most important is the presentation of the combined (serial) use of cluster and discriminant analyses to isolate clusters of cases, to collapse clusters, and to add unclustered cases to the clusters. This is the technique that permits discovering the number of individuals represented in a collection of items when this is not known *a priori*. The technique, including the all-important procedures for knowing when to stop the cluster collapsing, was developed by Mary Ann Hill specifically for this study (see under Acknowledgments). The interesting idea of using factor analysis prior to cluster analysis to reduce redundancy among the variables and create better ones was suggested by Dwight W. Read (see under Acknowledgments). Although it is possible that this combination of analytic techniques is not new, I am not aware of its previous usage. In any event it is important, especially since it should be found useful in discovering attribute clusters in *any* data set where interval-scale measurement is employed. The significance of this in terms of discovering artifact types is obvious.

A further technical contribution is the discovery that the works of individuals can be distinguished using very few attributes (variables); all four of my experiments indicate that between two and four attributes will usually be sufficient. If so, this will greatly reduce the measuring effort involved, thus helping to make this kind of research more practical in terms of research time. I would think, however, that the number of variables would have to be increased somewhat as the presumed number of craftsmen to be distinguished increases.

Another discovery, a rather surprising one, is that the means of most of the variables were more significant than either the standard deviations or transformations (see especially Tables 5.4 and 5.5). I do not understand why this is so, since I had thought that the standard deviations would have worked best in isolating interindividual variation.

I also discovered that both nominal and interval scales of measurement can be used successfully in research of this nature. Although most of the experiments employed the latter, the 3 × 5 card study used the former as well. My feeling is that nominal measurement will be found most suitable in the long run, since nominal attributes are often *peculiar* to the works of individuals; they are clear and unequivocal marks of individuality. They are also easy to measure. Moreover, the works of any given individual might often be recognized by only a single such attribute! Art historians and suspect-document examiners have found nominal-scale measurement useful, although they have given little or no consideration to other scales as yet.

I think that in some instances it will simplify the measuring process to use ordinal measurement. For example, if one has fewer than 200 cases of a given attribute to compare (say line width), one can simply line up all the cases on a table in order from the lowest to highest values and use the *rank* values as input into the analyses.

Although the results of this research are thus far gratifying, they must be considered preliminary. Some important research still must be done:

1. There should be further experimentation isolating the works of individuals in controlled situations where the individuals involved are known. We must learn more about the nature of the attributes that can be ascribed to individual performance (as distinguished from intra- and extraindividual variation). If we can establish a reliable relationship between specific kinds of variation and individual motor performance, we can then simply *apply* the results to prehistoric data without using independent archaeological data to test the relationship itself.

2. We must devise further experiments to learn more about the effects of heredity and learning environment on motor performance.

3. Additional experimentation is needed to test my conclusion that changes through time in individual motor performance are small, and of minimal importance in this kind of research. The effects of extreme youth and old age on motor performance should also be examined.

4. There is need for further testing of the effects on motor performance of the tools and materials used in craft production, as well as the effects of variations in speed, carelessness, fatigue, illness, and the like.

5. As previously indicated, it would be useful to find a quick and easy way to measure motor-performance variables.
6. The quantitative techniques employed to discover variable clusters can probably be improved.
7. All the problems listed on pages 98–99 should be given further consideration.

All in all, however, the results of these experiments have been remarkably good.

In closing, I want to suggest that the kind of research reported here may lead to two interesting and useful extensions. The first of these is the likelihood that in addition to isolating the works of *individuals*, we can use a similar general approach for identifying the products of *machines* or manufacturing equipment of any kind. This can in fact be done, since all such machines produce minute differences in their products, even when they are producing the same products (see Harrison 1958:242–287). This is true of both simple machines like the potter's wheel, and complex machines like the typewriter or printing press. Although we would not be dealing with individuals, motor performances, subconscious attributes, and so forth, it is nonetheless evident that we can identify the "manufacturers" of craft products regardless of how they were made. This means, of course, that similar kinds of analyses can be done in complex societies where many artifacts may be made by machine or other nonhuman equipment. One can also identify the products of different craft guilds or workshops, since different workshops presumably employ different machines or equipment *and* individuals (see Johnson 1973:27–28, 90, 92, 107, 113).

My second, though more tenuous, suggested extension of the research is that it may ultimately lead to the serious study of paleophysiology and/or paleopsychology. There is clear indication that changes occur in the motor performances of individuals under physiological and psychological stress. As already indicated, however, these changes are (for given individuals) usually short-term changes in response to short-term stress (natural variation). But there is also support for the idea that in the relatively rare instances in which stress or trauma is long term and continuous, the resultant changes in motor performance may also be long term (i.e., no return to normal). (See Bell 1948:291; Gottschalk 1973; Harrison 1958:407; Kanfer and Casten 1958:1–19; Myers 1963: 151; Steinert 1975:6–8.) If this is so, then we may find that where entire prehistoric populations have been subjected to long-term stress, there is a concomitant long-term change in the average motor performances for such populations. That is, more artisans may exhibit the symptoms of deteriorated motor performance more of the time—and this could be reflected in the archaeological record by such things as more mistakes in execution, shakiness or sloppiness of execution, and so on. If this proposition is correct, we may be able to develop quantitative measures that will allow us to measure spatial and temporal variability in the physiological and psychological states of prehistoric populations, and relate these states to environmental causes. I am attempting research akin to this myself.

ACKNOWLEDGMENTS

I am grateful for the assistance of numerous UCLA students, especially Cheryl Acker, Karen Canfield, Michael Carmona, Gelya Frank, Mary Ann Hill, Denise Knopp, Sheree Levin, Janet D. Orcutt, Mathilda Schulte, Louis J. Tartaglia, and W. Nicholas Trierweiler. Statistical and computational advice were given by Mary Ann Hill (Department of Biomathematics, UCLA) and Dwight W. Read (Department of Anthropology, UCLA). Mary Ann Hill did the statistical work for the Tijuana ceramic study; Cheryl Acker did much of the Rainbow Bridge ceramic study; and W. Nicholas Trierweiler performed much of the analysis of handwriting. Timothy K. Earle (Department of Anthropology, UCLA) provided useful ideas and editorial suggestions. An earlier and less complete version of this chapter was presented at the Thirty-eighth Annual Meeting of the Society for American Archaeology, in Miami Beach, Florida (1972).

REFERENCES

Afifi, A. A., and S. P. Azen
    1972   *Statistical analysis: A computer oriented approach*. New York: Academic Press.
Allport, G. W., and P. E. Vernon
    1933   *Studies in expressive movements*. New York: Macmillan.
Beals, Ralph L., G. W. Brainerd, and Watson Smith
    1945   Archaeological studies in northeast Arizona. *Publications in American Archaeology and Ethnology* **44** (1). Berkeley: University of California Press.
Bell, John E.
    1948   *Projective techniques: A dynamic approach to the study of personality*. New York: Longmans, Green.
Berenson, Bernhard
    1962   *Rudiments of connoisseurship: Study and criticism of Italian art*. New York: Schocken Books. (Published in 1902 as *The study and criticism of Italian art*. Second series. New York: Schocken Books.)
Brownlee, K. A.
    1965   *Statistical theory and methodology in science and engineering*. 2nd ed. New York: Wiley.

Bunker, Milton
1963   *Handwriting analysis.* Chicago: Nelson Hall.
Bunzel, Ruth L.
1972   *The Pueblo potter: A study of creative imagination in primitive art.*
New York: Dover. (Originally published, 1929.)
Christenson, A. L., and D. Read
1977   Numerical taxonomy, R-mode factor analysis, and archaeological classification. *American Antiquity* 42:163–179.
Cratty, Bryant J.
1973   *Movement behavior and motor learning.* Philadelphia: Lea and Feb-
iger.
Deetz, James
1967   *Invitation to archaeology.* Garden City, New York: Natural History
Press.
DeGarmo, Glen D.
1975   Coyote Creek Site 01: A methodological study of a prehistoric Pueblo
population. Unpublished Ph.D. dissertation, Department of Anthropology, University of California, Los Angeles.
Dixon, W. J. (Ed.)
1970   BMD biomedical computer programs. *University of California Publications in Automatic Computation,* No. 2.
1975   *BMD-P biomedical computer programs.* Berkeley: University of California Press.
Donnan, Christopher B.
1976   Moche art and iconography. *UCLA Latin American Center Publications,* Vol. 33. University of California, Los Angeles.
Dunn, Olive Jean, and Virginia Clark
1974   *Applied statistics: Analysis of variance and regression.* New York:
Wiley.
FBI Laboratory
1973   They write their own sentences. In *FBI Law Enforcement Bulletin* (revised April 1973). FBI Laboratory, U.S. Department of Justice, Washington, D.C.
Gottschalk, Marina
1973   Your character is in script. *Oakland Tribune,* March 7, 1973.
Grenzeback, Jeanne A.
1958   Individual differences in movement: A critical survey of the research.
Unpublished Ph.D. dissertation, Department of Kinesiology, University
of California, Los Angeles.
Gunn, Joel
1975   Idiosyncratic behavior in chipping style: Some hypotheses and preliminary analyses. In *Lithic technology: Making and using stone tools,*
edited by Earl Swanson. The Hague: Mouton. Pp. 35–61.
Harris, Theodore L., and G. Lawrence Rarick
1955   *Pressure patterns in handwriting.* The Committee for Research in
Handwriting, Department of Education, University of Wisconsin.
Harrison, Wilson R.
1958   *Suspect documents, their scientific examination.* London: Sweet and
Maxwell.
Hill, James N.
1970   Broken K Pueblo: Prehistoric social organization in the American

Southwest. *Anthropological Papers of the University of Arizona*, No. 18.

1972   Inferring prehistoric social organization through ceramic pattern recognition. In *Interdisciplinary Colloquium on Mathematics in the Behavioral Sciences, Colloquim Documents, 1971–1972*. Western Management Science Institute, University of California, Los Angeles. Pp. 7.1–7.7.

1974   Individual variability in ceramics, and the study of prehistoric social organization. Paper presented at the 1974 meeting of the Society for American Archaeology, Washington, D.C.

1977   Hill, James N. (Ed.) *Explanation of prehistoric change*. Albuquerque: University of New Mexico Press.

Hill, James N., and Robert K. Evans
1972   A model for classification and typology. In *Models in archaeology*, edited by David L. Clarke. London: Methuen. Pp. 231–273.

Hofsommer, W., R. Holdsworth, and T. Seifert
1965   Reliabilitats fragen in der graphologie. *Psychologie und Praxis* 9:14–24.

Huse, Hannah
1976   Identification of the individual in archeology: A case study from the prehistoric site of Kawaika-A. Unpublished Ph.D. dissertation, Department of Anthropology, University of Colorado.

Johnson, Gregory Alan
1973   Local exchange and early state development in southwestern Iran. *Anthropological Papers, Museum of Anthropology, University of Michigan*, No. 51.

Jones, Harold E.
1949   *Motor performance and growth: A developmental study of static dynamometric strength*. Berkeley: University of California Press.

Kanfer, A., and D. F. Casten
1958   Observations on disturbances in neuromuscular coordination in patients with malignant disease. *Bulletin of the Hospital for Joint Diseases* **19**: 1–19.

Lewinson, Thea Stein, and Joseph Zubin
1942   *Handwriting analysis*. Morningside Heights: King's Crown Press.

Longacre, William A.
1970   Archaeology as anthropology: A Case study. *Anthropological Papers of the University of Ariozna*, No. 17.

Lothrop, Samuel K.
1942   Coclé, an archaeological study in central Panama, Part II. *Memoirs of the Peabody Museum of Archaeology and Ethnology, Harvard University*, No. 8.

Malespine, E.
1951   Graphology and its applications. *International Criminal Police Review* **51**:266–273.

Modlin, H.
1969   Use of graphology in psychiatric evaluation. *Journal of the American Medical Association* **210**:240.

Myers, Emma Harrison
1963   *The whys and hows of teaching handwriting*. Columbus: Zaner–Bloser.

Osborn, Albert S.
    1910   *Questioned documents.* Rochester: Lawyers' Co-operative Publishing
            Company.
Oxnard, Charles E., and Peter M. Neely
    1969   The descriptive use of Neighborhood Limited Classification in func-
            tional morphology: An analysis of the shoulder in primates. *Journal
            of Morphology* **129**:127–148.
Plog, Fred
    1977   Explaining change. In *Explanation of prehistoric change*, edited by
            James N. Hill. Albuquerque: University of New Mexico Press.
Shapiro, S. S., and M. B. Wilk
    1965   An analysis of variance test for normality (complete samples).
            Biometriks **52**:591–611.
Siegel, Sidney
    1956   *Nonparametric statistics for the behavioral sciences.* New York: Mc-
            Graw-Hill.
Singer, Robert N.
    1968   *Motor learning and human performance.* New York: Macmillan.
Sonnemann, V.
    1950   *Handwriting analysis as a psycho-diagnostic tool.* New York: Grune
            and Stratton.
Steinert, George D.
    1975   Graphology debunked and the science of graphoanalysis. Paper pre-
            sented at the 1975 Convention of the California Personnel and Guid-
            ance Association.
Welford, Alan
    1958   *Aging and human skill.* London: Oxford University Press.
White, J. P., and D. H. Thomas
    1972   Ethno-taxonomic models and archaeological interpretations in the
            New Guinea Highlands: What mean these stones? In *Models in
            archaeology*, edited by David L. Clarke. London: Methuen. Pp. 275–308.

6

Individual Style in
San José Pottery Painting:
The Role of Deliberate Choice[1]

MARGARET ANN HARDIN

The study of individual style within contemporary anthropological archaeology has begun to raise questions that cannot be satisfactorily dealt with through the study of archaeological materials. Although earlier reconstructions of social groupings involved considerations of the response of the individual level of style to its social context, there was relatively little interest in the direct investigation of the nature of individual style (Deetz 1965, 1967: 109–116; Hill 1970; Longacre 1970); a related projected ethnoarchaeology of pottery making also reflects these concerns (Longacre 1974). In contrast, current discussion of individual style focuses on the question of whether there are immutable markers of

[1] This chapter is based on ethnographic fieldwork conducted in 1966–1967 under a Public Health Service predoctoral fellowship (5F1-MH-32, 844—02) from the National Institute of Mental Health and on subsequent museum research supported in part by a Wenner–Gren museum research fellowship at the Field Museum of Natural History in Chicago.

individual style, (see Chapter 5 by Hill in this volume) and whether it is feasible to demonstrate conclusively the existence of individual style in an archaeological context (see Chapter 4 by Redman in this volume). Although the archaeologist's interest in individual style is of an understandably practical nature, these investigations do raise questions of general anthropological interest about style and material culture.

In this chapter I seek to examine, in the light of ethnographic evidence, some of the questions raised by the current interest in individual style. One problem is whether, in fact, the work of individual artisans is marked by minute variation in the way a style is rendered. A second and related question is whether painters are able to change their execution of design deliberately and thus change the patterns of microvariation investigators tend to identify with individual style.

Investigating individual differences in the execution of design in an ethnographic context offers two advantages. The first, and most obvious, advantage is that the association of individuals and their products is known. The second, and equally important, advantage is that the cognitive structure underlying pottery decoration is available for study. More specifically, we can identify a minimal conceptual unit of design structure and then focus the study of individual style on variation in its execution. Once the problem to be investigated has been phrased in terms of the ethnographically known style, it may be approached in several ways. The role of design execution can be examined in the context of the full range of factors contributing to the distinctiveness of personal style. The work of individuals can be examined for distinctive patterns of variation in the execution of minimal conceptual units. If specific cases in which painters manipulate variation in the execution of these minimal units are found, the mechanisms involved can be studied.

ETHNOGRAPHIC BACKGROUND

My understanding of the system of design that I discuss in this chapter is based on ethnographic fieldwork conducted over a period of 14 months in San José, Michoacán, Mexico, a small village in the foothills of the Tarascan Sierra. The village consisted of about 40 households; total population was about 300 persons. Most village residents were bilingual, speaking both Tarascan and Spanish.

Most households engaged to some extent in pottery making on a regular basis. The kind of pottery most commonly made was a red utility ware. Also common, and considered typical of the village, was the green-glazed ware upon which my studies focused. A white slip was used to paint intricate designs on the most visible surfaces of the vessels. These areas were then covered with a clear green glaze, producing bright green designs on a blackish background; however, most of the vessels discussed in this study were collected after the first firing, as the glaze can obscure the painted designs.

The major focus of my study was upon design as a cognitive structure (Hardin in press) and upon variation in family and individual style that was related to differences in design structure (Hardin 1970). The study yielded general information about individual style as well. The examples given are based on two kinds of observation. Many of the markers of painters' personal styles were isolated during the period of fieldwork. Because I wished to learn in detail how each painter used the San José pottery painting system, I spent a large portion of my time watching people paint. In order to make my purpose obvious and as an aid to my own learning process, I drew each vessel as it was being painted. From the beginning of the study I made frequent note of features of design that might serve to distinguish individual or group style. Further information about the markers of individual style was gained from examining vessels collected during my stay in the village. This collection includes about 250 painted vessels, representing the work of all 16 major painters and most of the occasional painters.

The markers of individual style were of three kinds: (1) differences in the organization of decoration; (2) differences in the content of decoration; and (3) differences in the order used in the painting process. The first and second markers could be abstracted from the data available, but the third marker, differences in painting order, requires further explanation. Because I felt that order of execution might provide valuable insights into the organization of stylistic variation, I recorded the order of brushstrokes on my drawings of painters' work. In addition, it was possible to glean information about individual painting technique from the collection although its basic purpose was to represent the range of designs used by each painter.

Three properties of San José painting made it possible to reconstruct the order and direction of brushstrokes from completed vessels. When the paint was thin, overlapping was obvious. It was possible to see or feel the edge of a brushstroke when thick paint was used. The brushes were characteristically used in ways that built up distinctive accumulations of paint at particular points in the brushstroke; similarly, the ends of brushstrokes were distinctive.

The illustrations in this chapter were largely drawn from the collected vessels, although some field drawings are shown. For the convenience

TABLE 6.1
Representation of San José Painters in Illustrations

	Drawings and photographs of vessels	Design element series			
		Curved leaf	Arc-shaped leaf	Repeated petal	Straight line
Painter A	X			X	
Painter B	X				
Painter C	X	X	X	X	X
Painter D		X	X	X	
Painter E	X	X	X	X	X
Painter F	X	X		X	X
Painter G	X	X	X	X	X
Painter H	X	X			
Painter I	X	X		X	X
Painter J	X			X	X
Painter K	X	X	X	X	X
Painter L		X			
Painter M	X	X		X	X
Painter N		X			
Painter O	X				

of the reader, each painter's representation in drawings and photographs of vessels and in the design element series is listed in Table 6.1.

SOURCES OF DISTINCTIVE CHARACTERISTICS IN PERSONAL GRAPHIC STYLE

In San José, the work of each painter is distinct. The outside observer learns quite readily to recognize the work of each artisan, usually without consciously stopping to construct checklists of the markers of the various individual graphic styles. Upon questioning, San José painters display similar competences. Their ability to recognize the work of other painters does, however, reflect patterns of communication within the village; that is, they can identify the hand of those painters whom they regularly observe at work but not that of others whose work areas they rarely enter for reasons of physical and social distance. Even the most knowledgeable painters tend to be at a loss when asked how they are able to identify the painter of a particular vessel.

Closer examination of the characteristics of graphic style that identify the painter of a vessel reveals that these features are of three kinds:

differences in (1) painters' knowledge or theory of design, (2) painters' preferences for equivalent decorative alternatives, and (3) painters' execution of vessel decoration.

Each painter possesses an individual, and to some extent unique, design structure. That is, differences in the individual's knowledge or theory of design may result in a treatment of space or the use of a design unique to that painter. Differences in the organization of space may be illustrated by comparing the work of three painters (Figure 6.1). The first vessel (Figure 6.1, parts a and b) is the work of Painter A, a competent craftsman, whose organization of space is typical of that used by most San José painters. In contrast, the second and third vessels are the work of two painters whose organization of space includes idiosyncratic features. Painter B is quite skilled; however, his work, unlike that of painters of equal skill, exhibits a number of individual peculiarities (Figure 6.1, parts c and d). He is the only painter who routinely places designs inside the rim, thus extending the decorative field to the inside of the vessel (Figure 6.1, part c). He uses a unique division of space, dividing the vessel into three main areas rather than two. The bottom of the vessel is made into a separate major subdivision, which is marked

Figure 6.1. Individual variation in the organization and content of pottery decoration: (a, b) Painter A; (c, d) Painter B; (e, f) Painter C.

off with a thick band of paint (Figure 6.1, parts c and d). In the work of
other San José painters, thick bands occur only as optional markers of
the major division between the vessel's neck and body. Painter C makes
optional use of two lower bands rather than the usual one (Figure 6.1,
parts e and f). Other painters who use only one band in this position
fall into two groups, each of which uses a different approach to defining
the lower band. Painter C associates closely with painters from both
groups and apparently employs both sets of rules, sometimes simultaneously, producing two bands on the same vessel. The work of Painter B
also provides an example of idiosyncratic design content; that is, he
uses designs that do not occur in the work of other painters (Figure 6.1,
part c).

Many of the distinctive characteristics of a painter's personal style
stem from the fact that the design structure, which is largely shared by
all the painters in the village, offers a number of alternative choices at
almost every step of the painting process. Some alternatives are typically
although not exclusively taken by certain painters. One example of this,
consistent choice of a favorite design, affects only part of the vessel.
Other choices involve decisions about how the entire vessel is to be
painted. For example, a painter may prefer a particular pattern of spatial
division. Consistent application of a particular criterion in choosing designs to fill the areas defined will give the vessel's decoration a uniform
and in some cases distinctive appearance.

The unique quality of a painter's work may be in part related to his
execution of painted elements. He may handle materials and tools in a
way that makes his work look different from the work of others. Widely
distributed designs, differently rendered, may thus provide a source of
markers of individual style.

Knowledge of design structure and selection of alternatives in decoration both involve explicitly held information; that is, San José painters
can and do discuss the organization and content of vessel decoration, as
well as their variation. Because patterns of variation in graphic style
involving these aspects of design are subject to the deliberate manipulation of painters, it is useful to examine those factors external to the
design structure that affect artisans' decisions about their painting. Two
kinds of considerations, aesthetic and economic, play particularly important roles in the San José painter's decisions about design.

For the San José painter, aesthetic evaluation constitutes a separate
cognitive domain, involving judgments about how well vessel decoration is rendered. This domain may be contrasted with that of design
structure, which involves the organization and content of decoration. A
painter's aesthetic preferences, reflected in his choice of designs and

manner of rendering designs, may have a pervasive effect on the vessel's entire decorated surface. The system of evaluation used involves both a general notion of *well-paintedness* and two specific concepts, *coveredness* and *fineness*. The last two values constitute the positive poles of two logically independent dimensions. Even though San José painters share this aesthetic framework, they place different priorities on the two specific dimensions. Painters who emphasize coveredness at the expense of fineness make liberal use of the broad brush in their painting. Those painters who sacrifice coveredness for fineness use characteristically small, delicate designs, which do not always properly fill the areas marked off on the vessel's surface.

Many San José painters practice patterns of economically motivated style switching, which are related specifically to an economy of means. Painter A uses three distinct styles depending upon the economic circumstances involved (Figure 6.2). When he is not rushed and expects a good price, he uses a variety of complicated designs, one of which is shown in parts a and b of Figure 6.2. The second design, or another of similar complexity, is used on vessels intended for most markets, and for that matter, on most of the pots he paints (Figure 6.2, parts c and d). The third design is used when he is pressed for time, typically when he

Figure 6.2. Economically motivated style switching by Painter A: (a, b) vessel painted with care; (c, d) vessel painted in usual manner; (e, f) vessel painted hastily.

needs to complete a kiln load in time for market (Figure 6.2, parts e and f). This economically motivated variant is notable for its efficiency, due to the exclusive use of a broad brush. The third vessel also illustrates a common alternative to a simplified painting style, the use of molded decoration, in this case the face, which can simply be covered with paint. The strategy used to paint designs on the third vessel is employed only by Painter A and his son, Painter L.

Other painters employ their own efficient designs, which may for several reasons serve as markers of their painting styles (Figure 6.3). These alternative styles frequently represent idiosyncratic departures from the design structure underlying the common village style (Figure 6.3, parts a–c). In the first example, part a, Painter G uses a common design in an inappropriate context. In the second example (part b), Painter H uses the S-shaped element, which normally does not appear alone, to fill an entire area. The third example (part c), which only appears in the work of Painter I, employs an atypical subdivision of the wide central area by single lines into three narrow bands, which are then filled with easily painted designs. The fourth example (part d), shows a design of somewhat more complex appearance; it can actually be produced quite rapidly. Although used by several painters, it is greatly

Figure 6.3. Examples of efficient vessel decoration employed by various San José painters: (a) Painter G; (b) Painter H; (c) Painter I; (d) Painter J.

favored by Painter J. His more economical style is thus marked by a high incidence of this design. Economically motivated decisions, like aesthetic preferences, have a pervasive effect on the whole of the vessel's decorated surface. In many cases, a painter's modification of his graphic style represents a compromise between aesthetic standards and economic considerations. The study of individual style thus becomes in part a comparison of individual painters' assessments of these factors and the adjustments they occasion in painted decoration.

Variation in the execution of design poses a different problem for the analyst. It is not clear whether painters are able to change deliberately those features of execution significant in marking their personal styles. The extent to which the patterning of individual stylistic variation can be modified is at this time largely unknown. It poses a question that is susceptible to empirical investigation, either through imitative experiment or ethnographic observation.

INDIVIDUAL VARIATION BELOW
THE LEVEL OF NAMED UNITS

The role of deliberate choice in the execution of design is best approached through the study of certain aspects of painted design. Both the complexity of the unit of design chosen and its relation to the cognitive structure underlying vessel decoration are important. Ideally, the aspect of design upon which the study focuses should be the smallest and simplest kind of unit explicitly recognized in painters' discussions of design. The reason for this choice is twofold. On the one hand, variation involving the combination of units of this order is subject to the deliberate choices of painters. On the other hand, patterned variation in the construction of these units cannot be assumed to be the product of deliberate choice. In an ethnographic context, it is possible to ascertain what portion of the vessel's decoration should be isolated for further study. For the San José painter, the design element, which will be discussed in the following section, is the minimal cognitive unit.

Once the painted reflex of the minimal underlying cognitive unit has been isolated, one may examine variation in its execution. Three factors are involved: materials, tools, and patterned movements. Each factor must be examined so that its contribution to the observed pattern as well as its potential role in the deliberate manipulation of stylistic variation can be assessed. In the San José case discussed in the following section, the respective roles of the paint and brushes used are assessed; however, present evidence does not include the direct observation of minute differences in painters' patterned movements. The detailed examination of variation in the product of these factors, the design elements themselves, provides a second approach to the problem of the effect of deliberate choice on individual style.

Design Elements

The painted designs used to decorate San José pottery regularly exhibit two levels of organization. These are the design element and the design configuration. The design element may be defined as a minimal bounded unit. For example, each of the scallops used to form the design illustrated in Figure 6.1, part d, is a design element. The design configuration is an arrangement of design elements of sufficient complexity to fill one of the bounded areas into which the vessel's decorative field is divided. The series of scallops shown in part d of Figure 6.1 constitutes a simple configuration, used to fill the band-shaped area encircling the vessel's base. Configurations of greater complexity, involving more than one kind of element, also occur. Part b of Figure 6.1 illustrates a two-element configuration, using scallops and leaves; the configuration used in the wide central area of the vessel shown in part d of Figure 6.3 employs three design elements: thin lines, repeated petals, and hooked leaves.

The design element is the smallest unit of design named by painters. Painters' discussion of design, however, focuses on design configurations. The classification of designs is organized in terms of configurations, of which there are a great number. In contrast, there are relatively few design elements. Eighteen of these minimal units are widely distributed within San José; seven more are only used by a few painters. The complexity of design lies in the organization of configurations; most design elements play many roles in the structure of design configurations.

Design elements are manipulated and used in configurations as if they were single, indivisible entities. Their execution, however, is in itself complexly patterned. Many design elements are constructed from more than one brushstroke; furthermore, the number of brushstrokes used to render certain design elements may vary. Painters do not talk about the construction of design elements, nor do they systematically discuss variation in their execution.

The Execution of Design Elements:
Materials, Tools, and Patterned Movements

Several factors affect technique in San José pottery painting. In addition to the patterned movements he or she normally uses, a painter's technique is also a function of his materials and tools. In the San José case, it is possible to vary both paint and brushes independently in ways that may change the patterning of the painter's movements and certainly change the appearance of the designs painted.

The designs are painted with a white slip. As this is mixed with water and ground in each household, the thickness of the paint varies. Thin paint is an economizing measure, although a minor one. In addition, the ground material tends to settle out, so a painter who stirs his slip infrequently uses a thinner paint.

The brushes used in San José are made by binding squirrel-tail hairs to a small twig with thread (Figure 6.4). The motor habits required to use them properly are considerably different from those to which we are accustomed. These differences are clearly related to three properties of the tools and materials used: the softness of the hairs in the brushes, the heaviness of the paint, and the shape of some brushes. Each brush has different properties and limitations. In addition, painters differ not only in the kinds and numbers of brushes they use but also in the precise range of tasks they carry out with a particular brush.

Two kinds of brushes are basic to San José painting and are used by all painters. The first of these is a relatively fat, tapered brush, used for thick or curved designs (Figure 6.4, part a). Its use requires a rather light hand; important effects are gained by varying the pressure applied. The second brush is very long and thin (part b). It is reserved for lines, which are made by covering the entire length of the hair with white paint, laying this entire working length on the surface of the vessel, and drawing it through the line being painted.

Some painters add other brushes. The simplest addition is a smaller, thinner version of the fat brush, which is employed for more delicate flat designs (Figure 6.4, part c). Similarly, a second, narrow version of the long, thin brush may be added (part d). In this case, the slighter

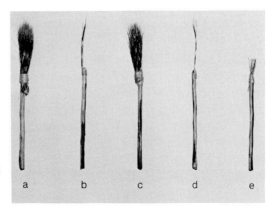

Figure 6.4. Set of San José brushes.

brush is used for cross-hatching; the thicker one is reserved for boundary marking lines. In two households, a third major brush type has been added (part e). It is made by cutting a thin brush off short; it paints short, curved lines with greater precision than the flat brushes. The three best painters in San José, Painters E, F, and K, live in the household where it was first used. It was later adopted by the older brother of Painter K, the head of that household. The set of brushes shown was made by the older brother and are representative of the range of brush types used in his household. Painters in the household of the younger brother use a wider variety of brushes than those shown, although they are all related to the three basic types. Many of these are small, delicate, and for San José painting, quite task-specific. Each painter in the household favors certain brushes.

Most painters use a few simple brushes, and they are quite attached to the ones they have. Painters, working on the spur of the moment in another household, may stop to make brushes that will do what they want. The most skilled painter in San José, Painter E, felt she could not make some designs without a specific brush. My attempts to collect from each painter a sample of pots together with the brushes used to paint them met with failure. Painters did not want to give up their brushes; in fact, their reactions to my request were sufficiently negative that I felt that further insistence would jeopardize the rest of the study.

Individual Characteristics in the Rendering of Design Elements

In this section I shall detail patterned variation in the execution of design elements, including differences in the production of elements and differences in the appearance of completed elements. The length of the series illustrating each element is limited by two factors. It was necessary to restrict the choice of illustrations of an element to one kind of configuration, for some painters vary the form of an element with its context. The number of painters represented in each series is in part a function of the fact that illustrations were drawn from the unglazed vessels in the collection. This was necessary in order to use techniques of illustration, tracings, and photographs that would present the variability as fully as possible. Four design elements are represented in the series that follows: (1) the curved leaf, (2) the arc-shaped leaf, (3) the repeated petal, and (4) the straight line.

The curved-leaf element has many uses in San José painting. The series of examples shown in Figures 6.5 and 6.6 is drawn from a fourfold arrangement, which is the configuration most commonly used to decorate the bottom of the vessel (see Figure 6.2, part d). All painters execute

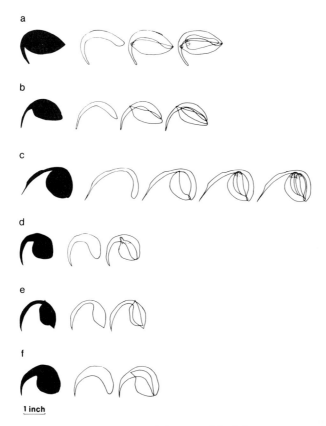

Figure 6.5. Variation in the execution of the curved-leaf element, part 1: (a) Painter E; (b) Painter F; (c) Painter K; (d) Painter L; (e) Painter G; (f) Painter H.

this element with essentially the same large, fat brush (Figure 6.4, part a). They differ not only in the number of brushstrokes they use but also in the order in which these occur.

Painters E, F, and K all construct the curved leaf in three steps (parts a–c, Figure 6.5). A single brushstroke makes the element's tail and defines one of its sides. Another brushstroke defines its other side. Finally, the center of the element is covered over. For this Painter E, the mother (part a), and Painter F, the son (part b), use a single brushstroke; Painter K, the father (part c), uses two and occasionally three brushstrokes. All three members of this skilled family place the tail at a relatively sharp angle to the leaf; however, individual styles may be distinguished by the proportions of the element, especially of the tail. The ways in which the brushstrokes in the second two steps are terminated are also distinctive.

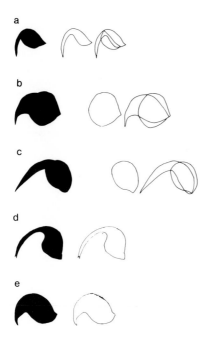

1 inch

Figure **6.6.** Variation in the execution of the curved-leaf element, part 2: (a) Painter M; (b) Painter C; (c) Painter D; (d) Painter N; (e) Painter I.

Most San José painters use two brushstrokes for the curved leaf. Normally the longer part is painted first. The work of the next four painters in the series varies in the proportions of the element and the degree to which the two brushstrokes overlap (Figure 6.5, parts d–f; Figure 6.6, part a). Distinguishing features of Painter L's work are the squatness of the element and the manner of terminating the second brushstroke (Figure 6.5, part d). Painter G's work is marked by the extreme overlap of the two brushstrokes, which causes the second brushstroke to extend beyond the far side of the first brushstroke (part e). Painter H uses two long brushstrokes, which begin closer together and exhibit a lesser degree of overlapping than do the previous two examples. The narrower shape of the first brushstroke is also distinctive (part f). Painter M's work is marked by the relative shortness of the tail portion of the element and by the way the second brushstroke is terminated (Figure 6.6, part a).

Painters C and D, daughter and father, use an abnormal order in constructing the curved leaf (Figure 6.6, parts b and c). The second brush-stroke is the longer and includes the element's tail. In Painter C's work the first brushstroke is proportionally shorter and may stick out on both sides of the second brushstroke. In addition, the entire element is shorter (part b). Painter D's work has a longer and thicker tail (part c).

Painters N and I, who live a block apart, use only one brushstroke. Their work may be distinguished by the proportions of the elements (Figure 6.6, parts d and e). In the work of the former, the tail portion of the element is more prominent (part d); in the work of the latter, the tail is short, and the base of the element is noticeably twisted (part e).

The most common use of the arc-shaped leaf is as the major element in an overlapping linear arrangement (Figure 6.3, part a). The examples were drawn from this kind of configuration (Figure 6.7). In executing this element, painters vary in both the number of brushstrokes used and in the brush type employed.

Most painters who execute this element with a single brushstroke use a large, broad brush (Figure 6.4, part a). They begin the element with its stem; more pressure, suddenly released, produces the leaf. Although brush size is clearly important, variation in the results gained by differ-

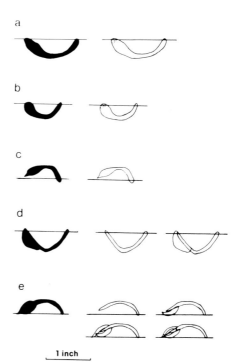

Figure 6.7. Variation in the execution of the arc-shaped-leaf element: (a) Painter D; (b) Painter C; (c) Painter E; (d) Painter G; (e) Painter K.

ent painters cannot be attributed to brush choice alone. Painters D and C use the same set of brushes; the examples shown were painted with the same brush. Although both painters produce a leaf with a blunt tip, the proportions of the elements differ. Painter D's leaf has a more elongated blade (Figure 6.7, part a); Painter C's leaf has a rounder blade (part b). Also, the buildup of paint at the end of the brushstroke is proportionally larger in the work of Painter C. Painter E uses a more delicate brush of the same form; her leaves have a distinctively pointed tip (part c).

Three painters use more than one brushstroke to construct this element. Painter G uses the large, broad brush (Figure 6.4, part a). His procedure has two steps (Figure 6.7, part d). First, the arc-shaped stem is painted; a second brushstroke produces the blade of the leaf. Painters K and F use the short, fine brush (Figure 6.4, part e), and a more elaborate procedure to render this element. The example of Painter K's work shown in Figure 6.7, part e, exhibits a four-step construction sequence:

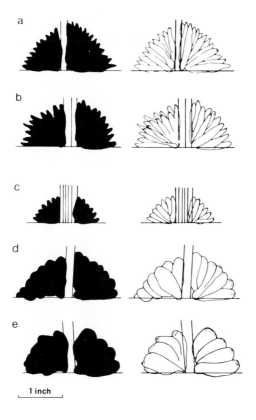

a

b

c

d

e

1 inch

Figure 6.8. Variation in the execution of the repeated-petal element, part 1: (a) Painter K; (b) Painter F; (c) Painter E; (d) Painter D; (e) Painter C.

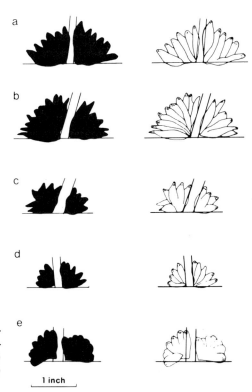

Figure 6.9. Variation in the execution of the repeated-petal element, part 2: (a) Painter G; (b) Painter A; (c) Painter M; (d) Painter J; (e) Painter I.

(1) the stem is drawn, (2) the lower side of the leaf is defined, (3) the upper side of the leaf is added, and (4) the interior of the leaf is filled in.

The repeated-petal element occurs in a number of contexts in San José painting. One of its more common uses is to fill the angles created by the intersection of thin lines (Figure 6.3, part d). The examples shown are drawn from this context; whenever possible, configurations with pairs of intersecting lines were used (see Figures 6.8 and 6.9). Painters vary in the kind of brush they employ for this element; the number of brushstrokes used is in part a function of brush width. Frequently, so much overlapping of brushstrokes occurs that it is impossible to ascertain their order.

Painters K, F, and E use the thin, short brush (Figure 6.4, part e). Their flowers have many petals, the tips of which are clearly defined. Painter K controls his petal length very well; the curve defined by the petal tips is flattened out (Figure 6.8, part a). Painter F does not control petal length as well (part b). Painter E produces shorter and proportionally thicker petals (part c).

Painters using the larger brush (Figure 6.4, part a) vary in the effects they obtain. Painter D (Figure 6.8, part d) and Painter C (part e) produce heavy, rounded petals with a clearly defined dot of paint at the tip; however, Painter C uses fewer and larger petals than Painter D. The work of Painter G is marked by pointed petals, the tips of which are clearly defined by a dot of paint (Figure 6.9, part a). Painter A uses two petal shapes at random (part b). Painters M and J, a wife and husband, both use smaller petals. Painter M's petals exhibit noticeable variation in length and shape (part c); her husband's are very evenly painted (part d). Painter I paints rounded petals of various lengths; his work shows great variation in the extent to which brush strokes are run together (part e).

All painters use the long, thin brushes (Figure 6.4, parts b and d) to paint thin lines. Both the brush width selected and the amount of paint

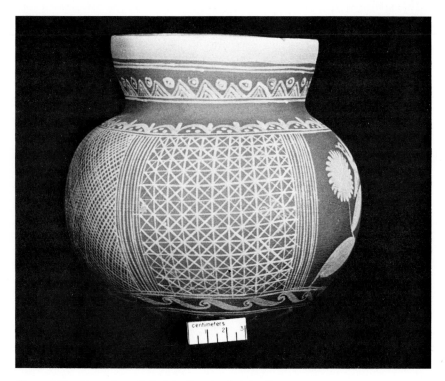

Figure 6.10. Execution of straight lines by Painter E.

Figure 6.11. Execution of straight lines by Painter K.

used affects the appearance of the line. It is difficult to use these thin, floppy brushes and, in particular, to control the exact path and terminations of the lines. The kind of cross-hatching used in the illustrations was chosen because its execution is particularly demanding. The painter's control over the brush is displayed in the accuracy with which he or she is able to match up the junctures of the two sets of crossed lines. Frequently, painters make characteristic errors.

Painter E (Figure 6.10), Painter K (Figure 6.11), and Painter F (Figure 6.12) exhibit the exceptional control typical of their painting. Variation in fineness of line, amount of bare space, and paint thickness reflects individual preferences within the family.

The work of other painters shows characteristic problems. Painter C's lines do not match up in the lower right-hand corner of the area being filled (Figure 6.13). Painter G uses heavier horizontal lines in this pattern (Figure 6.14). In addition, he begins one set of diagonal lines at the top of the area and the other set at its bottom. The most obvious result of

Figure 6.12. Execution of straight lines by Painter F.

this procedure is that his left-to-right diagonal lines begin outside the upper boundary, which should be their beginning point. Painter I has little control over the placing of diagonals and trouble in ending lines at the boundary (Figure 6.15). His diagonal lines do not always meet at the juncture of the other lines; furthermore, some diagonal lines are omitted. Painter M has trouble placing diagonal lines in both of the lower corners of her area (Figure 6.16). Painter J matches up his diagonal lines with the junctures of the lines painted earlier only in the center of the area being filled (Figure 6.17).

Special Problems: The Effect of the Brush

The painter's choice of brush is, as has been shown in the series of examples presented, an important factor in the way an element is put together as well as in the form of the completed element. When painters use the same brush for a task, their work is more easily confused. Shared

Figure 6.13. Execution of straight lines by Painter C.

brushes and paint pots were an important factor in the two cases in which it was initially difficult to separate the work of two painters. In the first case, the error was occasioned by taking the effect of a particular brush for a typical characteristic of Painter H's hand. The brush, an unusually narrow example of the third brush illustrated (Figure 6.4, part c) produced a distinctively long and straight-sided leaf (Figure 6.18). When Painter O, his brother-in-law from a nearby town, used the brush, his work was taken for that of Painter H (Figure 6.19). In the second case, it was difficult to separate the work of the couple, Painter J (Figures 6.20 and 6.21) and Painter M (Figures 6.22 and 6.23). This confusion was due to the superficial similarity produced by shared tools and materials. More thorough inspection showed that their work differs in the content and organization of design as well as in the execution of shared elements. Differences of execution include those already discussed and the S-shaped element shown on the shoulders of Figures 6.20 and 6.22, which is oriented differently by the two painters.

Figure 6.14. Execution of straight lines by Painter G.

Figure 6.15. Execution of straight lines by Painter I.

130

Figure 6.16. Execution of straight lines by Painter M.

Figure 6.17. Execution of straight lines by Painter J.

131

Figure 6.18. Execution of straight-sided leaf by Painter H.

Figure 6.19. Execution of straight-sided leaf by Painter O.

Figure 6.20. First vessel by Painter J.

Figure 6.21. Second vessel by Painter J.

Figure 6.22. First vessel by Painter M.

Figure 6.23. Second vessel by Painter M.

134

It is not surprising that when San José painters wish to change their style, the brush is a mediating factor. Specific brushes are associated with particular results; the painter changes the brush in order to change the appearance of the painted design. Three factors underlie style switching in San José. The two factors previously discussed, aesthetic standards and economic requirements, frequently occasion responses that involve changing brushes. In addition to these patterns, there is a third, the deliberate copying of another painter's manner of execution. After a year of observation of painters at work, one instance of this pattern was noticed in the family of exceptionally skilled painters. Painter F was painting like Painter E, his mother. Upon questioning, he said that his father had asked him to paint some vessels in the style of his mother; he volunteered that he was using her brushes. It should be pointed out that deliberate style switching of this kind requires an exceptional control of painting technique; thus, it is not surprising that the single instance observed comes from the most skilled painters.

CONCLUSIONS

Individual style, marked in various ways and caused by several factors in addition to the patterned movements of the painter, is an important part of patterned variation in San José vessel decoration. The investigator working with archaeological materials should be encouraged by the fact that painters' execution of simple, commonly used elements is sufficiently variable that one can select unique sets of features that mark the work of individuals. The San José data do, however, suggest two reasons for caution. First, patterned variation at this level does not reflect only individual differences, for painters who are socially close, particularly through ties of coresidence or family membership, tend to share strategies for producing common design elements. Second, individual differences in the rendering of design elements cannot be assumed to be solely the result of differently patterned movement, and therefore, not affected by painters' deliberate choices. Other factors, particularly brush choice, may affect the form of elements. Furthermore, the use of a brush that will produce a given effect may represent a deliberate choice by the painter. Tool selection thus provides an avenue for conscious manipulation of graphic style below the level of design element.

These tentative conclusions imply a program for future research. It is not unreasonable to begin with the assumption that a highly patterned product of motor activity, like a painting style, results from a highly stylized set of actions. These patterned movements must, however, be observed directly. The technology and methods needed for this are available; either videotape or film could be used. The other factors that underlie variability in design element execution, namely tools, materials, and configurational context, must be carefully controlled while these data are being collected. Brush choice should be controlled or at least carefully recorded. Paint composition and use should be observed. Each painter should be asked to use the same popular designs. These measures should facilitate the isolation of that variation due to individual differences in patterned movement. It is only with this background that more complex patterns involving execution, such as learning between family members and style switching, can be understood.

ACKNOWLEDGMENTS

I am grateful to Henry Dybas, Phyllis Rabineau, Catherine Renne, and Judith Shapiro for reading the chapter in its earlier form and commenting upon it. I would like to thank Samuel H. Grove for reading the chapter, and for his invaluable advice on illustration strategy. Figures 6.1–6.3 are the work of Joanne B. Look and Figures 6.5–6.9 are by Susan Hopkins. The photographs used here are by John Alderson. I am grateful to Gloria Ramos for her editorial comments and typing of the manuscript.

REFERENCES

Deetz, James
    1965   The dynamics of stylistic change in Arikara ceramics. *Illinois Studies in Anthropology*, No. 4. Urbana: University of Illinois Press.
    1967   *Invitation to archeology*. Garden City, New York: Natural History Press.
Hardin (Friedrich), Margaret Ann
    1970   Design structure and social interaction: Archeological implications of an ethnographic analysis. *American Antiquity* **35**:3.
    in press The structure of Tarascan pottery painting. In *Artifact structure*, edited by William C. Sturtevant. Washington, D.C.: Anthropological Society of Washington, D.C.
Hill, James N.
    1970   Broken K Pueblo: Prehistoric social organization in the American Southwest. *Anthropological Papers of the University of Arizona*, No. 18.
Longacre, William A.
    1970   Archaeology as anthropology: A case study. *Anthropological Papers of the University of Arizona*, No. 17.
    1974   Kalinga pottery-making: The evolution of a research design. In *Frontiers of anthropology*, edited by Murray J. Leaf. New York: D. Van Nostrand. Pp. 51–67.

7

Style, Basketry, and Basketmakers

J. M. ADOVASIO
JOEL GUNN

The production of basketry is one of the oldest aboriginal crafts in North America. The antiquity of basketry manufacture is probably second only to the making of cordage and netting among the so-called "perishable fiber arts" (Adovasio 1974; King 1975). The term *basketry* encompasses several distinct kinds of items, including rigid and semi-rigid containers or baskets proper, matting, and bags.

Matting includes items that are essentially two-dimensional or flat; baskets are three-dimensional. Bags may be viewed as intermediate forms because they are two-dimensional when empty and three-dimensional when filled. As Driver (1961:159) points out, these artifacts may be treated as a unit because the overall technique of manufacture is the same in all instances. Specifically, since all basketry is woven, it is technically a class or variety of textile (see Emery 1966), though that term is sometimes restricted to cloth fabrics.

It has become increasingly apparent, through comparative studies of literally thousands of whole and fragmentary basketry remains (see Adovasio 1970a, 1971, 1974, in press a, b, c) that the study of prehistoric basketry is a tool of considerable use to the archaeologist on many levels. As Rozaire points out,

> woven objects of themselves have great cultural significance and constitute good sensitive criteria for comparisons; the importance of weaving can be better appreciated (especially in contrast to pottery) when one considers its antiquity in the Americas, . . . its frequency. . . , and its many diagnostic attributes [1969:184].

In a similar vein, though much earlier, Weltfish observed that

> Basketry . . . is peculiarly useful for comparative study. It can be approached and controlled from many points of view, because in the basketry art the fundamental mechanical factors involved in the technical process objectify themselves in the product *and are not lost in the process of making* [1932:108; emphasis added].

Likewise King, summarizing her extensive experience with archaeological textiles, noted,

> I have come to regard them (i.e., textiles and basketry) as perhaps the most culturally revealing of all categories of artifacts. These tiny fragments . . . once were a very important part of the lives of individuals in the past. . . . The intimacy of man's association with his textile production is far greater than that with pottery, tools, or other items he manufactures [1975:11].

In point of fact, few classes of artifacts available to the archaeologist for analysis possess more culturally and idiosyncratically determined yet still-visible attributes than does basketry. Whether the basketry is coiled, twined, or plaited, flexible, semirigid, or rigid, it appears to be an established fact that no two populations ever manufactured their basketry in precisely the same fashion. Not only is this ethnographically demonstrable, it also seems to be archaeologically valid (Adovasio 1972; Adovasio *et al.* in press a, b).

Though some of the technical attributes by which apparently similar basketry specimens can be distinguished are often very minor and seemingly inconsequential, they are nonetheless important because it is precisely these details that tend to be most localized in occurrence and most conservative. Thus, their potential value in delimiting the area of occupation or degree of interaction between prehistoric populations is great.

The analysis of archaeological basketry presents special problems. Although it is true that differences in weaving techniques are best detected in whole specimens, and that even in favorable areas of preservation these are not usually available, it is possible to extract a considerable amount of comparative data from very minute fragments.

Even the smallest fragment of a mat, bag, or basket may possess a great number of diagnostic attributes that can be isolated and compared to other such fragments. Unfortunately, most archaeologists generally ignore such attributes because they are simply unfamiliar with them and the potentialities inherent in their identification. As a result, many, though certainly not all, of the descriptions of basketry that have appeared in site reports note only the grossest and most obvious features of construction coded in a nominal form and analyzed either impressionistically or by limited statistical treatments. Some are even more concise, as witnessed by the following "classic" description: "A large number of coiled baskets were recovered from the cave, and they were nice [Anonymous 1956]."

If properly analyzed and described, prehistoric basketry from any part of North America or the world can yield rather specific information on a given population's general technological level, area of occupation or utilization, subsistence practices, intergroup relationships and movements, degree of conservatism, or conversely, capacity for innovation, and perhaps even something about kinship and social structure. Of course, connections between ethnographic and prehistoric populations may also be established through basketry analysis by examining technological and stylistic continuities. At the very least, basketry has proved to be as precise a time marker as any other artifact class (Gunn 1975:18), and its role in the establishment of regional chronologies and interregional relationships is great.

THE ISOLATION OF INDIVIDUAL BASKETMAKERS

It has been hypothesized that the selfsame "minor attributes" used to elicit the aforementioned information can also be employed in combination with quantified motor-skill data to isolate the work of individual basketmakers within any given prehistoric, or for that matter, ethnographic basketry assemblage (Adovasio 1974).

In order to test this hypothesis, a collection of 29 complete ethnographic Washo coiled baskets produced by "known" individual weavers was subjected to detailed attribute analysis. The collection included 13 baskets produced by the great Washo weaver Dat-so-la-lee, 5 baskets produced by a woman known only as Suzie, and 11 specimens in the

Parish Collection of the Nevada State Museum that are almost certainly the work of a single, though anonymous, hand (Don Tuohy personal communication). All were produced within the last 100 or so years.

The work of the individuals noted is readily distinguishable on casual observation of nominal attributes. Each employs a specific splice type, rim finish, and method of initiating the starting coil. Moreover, each evidences a slightly different variation of a given vessel form (e.g., globular bowl) as well as a particular combination of decorative motifs, the production mechanics as well as final form of which vary considerably.

The quantification of selected attributes shows that certain idiosyncratic motor-skill differences are also perceptible in the Washo sample. Each Washo basket was measured for four manufacturing attributes that, though controlled to some extent by cultural preference, are highly idiosyncratic. These include diameter of coil, number of coils per centimeter, width of stitch, and number of stitches per centimeter.

The four measurements were subjected to principal component analysis (modified version of BMD08M; J. Gunn 1975) and canonical analysis of discriminant function (BMD07M; Dixon 1973). The results of these analyses are shown in Figures 7.1 and 7.2.

As indicated, both the principal component and canonical discriminant analyses succeeded in separating Dat-so-la-lee from the other Washo weavers. Likewise, in both analyses, the work of Suzie appears as a tight cluster within the general range of variation of the Parish Collection.

When dimensional measurements of complete vessels were used in the analysis, the three groups were entirely distinct. However, because whole vessels are so rarely encountered in archaeological assemblages, we decided to delete these measurements from the example presented here.

Given the success of the Washo "case," we decided to ascertain whether the analysis was applicable to a series of archaeological basketry specimens recovered in the excavations of Antelope House, a multi-component though predominantly Pueblo III site in Canyon de Chelly, Arizona.

The archaeological sample consisted of 2 complete and 20 fragmentary specimens of Close Coiled, Two Rod and Bundle Bunched Foundation, Non-interlocking Stitch basketry from the three major architectural units of the site. These units include the North Room Block, North area, Central Room Block, South Room Block, and South Area and were designated N.R.B., N.A., C.R.B., S.R.B., and S.A., respectively (Figure 7.3). An immediate problem with an archaeological assemblage of this type is the level or order of contemporaneity of the sample. Although the site is known to have spanned at least 165 years of occupation, the

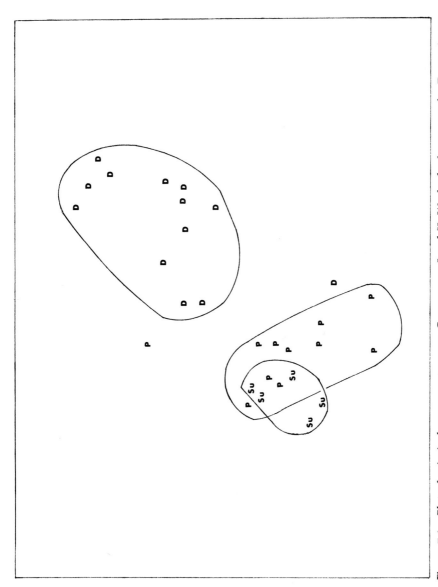

Figure 7.1. Plot of principal component scores, Components I and II, Washo basketry sample: D, specimens produced by Dat-so-la-lee; Su, specimens produced by Suzie; P, specimens in Parish Collection.

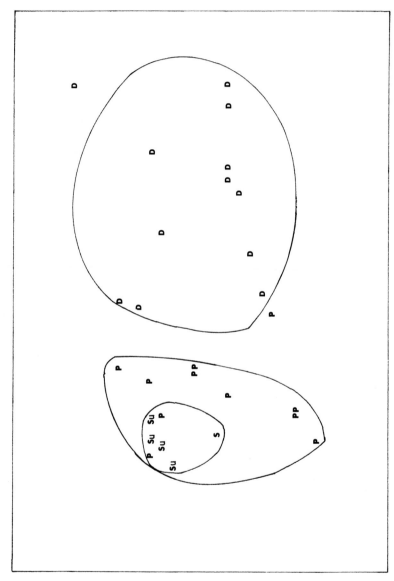

Figure 7.2. Plot of Canonical Variables I and II, Washo basketry sample. (See Figure 7.1 for symbol explanation.)

basketry sample was treated for analytical purposes as representing a synchronic collection.

This assumption may be questionable in a few specific cases, but the majority of the sample is ascribable to Early Pueblo III, a time period easily within the life span of a cohort of weavers. Once again, inspection of the nominal attributes suggests the existence of distinct clusters within the Antelope House assemblage. These included method of rod preparation (e.g., decorticated versus undecorticated), type and treatment of bundles (e.g., retted versus unretted), and most important, differences in manipulation of splices. Following the methodology employed with the Washo sample, the idiosyncratic measurements of the Anasazi basketry were subjected to principal component analysis and canonical discriminant function analysis.

The three architectural subdivisions of the site were used as prior groups. This appeared to be the maximum intra-site division that could be permitted without the danger of fragmenting the "domain" of any given weaver. We do not presume, however, that any weaver lived in a particular subarea of the site. Actual weavers were determined in a second step of the analysis. Once the program was run and component scores or canonical variables plotted, subgroups of baskets from any architectural unit occurring in any room or contiguous set of rooms were assumed to be from the hand of a single weaver, and further that said room(s) represented the residence of that weaver. The results of these analyses are presented in Figures 7.4 and 7.5.

Figure 7.4 represents the plot of component scores of Components I and II for the Anasazi Two Rod and Bundle Bunched Foundation, Non-interlocking Stitch basketry. The Central Room Block (C) specimens tend to cluster in the upper left-hand portion of the plot, and the North Room Block/North Area (N) and South Room Block/South Plaza (S) specimens tend toward the lower right-hand portion of the plot. The N specimens appear as a tighter cluster or subset within the S cluster. Canonical analysis of discriminant functions of this assemblage (Figure 7.5) more or less duplicated the results achieved in the principal component analysis while more successfully resolving C and N specimens into separate groups.

Three alternative explanations are possible for the apparent clustering observed in Figures 7.4 and 7.5. The clusters may represent temporal differences in a culturally homogeneous population; they may represent discrete groups of basketmakers or individuals within the Antelope House complex, or they may reflect functional variation between architectural areas of the complex. The first alternative may be tentatively discounted because of the tendency of the basketry fragments to cluster

S. A.   S. R. B.

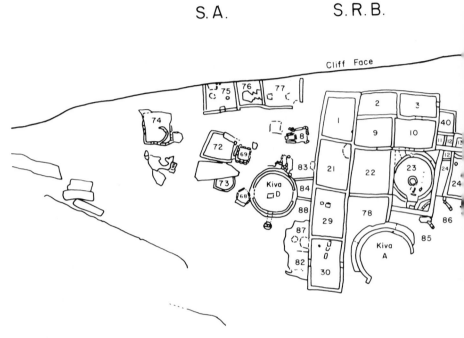

Figure 7.3. Architectural plan of Antelope House, Canyon de Chelly, Arizona. N.R.B., North Room Block; N.A., North Area; C.R.B., Central Room Block; S.A., South Area; S.R.B., South Room Block.

by architectural area. If the baskets represented the technical evolution of a homogeneous population of weavers through time there would be more variance within areas than between areas with a consequent masking or obscuring of areal distinctions. If the second alternative is correct, then the N baskets represent a tight grouping of specimens fortuitously located at the extreme of the more diverse range of variation of the S population.

These considerations suggest that there were indeed two basketmaking entities at Antelope House, one in the north and one in the south, with that in the north exhibiting a more restricted range of techno-manipulative variability. In other words, basketmakers from the northern precinct constructed a more standardized product than did those in the south.

The yet unanswered question is whether these basketmaking entities

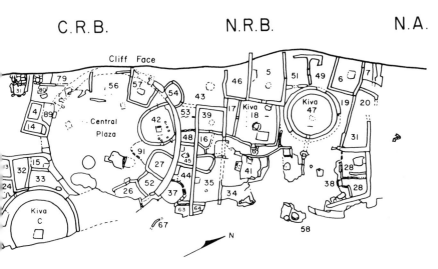

C.R.B.   N.R.B.   N.A.

ANTELOPE HOUSE RUIN

Canyon de Chelly National Monument

0 _____ 5 Meters

represent individuals or groups of individuals. Distinct subgroups *are* apparent in the south (see subgroups a, b, and c, marked by dashed lines in Figure 7.4). The possibility that these subsets represent three individuals can be readily tested (without resorting to inspection of nominal attributes) by checking the provenience of the specimens to ascertain if those from within groups are restricted to the same or immediately contiguous rooms. If we assume that an individual basketmaker lived in a given room or set of adjacent rooms, the restriction of the specimens in question to those rooms would seem to indicate that subgroups a, b, and c *are* individuals with more or less distinctive approaches to basketmaking. Significantly, the provenience data from Antelope House do appear to support this conclusion.

A third alternative remains to be considered. Specimens from architectural area C are clearly distinct from those in areas N and S. Several lines of analysis, however, indicate that the Central Room Block (C),

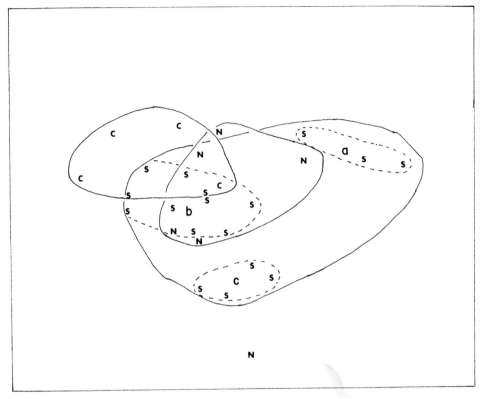

Figure 7.4. Plot of principal component scores for Antelope House, Components I and II, Two Rod and Bundle Bunched Foundation, Non-interlocking Stitch coiled basketry. Symbols N, C, and S are used here and in subsequent figures to refer to specimens from the North Room Block/North Area, Central Room Block, and South Room Block/South Plaza sectors respectively. Subgroups a, b, and c, marked by dashed lines, are distinct subsets of S.

dominated by ceremonial structures, is also functionally distinct from the more residential north and south precincts. Under these circumstances, it is not unreasonable to conclude that the C cluster of basketry specimens is distinct for functional reasons and may represent containers produced specifically for ritual activities. Canonical discriminant analysis places the C specimens more in the S than the N "tradition" and suggests that some component of the S population of weavers may have been responsible for the C specimens. Whatever the case, the C specimens *are* distinct and the reasons, as noted previously, may be related to functional factors.

It should be stressed that within each cluster certain groups of speci-

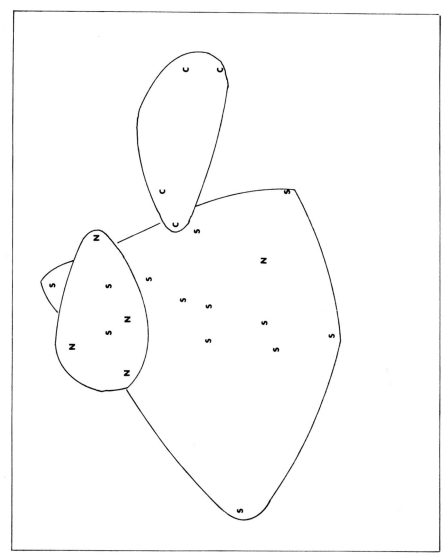

Figure 7.5. Plot of Canonical Variables I and II, Two Rod and Bundle Bunched Foundation, Non-inter-locking Stitch coiled basketry.

147

mens are so similar on purely nominal criteria that they must have been produced by the same hand. Careful examination of such attributes as splice manipulation, diameter of interior foundation rods, rim finish, and method of starting suggests that within groups located in areas C, N, and S at least six and possibly seven individual weavers can be positively distinguished. Significantly, the work of each of these individuals *is* confined to the same or to immediately contiguous rooms. Future research in this area of archaeological basketry analysis will be directed toward quantification of these highly diagnostic attributes as continuous variables. Alternatively, the problem may be approached through the analysis of nominal scales.

CONCLUSIONS

As a final test in the pilot study described here, the Washo sample and the archaeological sample were combined and analyzed as a single unit. Certain interesting trends emerged.

Table 7.1 shows an F matrix for the combined archaeological/ethnographic analysis. Though these figures are of no direct use in the isolation of individuals, they do afford a means of viewing the degree of overlap between the groups in question. In terms of the four variables measured in this study, most of the various "groups" are statistically distinguishable, with the exception of the North area, the Parish Collection, and the South Area, which exhibit varying degrees of overlap. Suzie is indistinguishable from the Parish Collection. Dat-so-la-lee and the Central Area have the highest F value as might be expected from inspection of the canonical variable in Figure 7.5.

The plot of Canonical Variables I and II for the combined Anasazi/Washo sample is presented in Figure 7.6. These variables vaguely sep-

TABLE 7.1

F Matrix for Combined Anasazi/Washo Sample[a]

	Central	North	South	Dat-so-la-lee	Parish Collection
North	4.33				
South	6.50	.50			
Dat-so-la-lee	14.14	8.71	11.38		
Parish Collection	12.81	1.79	2.77	12.84	
Suzie	13.33	2.84	4.97	14.03	1.14

[a] $p < .05$; coefficient of variation $= 2.45$.

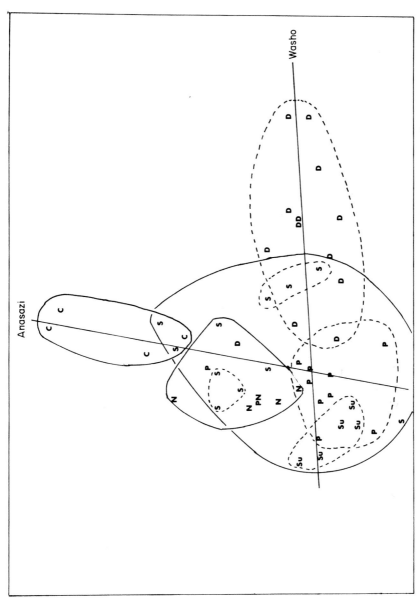

Figure 7.6. Plot of Canonical Variables I and II, combined Washo and Anasazi sample.

arate the majority of the weavers into groups in the lower left-hand corner of the graph. The southern precinct of Antelope House, as usual, generates as much variability as all the other samples combined and is therefore distributed throughout the plot. Again, there are distinct sub-groups in S.

Significantly, those samples from the two collections that may reasonably be considered "special," the work of Dat-so-la-lee and the C cluster, fall out on the extremes of different axes of the plot. This would seem to indicate that the weavers in question were operating on different underlying construction principles or parameters. This inference is supported by the distribution of the remainder of the sample. Specimens from the respective populations line up along the appropriate axes, Anasazi on the vertical axis and Washo on the horizontal axis.

This plot further suggests that Dat-so-la-lee and the C basketmaker(s) from Antelope House were not only practicing the "epitome" of the art of coiling in their respective weaving milieux but were also maximizing those quantities in coiling manufacture defined as "desirable" by their respective cultures.

If the axes in Figure 7.6 represent cultures (in the broadest sense of the term), then distributions along these axes represent the magnitude of an individual's skill in combining the requisite, culturally determined coiling production skills. This magnitude is measured by high correlations and constitutes an index of replicability on the part of the individual relative to other individuals in the same culture. We are not necessarily speaking only of adherence to an aesthetic standard or standards. Any normative aesthetic quality is ultimately incidental to an individual's ability to reproduce a pattern again and again. Rather, since aesthetic quality and manipulative consistency probably stem from the same set of psychological causal factors, these "phenomena" are no doubt highly correlated.

At this juncture, it is appropriate to consider the construction principles or production parameters that appear to have been operative among Washo and Anasazi basketmakers. While examining this question, we must remember that measurements taken on a coiled basket (or any other kind of basket) may or may not be important at "face value." In the present study, examination of the canonical coefficients indicates that the major variable that was paramount to Dat-so-la-lee and the other Washo women was the number of stitches per centimeter. Dat-so-la-lee, in particular, had the extraordinary ability to produce baskets with the same number of stitches per centimeter regardless of vessel form. Although this suggests that she may have been directly concerned with the production of a set number of stitches per unit of length, she may also have been influenced by some design elements, the reproduction of which incidentally and unconsciously resulted in great regularity in her stitch pattern. Even more complex is the possibility that she was concerned with several production elements simultaneously, which culminated in a given number of stitches per segment of coil. If Dat-so-la-lee was actually (i.e., consciously) concerned with the standardization of the number of stitches per unit of length, the measurements taken on her baskets serve literally as a measure of her intentions. In other cases, measurements are only an "indicator" of more widespread concerns. Thus, if we conclude that Washo weavers were principally interested in producing a certain number of stitches per unit of coil, we may also be defining a number of other, covert production parameters.

Despite the caveat just presented, the canonical analysis of the combined Washo/Anasazi samples *does* seem to indicate that the Washo valued stitches per unit length of coil, whereas the Anasazi were far more concerned with coil width. Approximately equal attention was given to the number of coils per centimeter and stitch width in both cultures.

The reasons for this differential emphasis are doubtlessly functional. Most Washo baskets, at least aboriginal ones, took the form of parching trays or watertight bowls that could serve as cooking vessels. In either of these forms, tight spacing of the stitches is an absolute functional necessity (see Adovasio 1974). Conversely, the Anasazi at Antelope House produced very few parching trays but manufactured a wide range of storage and carrying baskets. These latter forms require thick durable walls as certainly as parching trays necessitate tight stitches. In this light, the distribution of the Washo and Anasazi specimens along their respective axes is readily understandable, and to a great degree explainable by subsistence-related imperatives.

Although the combination of the Anasazi and Washo samples does not directly contribute to the isolation of individual weavers within their respective populations, it does demonstrate the utility of the present methodology in separating the products of discrete cultural entities and in extracting operational principles within or around which individual basketmakers practiced their craft.

In retrospect, two salient points emerge from the study reported here. First, the inability of the numerical measures alone to effectively and absolutely segregate clusters within the archaeological assemblage indicates the need to refine and expand the measuring process. Second, a way must be found to quantify the nominal attributes that, at present, provide far greater resolution than the continuous variables measured in this study. Despite the problems noted previously, it is patently obvious that the work of individual weavers *can* be distinguished and further-more that at least some of the cultural imperatives that conditioned or influenced basketry production in a given population can be identified. Presumably, with further experimentation, the methodology of isolation can be improved and standardized.

ACKNOWLEDGMENTS

We wish to thank David Clark, who provided measurements on the Washo sample used here, as well as Doris L. Rendall, research assistant, and Donald R. Tuohy, chairman, Department of Anthropology, the Nevada State Museum, for their cooperation and assistance in this project. We also wish to express our appreciation to Andee Ferenci and Elaine Springel, who typed this manuscript, Rhonda Andrews, who prepared the figures, and Ronald Carlisle who edited the original manuscript.

REFERENCES

Adovasio, J. M.
    1970a   The origin, development and distribution of Western Archaic textiles. *Tebiwa* **13**:1–40.
    1970b   Textiles. In Hogup Cave, by C. M. Aikens. *University of Utah Anthropological Papers*, No. 93:133–153.
    1971   Some comments on the relationship of Great Basin textiles to textiles from the Southwest. *University of Oregon Anthropological Papers*, No. 1:103–108.
    1972   Basketry as an indicator of archaeological frontiers. Paper presented at the Thirty-seventh Annual Meeting of the Society for American Archaeology, Miami Beach.
    1974   Prehistoric North American basketry. *Nevada State Museum Anthropological Papers*, No. 16:100–145.
    in press a   Prehistoric Great Basin textiles. In *The handbook of North American Indians*, Vol. X, *Great Basin*, edited by W. D'Azevedo.
    in press b   Basketry. In *The handbook of North American Indians*, Vol. XVI, *Technology and visual arts*, edited by W. C. Sturtevant.
    in press c   Prehistoric basketry . . . Mexico. In *Early Americans, ecology and Eskimos*, edited by David L. Browman. World Anthropology Series. The Hague: Mouton.
Adovasio, J. M. *et al.*
    in press a   Basketry from Antelope House. In *Antelope House*, by D. Morris *et al.* Publications of the National Park Service.
    in press b   Basketry from Dirty Shame Rockshelter. In Dirty Shame Rockshelter, by C. M. Aikens and D. Cole. *University of Oregon Anthropological Papers.*
Dixon, W. J. (Ed.)
    1973   BMD: Biomedical computer programs. *University of California Publications in Automatic Computation*, No. 2.

Driver, H. E.
1961   *Indians of North America.* Chicago: University of Chicago Press.
Emery, I.
1966   *The primary structure of fabrics.* Washington, D.C.: The Textile Museum.
Gunn, J. D.
1975   An envirotechnological system for Hogup Cave. *American Antiquity* **40**:3–22.
King, M. E.
1975   Archaeological textiles. *Proceedings of the 1974 Irene Emery Roundtable on Museum Textiles.* Washington, D.C.: The Textile Museum.
Rozaire, C.
1969   The chronology of the woven materials from the caves at Falcon Hill, Washoe County, Nevada. *Nevada State Museum Anthropological Papers*, No. 14:181–186.
Weltfish, G.
1932   Problems in the study of ancient and modern basketmakers. *American Anthropologist* **34**:107–117.

8

Computer Mapping of Idiosyncratic Basketry Manufacture Techniques in the Prehistoric Ozette House, Cape Alava, Washington

DALE R. CROES
JONATHAN O. DAVIS

In order to discover traits in a site that reflect different individuals, most prehistorians would benefit immeasurably if they could employ a full-time cartographer to draw map after map of the distributions of different artifact characteristics. But limited time, skills, money, and other resources usually force the analyst to restrict drawings to only a few crucial maps and he does not further manipulate the data graphically. In fact, however, facilities and resources are available at most universities to do much more distributional analysis. The high-speed digital computer can be an excellent cartographer and artist, drawing any projection: horizontal, vertical, or perspective. This is the idea we have pursued to map the prehistoric Ozette basketry. The program is developed now and can be used to approach several different problems, and in this case to demonstrate whether certain basketry distributions in the Ozette village area reflect individual idiosyncrasies in basketry manufacture. The facilities for this work and direction were provided by Henry T.

Irwin of the Department of Anthropology, Washington State University (WSU).

For this study we have used the WSU on-line Calcomp 663 drum plotter, and a system of FORTRAN subroutines developed by Stanford University (n.d.), called OPS (On-line Plotting System) which we have modified (Croes, Davis, and Irwin 1974). It is relatively simple to modify this programming to produce a drawing of a typical artifact rather than a letter. (Davis modified the program and Croes provided the data and representative drawings of the basket type symbols.)

Basketry artifacts from a single prehistoric house excavated at the Ozette Village Archaeological Site (45CA24) on the coast of Washington comprise the universe of study. The Ozette Site is being excavated through the cooperative efforts of the National Park Service, the Makah Tribal Nation, and Washington State University under the direction of Richard D. Daugherty. Ozette consists of a section of a prehistoric Northwest Coast Indian village that was encased and preserved by a massive mudslide about A.D. 1400 (Daugherty and Kirk 1976; Gleeson and Grosso 1976). The first excavated house is large, measuring about 40 × 70 feet. It housed several families, each living in a distinct corner or wall area of the house. Because of the waterlogged condition of the site, the basketry artifacts have been perfectly preserved in their general spatial relationship in the house, though some disturbance was caused by the mudslide. The unique distributions of certain basketry modes and types in the Ozette house may be indicative of unique family and/or individual basketry styles. The task performed by the computer is the plotting of the distribution of these basketry artifacts in the house according to any specified criteria.

BASKETRY TYPES AND COMPUTER SYMBOLS

For this distributional analysis we used paradigmatically defined basket, mat, and hat types defined by the combination of these selected modes: material, shape, body weave, bottom weave, and basket extensions (Croes 1972). These explicit basketry types provide ideal units for computer mapping.

A representational symbol was created for each basketry type. We could have simply used numbers or letters in this manner, yet the elegance and interpretative content of the map is vastly improved by the use of representational symbols. Such symbols communicate additional attribute information about the artifact types depicted. In this case, the symbol conveys the important basket modes of shape (rounded rec-

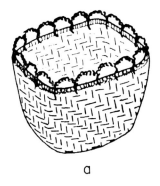
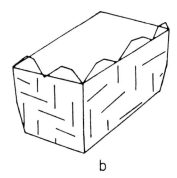

a   b

Figure 8.1. (a) Illustration of Ozette Basket Type 20; (b) computer drawing representing Ozette Basket Type 20.

tangular), body weave (twill), and handle extensions (continuous loop handle). (See Figure 8.1.) In maps, this additional information allows the reader visually to discover unique distributional patterns of both basketry modes and types. Fifty-nine basketry types have been delineated and programmed. The repertoire of symbols presently available is shown in Figure 8.2. Note that these are type-class symbols and are not representative of individual baskets. The baskets themselves are positioned in their proper places in the classification and the type symbols occur on the map as defined basket, mat, or hat classes reoccur in the Ozette house area.

THE MAPPING PROGRAM

The essential data recorded for each basket consist of its site location and its type-class designation. Also the artifact completeness is recorded; a broken basket may have a slash drawn through its symbol. (Many of the baskets outside the house seem to have been broken and discarded.) These are the minimum data required by the program; much more information needs to be coded for each artifact in order to permit detailed manipulation of the program for different distributional problems. The additional data recorded for each of the baskets include its elevation, stratigraphic unit, catalog number, materials, shape, body weave, bottom weave, extensions in the form of handles, flaps, and tumpline loops, rim construction, size, ornamentation, gauge of weave—and any other important artifact mode information that can be added. These will be important when the unique distributions of artifact modes, rather than artifact types, are desired.

Additional features may be incorporated in the programming to com-

BASKETS   HATS MATS

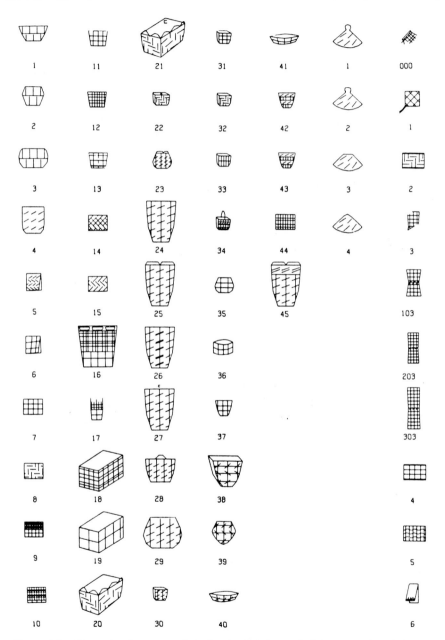

Figure 8.2. Computer-drawn symbols for basket types, hat types, and mat types from the Ozette Site.

prise a finished map; the plan view outline of the first Ozette house is our framework, and a border, title, north arrow, and legend are drawn by the plotter. Grids, trench wall outlines, grid stakes, and grid line numbers could also be added.

ILLUSTRATED COMPUTER MAPPING PROBLEMS

This mapping program can now do our cartographic work at low cost. Various possibilities are available. First, all the baskets, mats, and hats can be drawn by class onto a finished map (Figure 8.3). This first map indicates that most of the activities involving basketry took place along the wall areas of the house; less use of these artifacts took place in the central area (the concentration of basketry along walls also corresponds to family living areas, Drucker 1951:71). Now, for a hypothetical example: Suppose we wanted to see whether there is a unique distribution of plain twined weave with a narrow gauge (regardless of basketry type, but drawn with the type symbols). Insertion of a sorting routine produces a map showing only those baskets. Several possibilities now present themselves, and with the computer plotter, we are now equipped to search out unique distributions of basketry modes or types systemati-

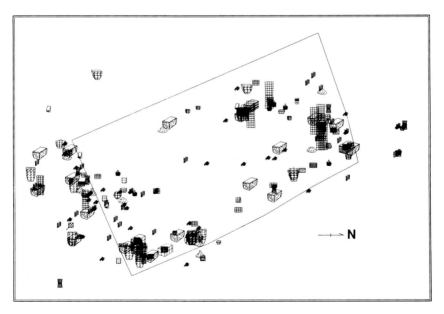

Figure 8.3. Computer plot with all Ozette basketry types located (as of 1973). Scale: North arrow is 2 m in length (basketry symbols not to scale).

cally. These unique distributions in the Ozette house, at this single point in time, may be indicative of idiosyncratic, individualistic styles. This possibility can only be presented as a hypothesis, and certainly is not the only possible explanation. Several alternative explanations can be given for these unique distributions, but the value here is being able to search for and discover unique distributions, if they exist. A hypothetical explanation can be given, and, as long as the means are explicit, the hypotheses can be further tested and evaluated. Some steps taken concerning Ozette basketry and this problem will be demonstrated.

First, computer maps were drawn according to different types of rim construction on baskets. Rim construction is not a dimension for defining the basket types, since it often crosscuts general type definitions; several baskets of the same type will have several different rim constructions. We posited the hypothesis that different rim constructions on the same types of baskets might be indicative of individually preferred or learned rims. If different rim construction techniques cluster in distinct living areas of the house (and on the same general types of baskets) then this may be indicative of individualistic traits. Three maps were drawn of the three most common rim types. Each map showed a random distribution of these rim techniques, and therefore did not show a unique clustering in different areas in the house (Figure 8.4).

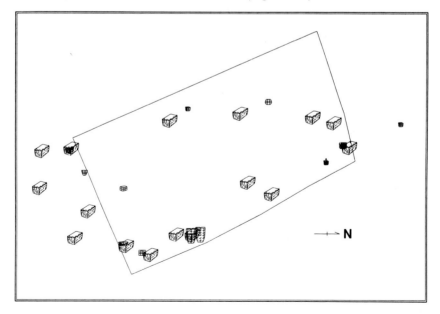

Figure 8.4. One example of the random distribution of a rim type (the hitched rim). Scale: North arrow is 2 m in length (basketry symbols not to scale).

Next, baskets were plotted according to defined ranges of weave gauge and distinct forms of ornamentation. Gauge of weave and forms of ornamentation could be indicative of individual tendencies. Again the basketry types according to these modes were randomly distributed throughout the house, and were not indicative of any unique distributions. These modes could still be the result of individual style, but their distribution in the house is random and this may need an explanation in itself.

Next, we compared basket types that were shown to have the same functional characteristics and similar type definitions, to see whether any unique distributions corresponded to the slight differences in definition. The equivalent functional basket types OB18 and OB19 are the same definitively except for their slightly different body weave; OB19 is plain checker weave and OB18 is a slight variant called checker II weave: The checker II weave has weft elements that alternate in width from wide to narrow strips, creating a form of structural ornamentation. The types are located at opposite ends of the house; the two OB18s are in the north end of the house and the three OB19s are in the south end of the house (Figure 8.5). This is a small piece of evidence for unique dis-

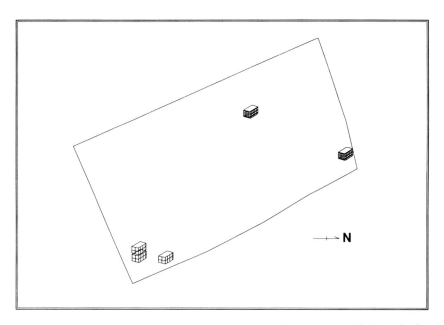

Figure 8.5. Distribution of OB19 basket types (southeast area) and OB18 basket types (north area). Scale: North arrow is 2 m in length (basketry symbols not to scale).

tributions, but it provided a possible indication for further testing. Plain checker weave is fairly common at Ozette but the checker II weave is rare, and so the next map drew baskets with only checker II weave (also drawing again the OB18 and OB19 baskets). All the baskets with checker II weave were in the north end of the house (Figure 8.6). Because of this unique distribution a hypothesis was posited that this could indicate that the basketweaver in the north area of the house used a slight variation of checker weave when weaving the associated functional class OB18–19 and also used this weave for other baskets; the weaver (or weavers) in other parts of the house (in particular the south) did not.

   With this possibility the map was searched for other unique north–south distributions. The same general mat types (OM303 and OM203) made in the north end of the house were found to be slightly longer than those in the south (about 7 versus 8+ feet). This difference possibly indicates that the mat weaver in the north area habitually made slightly

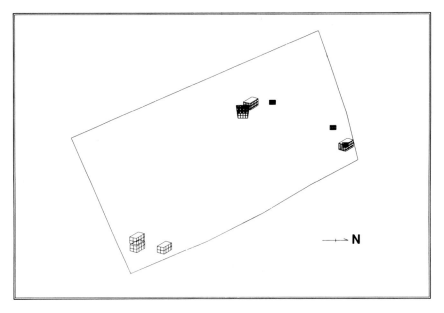

Figure 8.6. The distribution of checker II weave on baskets in the northern area. Also plotted are the OB18 and OB19 basket types. Scale: North arrow is 2 m in length (basketry symbols not to scale). Note the checker II basket inside the OB18 basket in the northeastern corner of the floor. Note also the two checker II baskets on top of one another in the northwest portion of the house.

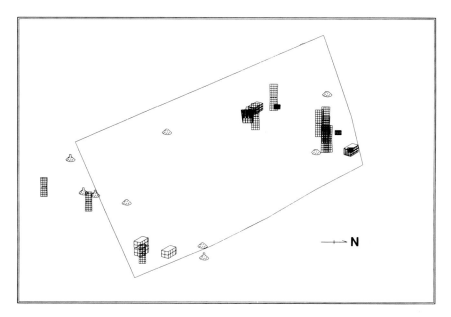

Figure 8.7. Distribution of checker II weave basket types, OB18 and OB19 basket types, mat types, and hat types. Scale: North arrow is 2 m in length (basketry symbols not to scale). Note the "onion" knob-type hats and medium-long mats that were relocated outside the south house wall by the southeast movement of the mudslide. Note also the single "biscuit" knob-type hat in the cluster of basketry items in the northwest portion of the house.

longer mats than those made in the southern and other areas of the house. (Figure 8.7).

Another distinct north–south distribution involves the basketry hats. The hats that are ethnographically attributed to male commoners (flat-top hats) are found in the north–northeastern areas of the house, and the majority of the high status indicative hats ("onion" knob-top hats) are found in the southern area of the house. A knob-top hat of a different stylistic type from those in the south ("biscuit" knob-top hat) was found in the north-northwestern area of the house associated with other high status equipment (whaling gear). With the exception of this specimen, the commoners' hats, possibly manufactured by the same individual, were in the northern area of the house, and the typical "onion" knob-top hats were in the southern end of the house (Figure 8.7).

In summary, the following basketry artifacts have unique distributions in the north and south portions of the house:

North	South
OB18 Baskets (only difference is checker II weave)	OB19 Baskets (only difference is plain checker weave)
Checker II weave (in other types than OB18)	No checker II weave
Long mat types only	Medium-long mat types only
Flat-top commoners' hats	No flat-top commoners' hats
One "biscuit" knob-type hat (OH2)	Three "onion" knob-top hats (OH1)

Several hypotheses could be posited for this north–south distribution. Some of these alternative possibilities include

1. Idiosyncratic traits of the basketweavers in the north and south sections of the house
2. Traditional weaving techniques of different families
3. Class-status-indicative techniques and other permutations of the above

CONCLUSIONS

Similar Ozette basketry functional types have been shown to have slight variations existing in the weave techniques (checker versus checker II), sizes (the mats), and forms (the hats). These variations of the same functional types plus the consistent unique distributional characteristics of those noted variations provide the data for proposing possible individual idiosyncratic tendencies in the first of the Ozette houses to be excavated.

This hypothesis and others can be further tested and evaluated as new materials and houses are excavated at Ozette. Also, as other artifact categories (wood wedges, fishhooks, art motifs, arrows, boxes, bowls) are added to the program, other distributional problems can be economically and easily approached with completed and publishable maps. Some of the advantages of this computer mapping system are as follows:

1. It gives the analyst the flexibility and freedom needed to graphically manipulate data in order to discover unique distributional characteristics.

2. Mapping with type symbols lends itself more readily to analytical procedures than does the use of abstract symbols.
3. The program has the combined qualities of elegance, accuracy, speed, publishable results, and also economy.

The Ozette mapping system was used to discover idiosyncratic individualistic tendencies in basketry materials. We did not explicitly develop this program to approach the individual in prehistory, but the program can and has been used to seek out the Ozette individual. This computer mapping system can be used further for this kind of problem and for several other archaeological problems that deal with artifact distribution.

REFERENCES

Croes, Dale R.
    1972   An analysis of prehistoric baskets from the Ozette Site, Cape Alava. Unpublished M.A. paper, Department of Anthropology, Washington State University.
Croes, Dale R., Jonathan Davis, and Henry T. Irwin
    1974   The use of computer graphics in archaeology: A case study from the Ozette Site, Washington. *Reports of Investigations*, No. 52. Laboratory of Anthropology, Washington State University, Pullman.
Daugherty, Richard D., with Ruth Kirk
    1976   Ancient Indian village where time stood still. *Smithsonian* 7(2):68–75.
Drucker, Philip
    1951   The northern and central Nootkan tribes. Bureau of American Ethnology, *Bulletin 144*. U.S. Government Printing Office, Washington D.C.
Gleeson, Paul, and Gerald Grosso
    1976   Ozette Site. In *The excavation of water-saturated archaeological sites (wet sites) on the Northwest coast of North America*, edited by Dale R. Croes. *National Museum of Man Mercury Series*, Archaeological Survey of Canada, Paper No. 50, Ottawa. Pp. 13–44.
Stanford University
    n.d.   On-line plotting software. *Library Program* No. CO51. Computation Center, Stanford University.

9

Idiosyncratic Chipping Style as a Demographic Indicator: A Proposed Application to the South Hills Region of Idaho and Utah

JOEL GUNN

In a previous study, I tested the effect of environment on a subsistence trajectory at Hogup Cave (Gunn 1974, 1975b). It was apparent from regression residuals in that study that there were other factors for change that were not involved strictly with habitat. A highly probable additional source of cultural change was a shift in demographic patterns. In this chapter, I shall first present a method of detecting idiosyncratic behavior in bifacial chipping styles, and then examine the nature and scale of the prehistoric demographic system in the South Hills region of southeastern Idaho and northern Utah of which Hogup is a part. I shall model that system and select a set of theoretical operational alternatives, and finally, show that idiosyncratic style in chipping bifaces is a means of testing the model.

Demography and *cultural geography* are taken primarily to mean the density and distribution of populations relative to the material resources necessary to maintain life.

DISCOVERING THE PREHISTORIC INDIVIDUAL

The individual human being is the most elemental unit of social and cultural organization. Thus the products of individual minds and endeavors must be the basis of any data set designed to reveal social behavior. As a corollary it follows that the level of resolution at which social behavior is studied is directly dependent on how near the unit of study approaches that of the individual. For social scientists studying modern populations the highest possible level of resolution poses no problem. Issuing a statistically adequate number of questionnaires to a sample of people will reveal the behavior of a population with a known degree of reliability resolved to the individual level.

The study of prehistoric populations, on the other hand, is infinitely more complicated. There are no apparent individuals to study. Even the level of resolution is difficult to conceive or estimate. Is the researcher dealing with individuals or local societies or those broader social spheres we call cultures? Anthropologists have long assumed that *culture* was the level of resolution and it seemed for a long time that culture was as far as it was possible or necessary to resolve the past. Inevitably, however, questions that required higher resolution data bases began to be asked. By the late 1950s for instance, ceramic typologists were clearly grappling with the prehistoric individual. James C. Gifford notes that "variation as a recognizable reality can be thought of as the product of the individual or of relatively small social groups in human society [Gifford 1960:342]."

The individual is readily observable in some aspects of prehistoric technology. In ceramics, for instance, the individual seems almost to have forced himself into the typologist's consciousness. With other artifacts, such as stone tools, observation of prehistoric individuals may not be so easily accomplished. Lithics do represent, however, the largest and most complete continuous record of human development and sociocultural organization. As such they recommend themselves as a subject of idiosyncratic style analysis.

The study described here applies the technique of laser diffraction analysis to the study of scar orientations on bifaces (Gunn 1975a). I wanted to find out whether characteristics exhibited during the manufacture of bifaces could lead to the identification of prehistoric individuals. The research strategy designed used modern flint knappers so samples of artifacts from known makers could be secured. These artifacts were then analyzed by various linear models that accord with different archaeological situations likely to be encountered during archaeological research projects. The two situations foreseen are (1) assemblages without known knappers and (2) assemblages with some known knappers. In cases where knappers are not known the assemblage is treated as a population to be segregated systematically into subsets, each subset representing a prehistoric individual. Factor analysis followed by treatment of factor scores by a set of logicospatial criteria is used. In the second case, where knappers are known through association with caches and the like, discriminant function and canonical analyses are used to determine knappers of pieces not located with the associated group.

Individual Style Analysis:
Laser Diffraction of Biface Scar Patterns

A population of 30 bifaces produced by six knappers was collected. Five of the individuals were modern stone knappers. Each person was asked to make 5 bifaces according to an established procedure. Five more bifaces were analyzed from the Simons Site cache in Idaho (Muto 1971).

The bifaces were made according to the following specifications:

1. Material: obsidian (Glass Buttes, Oregon)
2. Chipping implement: soft sandstone hammerstone (Knapper 3 resorted to an antler billet occasionally.)
3. Product: semioval biface. The first biface made by the first knapper was used as the template. All succeeding bifaces were to be copies of it. The semioval shape, with one end expanded, was chosen to ensure a common orientation criterion for the pieces.
4. Extent of chipping: overall thinning flake scars
5. Flaking technique: percussion
6. Size: to approximate Biface 1
7. Shape: to approximate Biface 1

The work was done at the 1972 session of the Idaho State University Flintworking School.

In addition to the five sets of bifaces made by modern knappers, bifaces from the Paleo–Indian Simons Site cache were analyzed and five bifaces were selected for closeness to Biface 1. This was done to give a touch of prehistoric reality to the data, and to test a hypothesis put forward by Don Crabtree (personal communication). It is his opinion that prehistoric knappers, because they were practicing the same techniques and making the same tools every day, would produce tighter clusters of artifacts than would modern knappers. Modern knappers experiment with various techniques but seldom become master of any one. Crabtree regards the Simons knapper as very skilled on the basis of his experiments in replicating the Simons bifaces.

After the bifaces were collected, the scar patterns had to be converted into numerically analyzable data. In outline, the scar patterns were traced, inked, and photographed. The high-contrast negatives from this operation were placed in a laser diffraction apparatus. The orientation of scars could then be measured by machinery associated with the laser. Briefly, laser diffraction transforms the scar pattern into a target shaped pattern, or spectrum, like the one shown in Figure 9.1, part a. (The ap-

a

b   c

Figure 9.1. Making and measuring a laser diffraction spectrum: (a) scar outline of a quartzite hand axe made by F. Bordes; (b) idealized half-spectrum; (c) light-sensitive surfaces to measure spectrum. [Adapted from Idiosyncratic behavior in chipping style: Some hypotheses and preliminary analysis, by Joel Gunn (1975a), in *Lithic technology: Making and using stone tools*, edited by Earl Swanson (The Hague: Mouton), by permission of EDICOM N.V.]

paratus used for this experiment does not produce a photograph; the illustration is material from an earlier pilot study.) The outline in Figure 9.1, part a, is of the face of a hand axe made by F. Bordes. The outline was photographed and the laser diffraction spectrum, the star-like pattern to the right, generated. Longer rays in the spectrum indicate that more lines in the scar pattern are oriented in that direction. Shorter rays indicate fewer scars oriented in the same direction.

The process is not unduly complicated (Oxnard 1973:169–201; Preston, Green, and Davis 1970:23). A laser beam is directed through a set of lenses and the negative. Only the lines of the scar pattern let light through the negative. Beyond the negative, the focal point, the lenses form the spectrum. Either a camera or a light-sensitive surface may be located at the focal point to record the pattern of the spectrum. The spectrum is an optical Fourier transform of the scar pattern.

The apparatus used in this experiment had a light-sensitive surface at the focal point. This light-sensitive surface measured the concentrations of scar pattern orientations. Since the spectrum is symmetrical, only half of it must be measured, as in Figure 9.1, part b. The light-sensitive surface, Figure 9.1, part c, is divided into 32 wedges of 5° each. Each wedge measures the intensity of that part of the spectrum falling on it and thus the relative number of lines in the scar pattern oriented in its direction. These measurements were recorded and used as an indication of scar orientation. After the data were collected they were keypunched and processed as indicated later in this chapter.

A preliminary examination of the data from the laser diffraction analysis will point out some differences between knappers and act as a guide for interpretation of the multivariate analyses to follow. Both sides of each of the 30 bifaces collected were analyzed, yielding 60 spectra in all. A three-decimal number was read from the laser diffraction spectrum for each wedge (5° of arc). Thirty-two readings were taken from each scar pattern. To determine the distribution and dispersion of readings for each scar pattern, a mean, standard deviation, and coefficient of variation ($s/\bar{x}$) were calculated. The highest mean (Figure 9.2, part a) was .194 (scar pattern 23). The lowest mean was .081 (scar pattern 54). A high mean can indicate either of two conditions. First, the photo negative was generally letting more light through (many scars), or second, there were some arc segments registering very high readings, which raised the mean (many scars oriented in the same direction). The coefficient of variation (or c.v.), can serve as a tool to unravel these combinations (Figure 9.2, part b). It tells how much dispersion there is from the mean. In the case of our mysterious high mean, a high coefficient of variation would suggest the latter case, i.e., unidirectional orientations

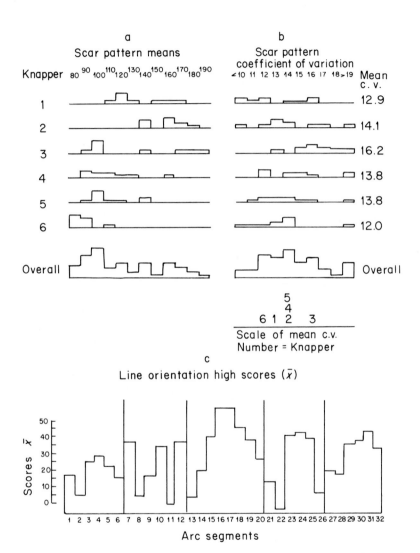

Figure 9.2. Distribution histograms for preliminary examination of the data. [Adapted from Idiosyncratic behavior in chipping style: Some hypotheses and preliminary analysis, by Joel Gunn (1975a), in *Lithic technology: Making and using stone tools*, edited by Earl Swanson (The Hague: Mouton), by permission of EDICOM N.V.]

yielding some very high and many very low numbers. Scar pattern 23 has the highest mean and coefficient of variation; inspection of the piece confirms the unidirectional orientation of scars. A low coefficient of variation indicates that there is no particular orientation to the scars. If the average of a knapper's coefficients of variation can be taken as an index of his tendency to orient scars in one or a few directions, the knappers studied can be scaled (from high to low) as 3, 2, 4, 5, 1, 6. Interestingly enough, the prehistoric knapper ranks lowest on this scale. If the prehistoric knapper is assumed to be the most experienced, then there is a negative correlation between consistently oriented scars and length of experience.

Another helpful preliminary observation would involve the locating of the part of the spectrum that shows the most variation between knappers. Inspection of the data after standardization showed that right-oriented scars are of a consistent nature on most pieces. A histogram of the scores greater than the mean (Figure 9.2, part c) shows that right-oriented scars also cluster about different modes. The left-sloping scars, however, were unpatterned and erratic, both as individual scars and in the histogram. I surmised from this that left-sloping scars would prove most valuable in distinguishing the tendencies of the various knappers. This observation will key interpretation of the multivariate analyses to follow.

With some idea of what can be expected of the data, we can now turn to a more thorough study of idiosyncratic patterns. In a prehistoric context, unless there is some reason, such as caches of projectile points in a study area, to suspect individuals, the assemblage of bifaces will be treated as a unit to be partitioned into subsets, with the assumption that each subset represents a knapper. Appropriate methods for this operation are global clustering techniques such as principal components analysis. Let us assume for now that our experimental data are from a series of sites in a study area.

The diffraction data were standardized by rows (scar patterns). A principal components program (Wahlstedt and Davis 1968) extracted eight components with eigenvalues greater than 1.0. The eight components accounted for 81% of the variance. As was mentioned earlier, the components accounting for variables on the left side of the laser spectra could be expected to discriminate among the knappers best because of the erratic behavior of that segment of the spectrum. These variables were strongly associated with Component II. As was expected, it separated the knappers best. A search through plots of component scores indicated that Component III was second in discriminatory powers. The others have little discriminatory power. The four most ex-

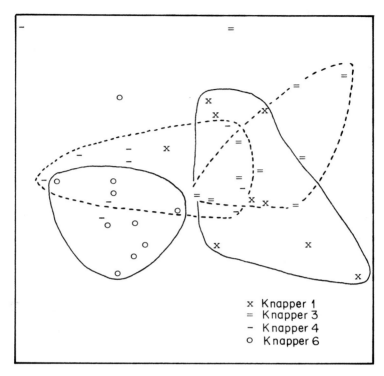

Figure 9.3. Plot of component scores for Components II and III for the experienced knappers. [Adapted from Idiosyncratic behavior in chipping style: Some hypotheses and preliminary analysis, by Joel Gunn (1975a), in *Lithic technology: Making and using stone tools*, edited by Earl Swanson (The Hague: Mouton), by permission of EDICOM N.V.]

perienced knappers are fairly well divided into two groups of two knappers each (Figure 9.3): Knapppers 4 and 6 are together on the left, and Knappers 1 and 3 appear on the right. There is some overlap of Knapper 4 into the other group (3 pieces).

The inexperience of Knappers 2 and 5 is apparent (Figure 9.4). Their scar patterns are spread over the entire area on the plot. Even so, the two inexperienced knappers seem to have distinctive enough styles; one appears at the top of the plot and the other toward the bottom, with little overlap in distributions.

If this particular sample had been drawn from an archaeological region it would be hard to separate one knapper from another. The fact that some knappers can be separated from others, however (e.g., Knappers 3 and 6, Figure 9.5) suggests potential utility for the method. The addition of further information on bifaces, such as other measurements,

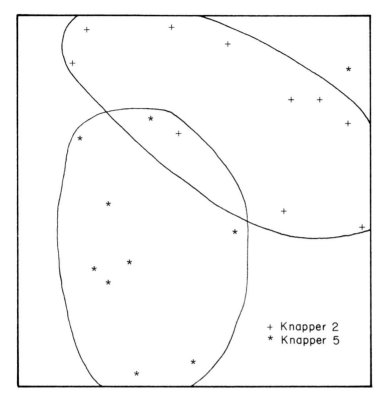

Figure 9.4. Plot of component scores for Components II and III for the inexperienced knappers. [Adapted from Idiosyncratic behavior in chipping style: Some hypotheses and preliminary analysis, by Joel Gunn (1975a), in *Lithic technology: Making and using stone tools*, edited by Earl Swanson (The Hague: Mouton), by permission of EDICOM N.V.]

would probably separate artifacts into groups attributable to distinctive knappers. Also, assigning site location to bifaces on the plots would indicate the affinity of the tools. Suppose, for instance, that the bifaces in Figure 9.5 were from four sites: A, B, C, and D. Analysis of Figure 9.5 shows that bifaces on the left side, associated with the area of Knapper 6, are from Sites A and B. All the bifaces on the right, in the area of Knapper 3, are from Sites C and D. The analyst would conclude that the A and B bifaces were knapped by a single person and his band traveled at least between Sites A and B. The same conclusions would be drawn for Sites C and D.

As Don Crabtree points out, the bifaces used in this experiment may be a particularly difficult sample to deal with. "Our replicas are usually patterned after a particular aboriginal artifact, while prehistoric man

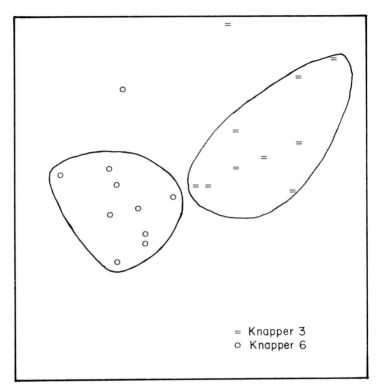

Figure 9.5. Plot of component scores for Components II and III; a clear case of separation. [Adapted from Idiosyncratic behavior in chipping style: Some hypotheses and preliminary analysis, by Joel Gunn (1975a), in *Lithic technology: Making and using stone tools*, edited by Earl Swanson (The Hague: Mouton), by permission of EDICOM N.V.]

made a specific artifact over a long period of time with little or no deviation. Since the purpose of the Bordes and Crabtree experiments has been to replicate a variety of techniques, I think we perhaps would show more variation due to constantly attempting to replicate various tool types of diverse industries [letter of January 2, 1972]." In support of Crabtree's judgment, I would say that the Simons knapper produced by far the tightest cluster of flake scar attributes of the six knappers used in the experiment. Such tight clustering would additionally contribute to identification of knappers from an archaeological context.

The principal components model is convenient because no assumptions have to be made about groups before the analysis is performed. Suppose, however, that two caches of bifaces were known from a study area. An analysis of the two caches leads to the belief that the two caches were made by different people. By use of a discriminant function program it would be possible to (1) determine a set of functions that would maximally separate the two groups or caches of tools into discrete numerical clusters and (2) classify all the bifaces excavated from the region with one of the caches, thus identifying it with the maker of that cache. Only step 1 is described here. Step 2 is demonstrated in an article on automatic classification by Gunn and Prewitt (1975). In this case caches would be substituted for projectile point types.

To demonstrate step 1, a discriminant function analysis was performed on the experimental data (BMD07M, Dixon 1973). Using the results of the discriminant function analysis, the program was able to classify all but one of the 59 scar patterns with its maker. Scar pattern 30 was mistakenly classified as being made by Knapper 1. Needless to say, this ability to classify scar patterns with knappers is quite impressive. Figure 9.6 is a plot of the first two canonical variables from an analysis performed on the diffraction data transformed by the discriminant functions. The plot is equivalent to the plot of component scores. The effects

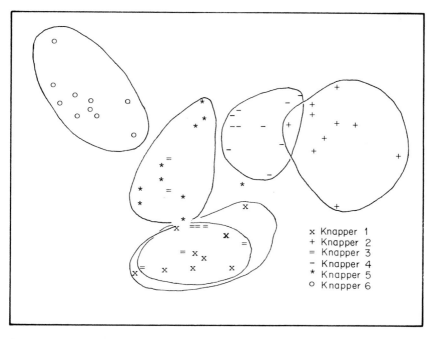

Figure 9.6. Plot of first two canonical variables. [Adapted from Idiosyncratic behavior in chipping style: Some hypotheses and preliminary analysis, by Joel Gunn (1975a), in *Lithic technology: Making and using stone tools*, edited by Earl Swanson (The Hague: Mouton), by permission of EDICOM N.V.]

of the discriminant function analysis can be seen in the clear separation between Knappers 2, 4, 5, and 6. Knappers 1 and 3 are together in the plot. The plot, however, represents only the first two dimensions (71% of the dispersion). Knappers 1 and 3 are separated by another significant canonical variable, which is not shown.

DISCOVERING THE WORLD OF THE PREHISTORIC INDIVIDUAL IN THE GREAT BASIN

Keeping in mind the numerical and conceptual technology by which idiosyncratic style can be discovered, we can now turn to an examination of the ethnographically known cultural system of the South Hills and demographic models relevant to the problem of shifting resources in arid regions.

From the ethnography we can acquaint ourselves with the scale and structure of the society in which the prehistoric individual lived in the eastern Great Basin. Relevant models are expected to retrodict the behavior of that social organization when it is faced with a known set of environmental circumstances such as would have been imposed by the Altithermal. Tracing the behavior of individuals in that circumstance will serve as a test of the proposed model, allowing either an outright rejection of the model or tending to support it.

In essence, the prehistoric individual can aid the social scientist only insofar as he is discovered in the context of a somewhat known social structure and cultural milieu, and as the information is treated within the bounds of an explicit theoretical framework.

The Ethnographic Picture

There are weaknesses in ethnographic analogy, but the Great Basin seems to be one of the places in the world where those weaknesses are most likely to be minimized. In particular, Julian Steward's studies of Shoshoni cultural geography can give insights into the scale and pattern of the populations being studied. Since the area around Hogup Cave is the center of interest in this study, I will review Steward's work north of the Great Salt Lake (Figure 9.7). Of areas verging on desert Steward noted that "people had to traverse enormous territories, modifying their itinerary considerably from year to year as local rainfall or other factors affected plant growth [Steward, 1938:233]." These wanderings may have been somewhat facilitated by the horse in historic times. There are numerous references, however, in Steward's study to travel by foot,

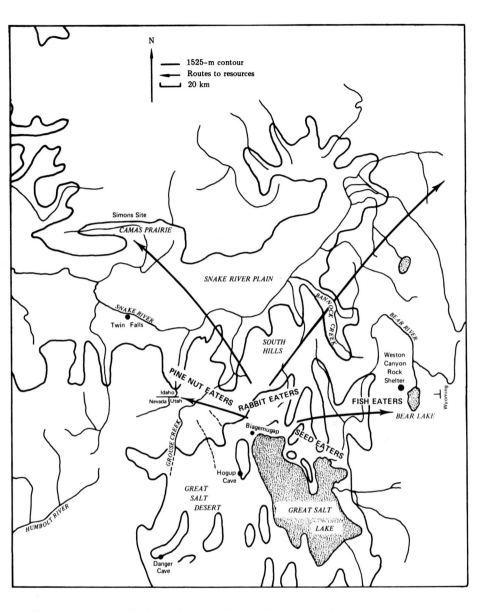

Figure 9.7. Map of the study area showing locations and also routes of travel. [Adapted from Steward 1938.]

which may well hark back to pre-horse periods. Also, archaeological evidence as interpreted by David H. Thomas (1974) indicates that subsistence patterns in the Great Basin have been essentially stable for 2500 years.

In the early 1800s most of the populations of southeastern Idaho, the Bannock and the Fort Hall Shoshoni, seem to have traveled by foot (Steward 1938:207). We can assume that at that time the old customs based on foot transport were largely undisturbed. The Bannock and Shoshoni ranged over southwest Montana, western Wyoming, all of southern Idaho to the Boise River, and into Utah north of the Great Salt Lake. The Shoshoni hunted buffalo in Montana at the time the animal was still to be had in Idaho. Those who had no horses walked across the Great Divide and sometimes wintered on the Plains in order to take advantage of the season's kill (Steward 1938:204). Alternatively, Steward (1938:206) cites a passage from observations by Leonard (between 1831 and 1836) who says, "They generally make but one visit to the buffalo country during the year, where they remain until they jerk as much meat as their females can bring home on their backs."

In addition, the Fort Hall-based Bannock and Shoshoni are reported to have made frequent visits to the Camas Prairie in the western sector of the Snake River Plain, which was an area so rich in vegetable resources that almost all the groups in the Snake River regions and environs as distant as Wyoming made an annual visit. Similar trips were made to Bear Lake near the Idaho–Wyoming–Utah border for roots, berries, mountain sheep, and other game [Stratham (1975) has surveyed Camas resources in southern Idaho]. Grouse Creek in extreme northwestern Utah was exploited for its abundant pine nuts.

In the South Hills on the Utah side are the Grouse Creek (Pine Nut Eaters), Kamuduka (Rabbit Eaters), and Promontory Point (Seed Eaters) districts. This area includes the archaeological site of Hogup Cave, which figures in the analysis to follow. Grouse Creek is about 60 miles northwest of Hogup Cave. Both Grouse Creek and Hogup Cave are on the Great Salt Desert, which seems to have prohibited traffic with the Gosiute to the south of the Great Salt Desert. They were also relatively isolated from westward contact by inhospitable desert (Steward 1938:173). These districts, then, including Hogup, were the southern periphery of a range centering to the north. The Grouse Creek district (1938:173–174) was occupied by people called the Pine Nut Eaters, so named because of the rich harvest of pine nuts to be had there. The pine nuts were known to and utilized by the people of the Snake River, the promontory district north of the lake, and other more peripheral areas. From Promontory

Point the trip is about 100 miles. The Seed Eater people, without horses, would traverse the distance four or five times a year to carry nuts back to their home villages. Grouse Creek was also unusually rich in antelope. Hunts were conducted both in the spring and fall when the animals migrated.

Immediately north of Hogup lived the Rabbit Eaters, the Kamuduka. Their territory covered Utah north of the Salt Lake and parts of south-eastern Idaho. Before the horse they were distributed in several independent villages over the district. Biagemugəp, which would have been near Locomotive Springs at the north tip of the Salt Lake, was the main village in the south (Steward 1938:217). It had 12–15 families. Winter encampments were sometimes made on Bannock Creek near the Snake River. During the summer, the Rabbit Eaters did not stay together but scattered into small family groups. They ranged from the Bear River to Twin Falls, Idaho, and the Camas Prairie.

Birdsell (1973) has proposed and tested a model that might well outline the dynamics and scale of populations of the South Hills. His research with Australian tribes in arid territories where all the available water is locally derived shows that there is a marked tendency for tribes to reach a size equilibrium of about 500 persons. Tribes are defined as a group of bands having the same language. Bands generally consist of about 25 people. This number is also found to be consistent over the world as a minimum viable social unit. Under the marginal circumstances of the eastern Great Basin, bands would tend to minimize unit size.

Tribal size is maintained by two opposing tendencies, both involving face-to-face contact. First, bands interact with other spatially contiguous bands within the tribe 70–90% of the time. Contact drops off to 10–20% with noncontiguous bands. There is almost no contact with bands outside the tribe. As the number of noncontiguous bands increases, groups in far reaches of the tribal territory tend to lose contact and develop regional peculiarities, which leads to the recognition of a new tribe. When the Aranda tribe of central Australia was contacted, it numbered about 1500, well over the 500-person ideal Birdsell suggests. The tribe was, however, in the process of dividing into three units of appropriate size, as was recognized by the tribesmen themselves (Birdsell 1973).

Second, when a tribe falls below 500 persons its bands will automatically be forced into contiguity with bands of other tribes. Language barriers and other ethnocentric forces will break down, paving the way for absorption of the bands of the diminished tribe into larger surrounding groups (Birdsell 1973).

These two tendencies act to maintain the size of the typical 500-person tribe, which Birdsell calls the Z-tribe. This hypothesis was tested against the diffusion of ceremonies across Australia, a process which fragmented tribes into small groups. The ceremony in question originated at a point in eastern Australia and radiated outward. As bands adopted the ceremony they split off from their old tribes to be associated with other bands that had changed to the new way of life. Birdsell's data show that after the disruptive influence passed, leaving tribes at below optimum, with the passage of time the 500-person equilibrium was restored (1973).

Steward's figures on populations in immediate post-European contact villages around the northern edge of the Great Salt Lake are scarce, but suggest a territory with three bands, Pine Nut Eaters, Rabbit Eaters, and Seed Eaters. These bands consisted of approximately 28, 15, and 27 families, respectively. If 5 individuals are taken to constitute the average family, about 350 persons occupied the region. This figure is somewhat lower than Birdsell's Z-tribe. Ethnic identity, however, would have to be fostered by strong isolating factors such as deserts, salt flats, and the Salt Lake. Additional numbers that would push the tribal size closer to the 500 mark are available if the Fish Eaters around Bear Lake are added to the South Hills Shoshoni, although little is known about their pre-horse habits (Hultkrantz 1974:24). Thus, taken as a whole, the Shoshoni north of the Great Salt Lake compose a Z-tribe of four bands. The area does meet the assumptions of Birdsell's model, especially in that all available water is locally derived.

Birdsell (1973:355) indicates that the techniques he used on Australian aboriginals were applied to the Shoshoni by M. Vorkapich. The attempt was apparently successful and indicated a generally higher density for Great Basin groups than for Australian tribes.

The foregoing discussion indicates that whatever groups used Hogup Cave undoubtedly included the highlands between the Great Salt Lake and the Snake River in their range of habitat (see also Aikens 1970a: 196) and thought nothing of trudging over a great part of this territory every year in order to gather a wide range of subsistence resources. The farthest point to which they traveled was the Camas Prairie. Judging from Steward's study, the population of southern Idaho would have been concentrated in small, independent villages of 15–30 families. Those "villages" would have been mobile, to some extent contingent on resource availability, and subject to reduction in certain seasons of the year. Under these circumstances tribal territories would have been necessarily fluid, but linguistically homogeneous tribal units would have consisted of about 500 persons.

Demographic Interaction with Environment

If we assume that the structure of social organization for the duration of human occupation in the eastern Great Basin was much as Steward and Birdsell describe it, we can proceed to an analysis of social and environmental interaction without fear of undue complication.

Two papers dealing with cultural system reaction to environment change and related areas have been published thus far. Ezra Zubrow's paper on population dynamics (1971) applies a Neomalthusian carrying-capacity model to prehistoric societies in the Hay Hollow Valley of Arizona. Zubrow explains the utilization of various ecological zones as a function of habitation density in most favorable, or optimal, zones. Initially, an optimal zone is occupied at or near carrying capacity. When carrying capacity is exceeded, or when carrying capacity drops, excess population will migrate to less favorable adjacent zones, or marginal zones, in a chain-reaction fashion. This process is illustrated in Figure 9.8.

The process operates as follows. A population moves into Zone A, the optimal zone in an area. It learns to exploit the resources of that zone, and the population increases to something short of carrying capacity. Should the population size overshoot the carrying capacity or the carrying capacity drop, excess population, line A–C, migrates to Zone B as indicated by the arrow in the figure. In a similar cycle, adaptations are made to Zone B and carrying capacity is reached. When it is exceeded, migration again ensues.

A second paper along similar lines was presented by James Adovasio and Gary Fry (1972). They attempt to show that the unstable ecological

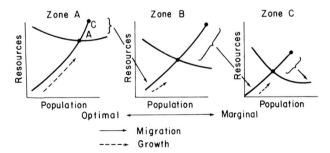

Figure 9.8. The dynamics of a Neomalthusian carrying-capacity model. [From Carrying capacity and dynamic equilibrium in the prehistoric Southwest, by Ezra B. W. Zubrow (1971). Reproduced by permission of the Society for American Archaeology from *American Antiquity* 36(2):130.]

conditions of the eastern Great Basin resulted in cultural change and adaptation. The eastern Great Basin is posited, following Binford (1968), as a marginal zone likely to receive population spillover from nearby optimal zones having too many people. The process is the same as that modeled in Zubrow's paper and shown in Figure 9.8. Since the addition of population to a marginal habitat results in disequilibrium between population and habitat, a means of restoring the balance must be found. The alternatives are population control by infanticide and senilicide, or technological innovations leading to the broadening of the subsistence base to support the population. Adovasio and Fry believe that the technological option was taken. There is no ethnographic evidence that infanticide and senilicide were practiced in the Great Basin. Also, there is evidence that advanced seed-processing methods were developed early in the eastern Great Basin (Adovasio 1970, 1974, in press). Only during later times did these innovations spread to the more optimal western and northern regions of the Great Basin. The improved technology included the use of coiled parching trays, which are the most efficient means of preparing small, hard-shelled seeds for consumption. In contrast, Coahuiltecans of northern Mexico are known to have practiced infanticide as a means of population control.

Although the constructs provided in these two papers may aid in an analysis of behavior at the level of populations and cultures, a model of behavior at the individual level might be instructive. I have used the word *individual* boldly in the previous sentence, to get the reader's attention, but now I would like to restate the proposition slightly. If one were to take the position that sociocultural behavior is a product of individual behavior and that therefore the same limitations and characteristics can be presumed for sociocultural systems as for cognitive systems, the difference between cultural and individual behavior would be diminished or would disappear, theoretically. In this context the old adage that suggests the cultural whole to be greater than the sum of its individual parts probably reflects our lack of understanding of the function of our own brains rather than the mysterious mechanisms of the cultural whole. At least this was the case two decades ago. Thanks to the revolution in psychology, neurophysiology, and related sciences after World War II, the function of the human brain need no longer be thought of as a total mystery (see Bolles 1974 and Powers 1973 for a discussion of the development of related theories). Regarding the brain in a systems context, researchers have developed reasonable and interesting hypotheses to explain the operation of cognition and motivation. I have been very much impressed by how these models can serve equally well as cultural adaptation models, and the following discussion demonstrates the application of one of these models to the problem of cultural adaptation.

The model needs to be bounded by two warnings. First, the system discussed is taken from an early work by William Ross-Ashby (1960, first published in 1951). Since then this basic idea has been considerably elaborated by writers such as William T. Powers (1973). The earlier Ross-Ashby model has the advantage of simplicity, which probably escapes reality more than its complex derivatives; but simplicity has advantages in a first try. If its expected potential usefulness is realized, elaboration of the scheme can follow.

Second, application of the model to societies of the lowest possible level of cultural complexity can be easily rationalized. The Great Basin aborigines lived in a "primitive democracy" (Spencer and Jennings 1965:281) in which the leader of a band very much represented the mind of the band. The behavior of the band probably expressed the motivations and concepts of the leader, perhaps slightly modified by the general population's marginal inputs to his thinking. The leader and the population were part of the same closely knit culture and they would have been more or less automatically in agreement as to the solution of most problems. The primary function of the head man of such an organization is to motivate the group along culturally accepted or culturally acceptable courses of action. Levi-Strauss (1974:307ff.) describes what is probably an analogous political situation in *Tristes Tropiques*. Under such circumstances the chief apparently has to be a virtual dynamo of motivation since he must lead by example rather than command. The continuous existence of low-complexity cultures over long periods of time is part of what stimulated my interest in aboriginal cultures of the Great Basin. Presumably these same principles can be applied to more complex societies (Flannery 1972).

William Ross-Ashby (1960) designed a cybernetic system to explain brain function. He called his design an *ultrastable system*. An ultrastable system is a goal-seeking system with two sets of feedback. In a version of the model modified to a cultural context, the goal is survival by adaptation to the environment, specifically, the maintenance of an adequate and balanced diet. The first feedback loop to an ultrastable system is feedback in the usual sense. Negative feedback goes directly from sensors to the system to maintain homeostasis. In the dietary situation such a feedback would be hunger, which motivates an individual to get food. Acquisition of food serves to maintain the favorable status of the individual and the social system of which he is a part.

The second feedback loop is by means of a continuous variable that monitors the more general status of the system. As long as the variable stays within acceptable bounds, the system pursues existing goals. When the variable is forced out of bounds by unfavorable changes in the system's status, however, a "step-mechanism" forces changes in the system's goals (Ross-Ashby 1960:132). The system then seeks equilibrium under a new set of priorities that may be more favorable to its stability and success. In a cultural adaptive system, starvation, as opposed to normal daily hunger, serves as a monitoring variable. Take as an example a fictitious band of hunters and gatherers. They are accustomed to eating meals composed of a combination of rabbit meat and pickleweed mush. This habit requires that pickleweed seeds and rabbits be harvested in a set ratio. For a period they easily meet their goal. After a time, however, climate, acting as an independent variable to the system, changes—resulting in an altering of the normal availability of rabbits and pickleweed seeds; subsequently there is more pickleweed and fewer rabbits. For a while our fictitious band tries to keep its standards. Hunting for the preferred number of rabbits, however, requires more and more time with less and less reward. Meanwhile the more abundant pickleweed resources go to waste. Unsatisfied hunger accumulates into starvation. Faced with the grim prospect of starvation's ultimate consequences the band decides to alter its dietary preferences and goals to meet the new circumstances. It becomes customary to eat rabbit only occasionally with pickleweed mush. Less time is scheduled for hunting rabbits and more time for harvesting pickleweed. This decision-making capacity is the step-mechanism that sets new goals and causes the system to seek an equilibrium around a new rabbit–seed ratio.

This process is illustrated in Figure 9.9, which consists of a graph with the amount of rabbit meat consumed per week on the horizontal axis and the amount of pickleweed eaten plotted on the vertical axis. A dot at any point on the graph will represent a seed–meat ratio. The total space on the graph represents all possible combinations of seeds and rabbits. This space was called by Ross-Ashby the *phase space* of the system. If a group has some point on that phase space as its dietary goal, its actual intake will probably fluctuate around that point as governed by the circumstances of the chase and gathering successes. In the situation posited the environmental change would have caused the band's effective location on the graph to drift away from Goal 1 toward the left as the input of rabbits decreased. The dotted lines mark the progress of the effective diet. Had the effective diet fallen into the critical region of the phase space where combinations do not constitute viable diets the population would have died of starvation. In order to avoid this calamity the goal was adjusted to location Goal 2 to match available resources in a more realistic manner. For the diner the effect would be an extra serving

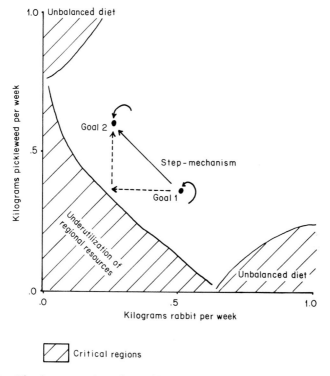

Figure 9.9.   The dynamics of an ultrastable system.

of pickleweed mush during meals except on Sunday when rabbit was also served.

Since the new goal moved the diet significantly toward the "unbalanced diet" critical region, adjustments on a third dimension would probably be necessary to increase protein input. This Z axis or third dimension of the graph could be pine nuts, deer, antelope, or whatever is available.

The visible consequences of this change of goals would be more time spent on the margins of the basin floor where pickleweed is abundant, and less time spent in the uplands where rabbits have become scarce. The ratios of artifacts used for the two different subsistence activities would change in a manner correlated to the change in the seed–meat ratio. This system could be simulated utilizing land area, population of rabbits, and areas good for pickleweed under varying moisture conditions.

In this section the social structure of Great Basin groups as they were observed ethnographically has been reviewed. The ethnographic picture of social structure and probable social behavior in the face of changing resource conditions has been "fleshed out" by a consideration of various models. In the next section the problems that arise as the through-time aspects of this system are observed archaeologically will be discussed.

THROUGH TIME, THE ARCHAEOLOGY

Ethnography has supplied a picture of the socioenvironmental system of the eastern Great Basin during a single moment in time. Archaeology, on the other hand, studies many such moments, effectively adding a third dimension to the picture of the social organization. Since archaeologists cannot "dig up" the territorial limits and social structures of the past, these features of the social system must be inferred from what is known or surmised from materials that are found. In this section we will be concerned with the temporal and spatial limits of the socioenvironmental system of the past. The boundaries can be fairly strong or impermeable, in which case the system is effectively closed, or they may be weak and permeable, leaving the system open to outside influences and population influxes.

Temporal Limits

Earl Swanson (1962) introduced the idea of dividing cultural diachrony into two types. *Cultural continua* he defined as occurring in regions where the same culture persisted through time aided by consistent environment. Among the characteristics of a cultural continuum would be relative cultural isolation and closure as a demographic system (see Binford 1968:437 for discussion of system closure). *Cultural sequences,* or "layer-cake sequences," on the other hand, occur in regions where there are breaks in the continuum. Analytically, there are six combinations of presence or absence of culture and population change, with or without environmental antecedents, that could underlie changes in a sequence. The three most probable combinations are these:

1. Environmental changes that caused the end of one population and its subsequent replacement by another group and culture
2. Environmental changes that caused cultural adaptation and consequent changes in the cultural inventory but no population change
3. Cultural changes without environmental causal factors

Demographically, under these various circumstances a system could be closed (options 2 and 3) or open (option 1) (Binford 1968:437).

The South Hills are on the Basin–Plateau interface, and as is the usual case with all transitional zones there are numerous points of view by various archaeologists on all archaeological matters of local prehistory. Whether the region can be considered an operationally temporal continuum or sequence will therefore be discussed in some detail.

Model I, Open System

There is linguistic and archaeological evidence that suggests breaks in the cultural continuum. The archaeological evidence is in the form of breaks in materials that indicate major changes in cultural orientation. At Hogup Cave, Aikens (1970a:190–192, 194–195; see Gunn 1975b for graphic presentation) infers breaks in the continuum at about 3150 B.P. and 600 B.P. The shift in artifact classes in the second or third millenium B.C. is fairly apparent. The shift around 600 B.P., however, is not readily apparent, as will be discussed in the next section.

The second set of evidence comes from linguistics in the form of lexicostatistical measures on the Numic languages. C. Fowler (1973) has recently reviewed the literature on the topic. According to lexicostatistical counts Numic probably split from a related language in southern California about 2500 to 3000 years ago. About 1000 years later Numic divided into its various subbranches. And about 1000 years ago there was southwest–northeast migration of Numic speakers (C. Fowler 1973:107).

Model II, Closed System

Alternative Model II involves evidence that the South Hills region can be treated as a closed temporal continuum.

Probably the strongest evidence in favor of an open system is the 3200 B.P. technological change at Hogup Cave. The environment–technology model now used to interpret such events is indeterminate (Gunn 1974) and the change could be interpreted equally well as a technological change without a population change. Note especially that the break occurs at the same time as the final drying of the Lake Bonneville marshes. This event would have fostered a functional shift in the tool assemblage without a necessary population change (option 2).

The next potential major break in the continuum is at the introduction of the Fremont agricultural complex into the region at about 1450 B.P. Population replacement has largely been discounted in the literature, however. The Great Salt Lake variant of Fremont is something of a curiosity in the Fremont milieu (Marwitt 1970:147). The environment in the vicinity of the Great Salt Lake is marginally suited for agriculture (1970:154). Artifacts, architecture, and ecological analysis indicate that horticulture never played a large part in the Fremont culture of the region (see Marwitt 1970:4 for sources). Aikens (1970a:192) notes a marked continuity from Unit II to Unit III (Fremont) at Hogup Cave.

The evidence, taken as a whole, seems to indicate that the Great Salt Lake variant of Fremont was derived from a Desert Archaic substrate (Aikens 1970a:154). New styles and approaches to subsistence were apparently introduced by stimulus diffusion. Subsistence, on the main, continued to center on hunting and gathering of wild seeds.

Finally, there is a strong current of opinion that there was a break in the continuum around 450 B.P. when Shoshonean peoples migrated into the region. As noted earlier, however, this movement is indicated mainly by linguistic evidence. Earl Swanson has long been of the opinion that the Bitterroot culture of eastern Idaho had a more or less unbroken life span from about 5000 B.P. "This culture is characterized by the appearance and persistence of side-notched points in an intergrading sequence, beginning in the Anathermal and lasting into the historic period in the Birch Creek of eastern Idaho [1962:155]." Evidence from the Birch Creek Project itself (Ranere 1971:49,54), and from other sources such as Mummy Cave (Husted and Mallory 1967) continues to support the proposition that the Shoshoni have been resident since the fifth millenium B.P.

Aikens (1970a:195) infers a sharp break in the Hogup Cave sequence between Units III (Fremont) and IV (Shoshoni). There is little in the artifact-count tables, however, to support this observation. All chipped stone and ground stone types are clearly represented in earlier units. There are two pieces of textile, one twined and one coiled. The types of which the two pieces are members are types that appear as early as Units I and II. Other artifact industries give similar impressions. When the general dearth of artifacts in Unit IV is considered, there are no cases where the observed and expected values in Unit IV are disparate enough to suggest a break in the continuum. The one exception to this trend is Shoshoni-ware pottery. Despite statements to the contrary, Shoshoni ware appears to have its origin in Unit III (Fremont). Other types clearly associated with Fremont persist into Shoshoni times. The overall picture is one of a classic battleship curve suggestive of cultural development, not population replacement.

In addition, at Newark Cave in eastern Nevada (D. Fowler 1968:30) Shoshoni diagnostics are fully present at about 2000 B.P. If it is assumed that Shoshoni ware is truly diagnostic of Shoshoni population movement, these data are incongruent with the proposed 1000-year-later migration of the Shoshoni into the Great Basin.

A recent and quite interesting addition to the evidence for a cultural continuum in the region north of the Great Salt Lake is the work of David Corliss (1972). Corliss's original intention was to discover when the bow replaced the atlatl by measuring projectile point neck widths. A total of 2712 neck widths were measured from 34 stratified samples (19 sites). The measurements seemed to show clearly enough the introduction of the bow. More important, and coming as something of a surprise, however, was that crosscutting the atlatl–bow relationship was another influence. Through the whole continuum from atlatl to bow were subareas of the region that showed internally consistent patterns. In the north, associated with the northern Rocky Mountain ecological zone and the Sahaptin ethnographic area was a small (.98 cm) projectile point neck width mean. In the south, in the Numic ethnographic area and northern Great Basin ecological zone, there was a larger mean (1.21 cm). Corliss reasoned that if there had been major disruptions in the cultural continuum as there would be with population movements, this continuum of what seems to be a sensitive indicator would have been interrupted. Corliss therefore concluded that territorial boundaries in Idaho were stable through the duration of the Holocene. Traditions within those territories, in like manner, seem to be continual and relatively undisturbed by migration.

In summary, then, although the evidence for a cultural continuum in the northeastern Great Basin may not be without weaknesses, some caution should be taken not to interpret the area automatically as the northern periphery of the classic Fremont area. The Great Salt Lake variant of Fremont is different from the variant further south. There is evidence for continuity from the Fremont to Shoshoni periods in stratified lithics and pottery samples. As was noted earlier, David Thomas (1974) sees a 2500-year continuum in the Reese River region of Nevada.

Spatial Limits

Melvin Aikens (1970b:69–70) has couched a set of commonly used spatial terms in the context of Great Basin archaeology in such a way that they form a good analytic model for organizing spatial relationships. *Patterns* (regional patterns of cultural ecology) are site components that can be grouped, or articulated, on a functional basis. They are culturally adapted to the same or similar environments.

Spheres (diffusion spheres) are site components that can be articulated by shared stylistic, diagnostic, or horizon-style traits. Since styles can easily crosscut ecological regions and areas, a sphere may overlap patterns or even several patterns. Likewise, a sphere may occupy only a small portion of the area of a given pattern.

Finally, a *culture* is defined when it is possible to show that a pattern
and a diffusion sphere are coextensive. "A *culture* would designate a
sociocultural group exploiting perhaps a number of ecological zones
within a given region in the course of a yearly round, and being inte-
grated by a set of shared stylistic traits which symbolize the group's
identity [Aikens 1970b:70]." A combination of Swanson's and Aikens's
models is presented in Figure 9.10.

Using this frame of reference, I shall attempt to determine plausible
boundaries for the South Hills region, and to determine whether those
boundaries justify an operationally open or closed system.

First, on strictly geographic terms, the region is somewhat isolated

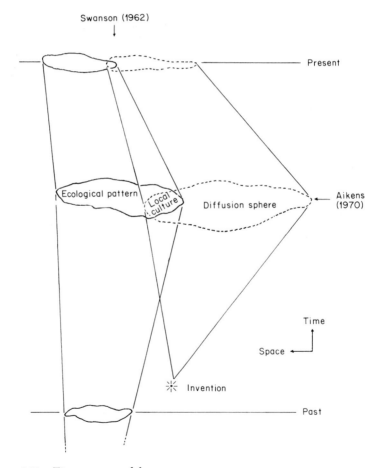

Figure 9.10.   Time–space model.

from the rest of the Great Basin. Judging from Steward's assessment of the travel patterns in ethnographic contexts (Figure 9.7) the Great Salt Desert and the desert to the west of the Grouse Creek district posed formidable barriers to travel and communication. To the north is the Snake River Plain. Travel across the Snake River to the Camas Prairie was apparently general and frequent. Likewise, travel to the east seems to have been relatively uninhibited to the Plains. To the north and east, then, relatively weak barriers to travel can be posited.

A strong southern boundary is confirmed by the archaeological record. Fry and Adovasio (1970) present an argument for occupation of Danger Cave and Hogup Cave by separate populations for most of the history of the two sites. The argument is based on lithic, textile, and coprolite data.

Similarly, Corliss's projectile neck width data (1972:6–7) indicate that there are two traditions in the northern Great Basin. One of these traditions includes Danger Cave. The other is indicated by a strong affinity between Hogup Cave and Weston Canyon Rock Shelter (extreme southeastern Idaho).

Combining the ethnographic and archaeological information, we can infer the following spatial situation. To the south the system has always been effectively closed by a relatively impermeable boundary of lakes, marshes, and deserts. To the north the relationships are less clear-cut. Corliss's neck width study indicates that Hogup Cave and Weston Rock Shelter are quite closely related, which may suggest that the Great Salt Lake side of the South Hills region was somewhat self-contained. This is a very interesting prospect. If the southern portion of the region proved to be a cultural entity, a territory and a "culture" in terms of Aikens's model, it could very well be the limits of the marginal zone of which Hogup was apparently a part. The contiguous optimal zone would be the upper reaches of the South Hills and the related northern slopes.

Otherwise Corliss's analysis suggests that the diffusion sphere of which the South Hills are a part extends to the Salmon River in central Idaho. There is some forbidding territory in the eastern Snake River Plain that may have prevented continuous habitation. Swanson and Bryan (1964) found evidence to suggest that it was abandoned during the Altithermal in particular. The eastern Snake River Plain, then, may have been inhospitable to continuous habitation, but it does not seem to have prohibited passage. It may have been something of a second boundary, or permeable boundary.

Corliss's data indicate that there may be an east–west trending boundary on his study area south of the Salmon River. The South Hills seem to be part of the eastern province of this as yet unclear division. This makes sense in light of the ethnographic data. People of the South Hills resorted to the Plains for subsistence. The Rocky Mountains would then be yet another permeable barrier.

On the surface, then, the system is closed to the south and west by effectively impermeable boundaries. To the north and east closure is less stringent. Only permeable barriers can be supposed.

Operational Model

The most manageable model for purposes of analysis would be one that is closed both spatially and temporally. Though such a system is highly unlikely in reality under any circumstances, a system is often closed enough that it can be assumed to be closed for purposes of analysis. That is to say, most influences on the system are internally derived. For instance, recall Birdsell's remarkable figures for different amounts of interaction between contiguous and noncontiguous bands. Those few influences that do come from the outside are negligible and will only cause a slight tendency to spurious conclusions about the structure and process of the system.

Therefore, I shall assume an operationally closed model. This model will be tested and if it fails to meet the specifications of the test data the alternative open model will be strongly implicated and subject to testing.

Assuming the closed model implies the following: Spatially the permeable barriers to the north and east will be treated as effectively impermeable barriers. Temporally a cultural continuum—a span of cultural development unbroken by intrusions of migrating populations—will be assumed. This assumption requires that the change from Mountain–Plains culture to Desert Archaic be an *in situ* development. Assemblages such as Hogup Cave, which change abruptly at the final drying of the western pluvial lakes and marshes, will *not* be treated as indicators of population change. It will be assumed that the same people came to the site before and after the event of drying. The continuity of the Elko series at Hogup is construed as an argument for population continuity. The altered assemblage is a product of that same group harvesting different resources and altering their tool kits to meet that contingency.

The alternative model would be unconstrained, both spatially and temporally. All barriers would be effectively permeable or nonexistent. Sharp breaks in assemblages would be indicators of population change. I will not deal with the open model beyond noting this general structure. An interesting test implication would be the breaking of the Elko series continuity by an as yet untried analytical procedure. This would show an across the board artifact inventory change at 3200 B.P. at Hogup Cave.

Relative to the optimal–marginal model, assuming the closed system implies the following: Adjustments to Altithermal reduction in optimal zone resources will *not* involve mass movements of population from one region to another. Populations will remain for the most part in their original territories. They will adjust population density. They will reconcentrate to be proximate to the changing resource pattern. They will in large part alter their seasonal round.

Hogup Cave is the most thoroughly investigated site in the South Hills relative to ecology and resources. Anathermal inhabitants might very well have included Hogup in their seasonal round for fowling, other water-related activities, and seed collecting. The Altithermal perhaps reduced the resources around marshes, particularly upland game birds and small mammals. Xeric plants, however, were little diminished, or perhaps even increased as new dry ground became available. The group continued to come to Hogup for dry plant subsistence, even increasing its concentration on developing better methods for exploiting them. Meanwhile highland habitats suffered proportionally greater reductions in resources. The net result was a greater reliance on the desert in drier times. Reeves (1973) has proposd a similar model for bison populations on the Plains in the Altithermal. Swanson (personal communication) warns, however, that high mountain environments will also be favorably affected by a decrease in precipitation. Thus, it appears that midrange altitudes will become donor areas during periods of decreasing moisture, whereas low (desert) and high (mountain) altitudes will become more open and productive and subject to more intensive subsistence exploitation and occupation.

Taking the optimal–marginal model as a conceptual frame, the South Hills proper can be regarded as a potential optimal zone. There is evidence indicating dwindling resources starting in the Altithermal (Swanson and Bryan, 1964). However, when the drought-resistant nature of desert plants is considered in the equation, the desert may have been less diminished as a habitat by drying than the lusher regions to the north. The desert may, in fact, have been enriched as new territory became available for desert-adapted food plants. Thus, the desert may have been a not altogether undesirable alternative for those foraging out of formerly rich upland zones in search of new resources. In addition, the area around Hogup Cave was marshy, because of a favorable water table, and had exploitable resources, during most of the time allotted to the Altithermal (in spite of detectable desiccation of upland environments).

Testing the System

The socioenvironmental system discussed in the preceding section had a certain, probably stable, structure, occupied a finite space whose boundaries were definable to some degree of permeability, and had an ongoing existence through time. The several models I have introduced show various points of view about how the social and environmental components of the system probably interacted.

Quite often the best way to observe the workings of a system is to represent its structure and processes in a series of mathematical formulas that contain the variables inherent in the system. This technique is known as *simulation*. A computerized simulation allows a researcher to observe the behavior of a system over long periods of time at a minimum of expense and effort. By controlling the behavior of some variable in the system the reaction of other variables to its changes can be observed and compared to what is known of the behavior of the system in the real world, even though the real-world data may be incomplete. A favorable comparison indicates that the system has been correctly modeled. An unfavorable comparison indicates that the system should be reworked until a favorable comparison is obtained.

The specifics of this case are that the effects of changing precipitation patterns on the population of the South Hills are to be studied. Once these effects have been simulated they can be checked against available archaeological data on how populations actually did react. Here the available data are limited, for the most part, to Hogup Cave, which provides the fullest long-term record of cultural reactions in the study area. Hogup alone can provide corroboration only for the desert part of the system. What actually happened in the hills needs to be worked out through examination of existing collections and further excavations. As will be pointed out later, individual style analysis will play a leading role in further testing of the model.

The present-day environment is the takeoff point for the simulation. The rainfall in the Great Salt Desert and the lowland immediately north of the Great Salt Lake is less than 25 cm (10 inches) a year. The Wasatch Range to the east of the Great Salt Lake receives 50–75 cm (20–30 inches) of rain a year. The great part of that falls in the winter. The South Hills are intermediate between these two extremes with 25–50 cm (10–20 inches) of rainfall annually. Precipitation is spread more or less evenly throughout the year.

The desert vegetation is dominated by shadscale, which occurs in patches. Intermediate elevations, including the South Hills, are covered by sagebrush grassland. Higher elevations, especially the Grouse Creek and Bear River districts, have areas of Pine–Juniper Woodland. A rough estimate of the territory in each of these ecological zones is as follows (see Figure 9.11, part a)

Desert   5,000 km²
Sagebrush grassland   45,000 km²
Pine–Juniper Woodland   10,000 km²

We will assume that this space supported a tribe of 500 persons divided into four autonomous bands. The population might have fluctuated through time but tended to stay at around 500 as a product of the sociostructural needs described earlier. As we have seen, the resources

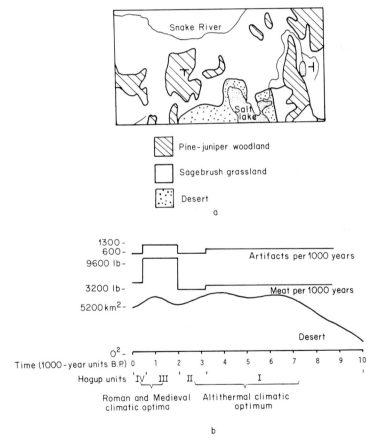

Figure 9.11. (a) Present vegetation of the study area (adapted from *Goode's World Atlas*, 10th ed.); (b) plot of desert area against occupation density indicators for Hogup Cave.

of the region are adequate to support this number under climatic conditions of the eighteenth and nineteenth centuries.

Let us further assume that under modern conditions a diet resembling Goal 1 described earlier is inherently the best for human populations given the usual distribution of resources in the area and their normal content of protein, carbohydrates, and so on. This situation does not need to resemble reality except in that the direction of the adaptation to a change has to move in the same direction on the graph (Figure 9.11, part b) as a real one would.

Now, how best can the element of climatic change be introduced into the system? There is no record of Great Basin climatic change refined enough to drive such a model. There is, however, a century-by-century record of world temperature changes based on the Greenland ice cap. W. Dansgaard et al. (1969) have reported on the concentrations of an oxygen isotope (^{18}O) deposited on the Greenland ice cap over the last 100,000 years. The amount of ^{18}O in the ice is thought to vary with world temperatures. If we assume that weather in the Great Basin is a transformation of worldwide temperatures, the trajectory of worldwide temperatures can be used to control the variation in rainfall over the term of the Post Pleistocene.

For purposes of this study we will assume that the area in the ecological zones changes directly in proportion to the percentage of present-day rainfall. The transformation may be much more complex than that. In this scheme desert will increase in direct proportion to the temperature at the expense of sagebrush grassland. Sagebrush grassland will increase at the expense of Pine–Juniper Woodland.

Figure 9.11, part b shows a plot of expanding and contracting desert along with Aikens's various indices of utilization at Hogup Cave. All three trajectories are relatively coarse on the time scale. The desert habitat available is averaged over 1000-year periods. Meat consumed and artifacts are per 1000 years for the duration of an archaeological unit at Hogup. Nevertheless, the curves do fluctuate in some semblance of unison. Utilization of Hogup increased both during the Altithermal climatic optimum and the Roman–Medieval climatic optima.

What is startling about the results and is the source of serendipity for this system simulation is that the amount of meat consumed over 1000 years also increased during dry periods. This may be showing that the desert serves more herbivores from its stock of xerophtic plants in dry times; both humans and animals subsist on the desert more and the uplands less. This would be parallel to, and support for, Reeves's findings for bison on the Plains during the Altithermal.

I conclude from the results of the simulation that the system is in broad outline correctly defined. Of course there will undoubtedly be refinement and restructuring as the archaeological facts become better known and as research continues into parameters of the environment such as climatology, hydrology, and vegetational zonation.

Probably the most controversial aspect of the archaeological data is the problem of continuum or sequence. Have the South Hills been occupied continuously by one population throughout the Holocene, or have there been cycles of occupation, each cycle representing a different stock of people? In the simulation the continuum was assumed. Thus, there was always one population that through time reacted to worldwide climatic conditions. As the simulation shows, this is one explanation of the data.

An alternative explanation, however, would be that there were sequential occupations of the South Hills by different populations. In this case the downs of the population density indicators at Hogup could be intervals when replacement populations were coming in and had not yet realized their density potential. This brings us back to the question of the open and closed system models.

The most apparent point in time to test the closed system model is at the 3200 B.P. culture inventory change at Hogup. When it became too dry at Hogup for fowling and fishing, did the Anathermal–Altithermal inhabitants move out of the South Hills to be replaced by others? If it can be shown that they did, the closed model is disproved and we are forced into the arena of open models. If, on the other hand, it can be shown that the same individuals (or "analytical individuals"; see Chapter 4 by Redman in this volume) occupied the hills and the desert before and after the change, the evidence supports a closed model. The closed model is only supported, however, to the extent that one more potential juncture of population change is eliminated. All such junctures have to be tested before across-the-board recognition can be given to the closed system for the prehistory of the Great Basin.

At the risk of belaboring the point, I would like to emphasize that I am not trying to say that there were no population movements in the history of the Great Basin. I am saying that each prehistoric juncture that shows a possible time of population movement—such as 3200 B.P. at Hogup—inferred from a shift in the artifact inventory must be tested to determine if the impression is valid or spurious. The artifact inventory could change as a result of adaptation to environmental changes at a station on a seasonal round as easily as it could change as a result of population replacement. The closed model is being proposed as a null hypothesis, which when disproved automatically implies the alternative hypothesis, the open model. Working with the closed model is a vehicle for testing for the open model while avoiding what statisticians call Type I error. Blindly accepting the open model because of changes in artifact inventory is inadequate and incomplete logic.

The second low-population juncture is in the pre-European contact period. It too needs to be tested to determine the fact of a population change. Tests will have to be engineered for each context at which a juncture is found. Since the area of interest in this study encompasses both dry and wet sites, a test will have to be designed around lithics because perishables are not universally preserved.

The means of detecting idiosyncratic behavior in chipping style described earlier can be applied to the problem. Naturally, early and careful selection of the appropriate artifact is important. Since a consistent artifact outline is important, some morphologically uniform type of biface will have to be selected. The Northern Sidenotch appears to be the best possible selection for several reasons. First, the type is spread over the study area. Second, there are large numbers of Northern Sidenotch in sites of the South Hills region. A large sample is needed to meet the minimum sample size requirements of numerical analysis techniques such as principal components. Also, having large samples increases the chance of getting several artifacts produced by the same individual. Although the prospect of getting numbers of tools made by the same person may seem unlikely at first thought, there is every reason to believe that there are lithic specialists in primitive societies, and some of those specialists are much more prolific than others. Also, if the analytical individual is given serious consideration, the increased possibility of getting very similar artifacts from a self-training, self-reinforcing group greatly increases the chance of a sample with the required characteristics. James Green, who is familiar with lithic replication experiments after the style of Don Crabtree, writes, "Northern Sidenotch are lenticular in cross-section with angular well formed notches and more consistent flaking pattern than Elko Sidenotch. Further study may indicate that Northern Sidenotch can be used as a general western type designation with Bitterroot and Elko Sidenotch designations for regional variants [1972:37–38]." Functionally, Swanson says, "At the Bison and Veratic Rockshelters there is an association of side-notch points with bison [1970:77]."

The third and most crucial reason for using the Northern Sidenotch is that it is a type that spans the period of possible population transition at 3200 B.P. If the same individuals made them before and after the change, both in the lowlands and the highlands, the closed model cannot be rejected. If, on the other hand, an open system were implied, the second stage of study would be to discover the demographic structure of the region by an extensive study of style distributions. From this structure the demographic and cultural geographic shift that accompanied the final desiccation of the swamps in front of Hogup Cave would be determined.

CONCLUSIONS

The material presented in the foregoing discussion seems to indicate that individual styles can be defined on the basis of a relatively limited range of continuous attributes measured from stone tools. These results combined with a logical consideration of spatial relationships may allow the archaeologist to approach the level of resolution of social scientists who study living populations.

As an attempt to lay some of the groundwork for such an effort, methodologies, models, and a region and problem of application were discussed. The proposed model was simulated with favorable results.

The artifact attributes involved in such a study need not be any different from those that numerically oriented archaeologists have been studying for years. Meeting prehistoric individuals appears to be hardly more difficult than admitting their existence and structuring our thoughts about the residue of their lives in such a way that we allow them to show us the nature of their lives and times.

ACKNOWLEDGMENTS

I would like to thank James M. Adovasio, Earl H. Swanson, Jr., and James N. Hill for critical and helpful reading of this chapter. The section entitled "The Ethnographic Picture" was taken from my dissertation (1974). Teresa Gutierrez typed the final manuscript.

REFERENCES

Adovasio, J. M.
    1970   Textiles in Hogup Cave. In *Hogup Cave*, edited by C. M. Aikens. *University of Utah Anthropological Papers*, No. 93:133–153.
    1974   Prehistoric North American basketry. *Nevada State Museum Anthropological Papers*, No. 16.
    in press   Prehistoric Great Basin textiles. In *Handbook of North American Indians*, Vol. X, *Great Basin*, edited by W. D'Azevedo.
Adovasio, J. M., and G. F. Fry
    1972   An equilibrium model for culture change in the Great Basin. In *Great*

Basin Cultural Ecology: A Symposium, edited by D. D. Fowler. *Desert Research Institute Publications in the Social Sciences*, No. 8:67–72.

Aikens, C. Melvin
  1970a   *Hogup Cave. University of Utah Anthropological Papers*, No. 93.
  1970b   Toward the recognition of cultural diversity in Basin–Plateau prehistory. *Northwest Anthropological Research Notes* 4(1):67–74.

Binford, Lewis R.
  1962   Archaeology as anthropology. *American Antiquity* 28:217–225.
  1968   Post-Pleistocene adaptations. In *New perspectives in archaeology*, edited by Sally R. and Lewis R. Binford. Chicago: Aldine. Pp. 313–341.

Birdsell, Joseph B.
  1973   A basic demographic unit. *Current Anthropology* 14(4):337–356.

Bolles, Robert C.
  1974   Cognition and motivation: Some historical trends. In *Cognitive views of human motivation*, edited by Bernard Weiner. New York: Academic Press. Pp. 1–20.

Corliss, David W.
  1972   Neck width of projectile points: An index of culture continuity and change. *Occasional Papers of the Idaho State Museum*, No. 29.

Dansgaard, W., S. J. Johnson, J. Møller, C. C. Langway, Jr.
  1969   One thousand centuries of climatic record from Camp Century on the Greenland Ice Sheet. *Science* 3903:377–380.

Dixon, W. J. (Ed.)
  1973   *BMD biomedical computer programs.* Berkeley: University of California Press.

Flannery, Kent V.
  1972   The cultural evolution of civilization. *Annual Review of Ecology and Systematics* 3:399–426.

Fowler, Catherine S.
  1973   Some ecological clues to Proto-Numic-Homelands, in Great Basin cultural ecology. In *Great Basin Cultural Ecology: A Symposium*, edited by D. D. Fowler. *Desert Research Institute Publications in the Social Sciences*, No. 8:105–122.

Fowler, D. D.
  1968   The archaeology of Newark Cave, White Pine County, Nevada. Technical Report N, Series S-H, *Social Sciences and Humanities*, No. 3. Desert Research Institute.

Fry, Gary, and J. M. Adovasio
  1970   Population differentiation in Hogup and Danger Caves, two Archaic sites in the eastern Great Basin. In *Five Papers on the Archaeology of the Desert West*, edited by D. Tuohy, D. Rendall, and P. Crowell. *Nevada State Museum Anthropological Papers*, No. 15:207–215.

Gifford, James C.
  1960   The type–variety method of ceramic classification as an indicator of cultural phenomena. *American Antiquity* 25:341–347.

Green, James Patton
  1972   Archaeology of the Rock Creek Site, 10CA33, Sawtooth National Forest, Cassia County, Idaho. Unpublished M.A. thesis, Department of Anthropology, Idaho State University.

Gunn, Joel
    1974   The Hogup system: A causal analysis of envirotechnological inter-
              action in the Desert West. Ph.D. dissertation, University of Pittsburgh.
              University Microfilms, Ann Arbor, Order No. 74–24, 174.
    1975a   Idiosyncratic behavior in chipping style: Some hypotheses and pre-
              liminary analysis. In Lithic technology: Making and using stone tools,
              edited by Earl Swanson. The Hague: Mouton. Pp. 35–61.
    1975b   An envirotechnological system for Hogup Cave. American Antiquity
              40:3–21.
Gunn, Joel, and Elton R. Prewitt
    1975   Automatic classification: Projectile points from West Texas. Plains
              Anthropologist 20(68):139–149.
Hultkrantz, Ake
    1974   The Shoshonis in the Rocky Mountain area. In American Indian eth-
              nohistory: California and Basin–Plateau Indians, edited by D. A. Horr.
              New York: Garland Publishing. Pp. 173–214.
Husted, W., and O. Mallory
    1967   The Fremont Culture: Its derivation and ultimate fate. Plains Anthro-
              pologist 12(36):222–232.
Levi-Strauss, Claude
    1974   Tristes Tropiques. New York: Athenium.
Marwitt, John J.
    1970   Median village and Fremont culture regional variation. University of
              Utah Anthropological Papers, No. 95.
Muto, Guy R.
    1971   A stage analysis of the manufacture of chipped stone implements. In
              Great Basin Anthropological Conference, 1970, selected papers, edited
              by C. M. Aikens. University of Oregon Anthropological Papers, No.
              1:109–118.
Oxnard, Charles
    1973   Form and pattern in human evolution. Chicago: University of Chicago
              Press.
Powers, William T.
    1973   Behavior: The control of perception. Chicago: Aldine.
Preston, F. W., D. W. Green, and J. C. Davis
    1970   Numerical characterization of reservoir rock pore structure. Final Re-
              port to the American Petroleum Institute Research Project No. 103.
              Center for Research, Inc., Engineering Science Division, The University
              of Kansas, Lawrence.
Ranere, Anthony James
    1971   Birch Creek Papers No. 4, Stratigraphy and stone tools from Meadow
              Canyon, eastern Idaho. Occasional Papers of the Idaho State Uni-
              versity Museum, No. 27.
Reeves, Brian
    1973   The concept of an Altithermal cultural hiatus in northern Plains pre-
              history. American Anthropologist 75:1221–1253.
Ross-Ashby, William
    1960   Design for a brain. New York: Chapman and Hall.
Spencer, Robert F., and Jesse D. Jennings
    1965   The native Americans. New York: Harper.

Steward, Julian H.
> 1938   Basin–Plateau aboriginal socio-political groups. *Bureau of American Ethnology Bulletin*, No. 120.

Stratham, Dawn
> 1975   A biogeographic model of Camas and its role in the aboriginal economy of the Northern Shoshoni in Idaho. *Tebiwa* **18**(1):59–80.

Swanson, Earl H., Jr.
> 1962   Early cultures in northwestern America. *American Antiquity* **28**:151–158.

> 1970   Ecology in the Great Basin–Plateau regions. *Northwest Anthropological Research Notes* **4**, No. 1:75–81.

Swanson, Earl H., Jr., and Alan Lyle Bryan
> 1964   Birch Creek Papers No. 1, An archaeological reconnaissance in the Birch Creek Valley of eastern Idaho. *Occasional Papers of the Idaho State University Museum*, No. 13.

Thomas, David H.
> 1974   An archaeological perspective on Shoshonean bands. *American Anthropologist* **76**:11–23.

Wahlstedt, W., and J. Davis
> 1968   Fortran IV program for computation and display of principal components. *Computer Contribution* **21**. State Geological Survey, Lawrence, Kansas.

Zubrow, Ezra B. W.
> 1971   Carrying capacity and dynamic equilibrium in the prehistoric Southwest. *American Antiquity* **36**:127–138.

10

A Technological Analysis of
an Aguas Verdes Quarry Workshop

L. LEWIS JOHNSON

During the 1970s, several attempts have been made to identify the individuals who made archaeological artifacts. Most of these studies have been aimed at identifying individuals responsible for the production of finished artifacts. It is argued that the work of an individual is often unique enough to detect and can be a source of information on prehistoric social organization and subsistence patterns.

My focus here is not so much on finished artifacts as on how they were manufactured. The artifacts I study, stone tools, lend themselves to this analysis, unlike those of other primitive technologies such as pottery, in that the manufacturing process involves reduction of mass into smaller mass; the by-products of manufacture remain available. My aim is to describe the steps, or production trajectory, by which an aboriginal knapper manufactured a finished artifact. Of particular note is that more information can be gained about variations in individual workmanship by examining the remains of knapping than by examining the finished products, since finishing an artifact involves removing obvious traits of manufacture.

THE SITE

Studying debitage to discover manufacturing processes requires careful consideration of the sites involved in the analysis. Since different individuals have different motor skills and since techniques develop through time, studying a large site could lead to an incorrect or too general view of the manufacturing process. Even if the results are technically valid, they may be too abstract to be useful. Thus, from studying two sites, RAnL 199B and RAnL 200B, belonging to the Aguas Verdes industry of northern Chile (Figure 10.1), I was able to say that points were probably made on blades or blade-like flakes by reduction knapping, but I could not trace the detailed manufacturing process the knappers followed. I knew that if I could be sure that I was studying the output of a single knapper, I could make a much more accurate analysis of his knapping patterns and discover variations in them.

A third site in northern Chile, RAnL 87XX (see Figure 10.1), evidenced a number of characteristics that led me to believe it would be appropriate for a study of individual variation: (1) It was a lithic workshop in which the products of the process of manufacture were preserved; (2) it was small, which suggested that only one or a few people worked at it; (3) it was reasonably undisturbed; and (4) as will be discussed at length, the knapper(s) was intent on making one type of artifact.

The site was collected in 1968 during the Columbia University Andes Project directed by E. P. Lanning. RAnL 87XX is located in the Atacama Desert on the crest of a ridge above the town of Chiu-Chiu in the province of Antofagasta. The ground surface is composed of sand, gravel, and limestone chunks. The light-green tuff of which the artifacts are made was probably transported from a tuff gravel plain just below and to the west. The site faces south and commands a view of the plain of the Loa River in a zone now desiccated though fertile, which was probably a valuable area for hunting and plant gathering in the past.

Site 87XX measures approximately 9×4.5, with the long axis running up and down hill (north–south). Its area is thus about $40m^2$. A small ceramic period cairn was built on the north end of the site, but the preceramic area does not seem to have been seriously disturbed, particularly the center section where the majority of artifacts were found (Figure

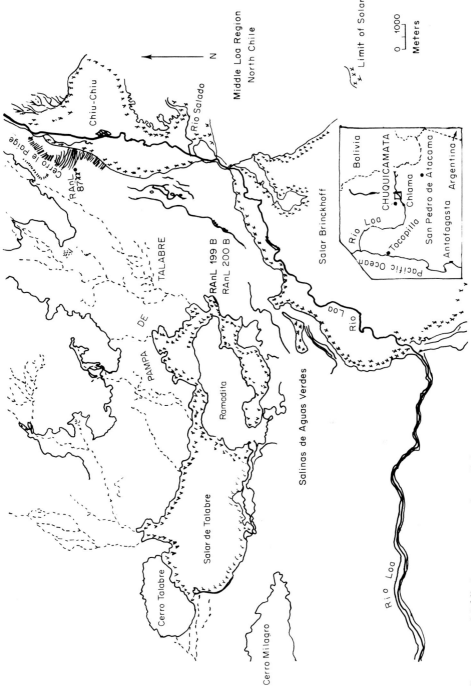

Figure 10.1. Middle Loa region, northern Chile.

Middle Loa Region
North Chile

N

Chiu-Chiu

Rio Salado

Cerro de Paige

RAnL
87

RAnL 199 B
RAnL 200 B

PAMPA DE TALABRE

Ramadita

Salinas de Aguas Verdes

Salar Brinckhoff

Rio Loa

Cerro Talabre

Salar de Talabre

Cerro Milagro

Río Loa

Limit of Solar

0   1000
Meters

Bolivia

CHUQUICAMATA

Chiama

Río Loa

Tocopilla

San Pedro de Atacama

Antofagasta   Argentina

Pacific Ocean

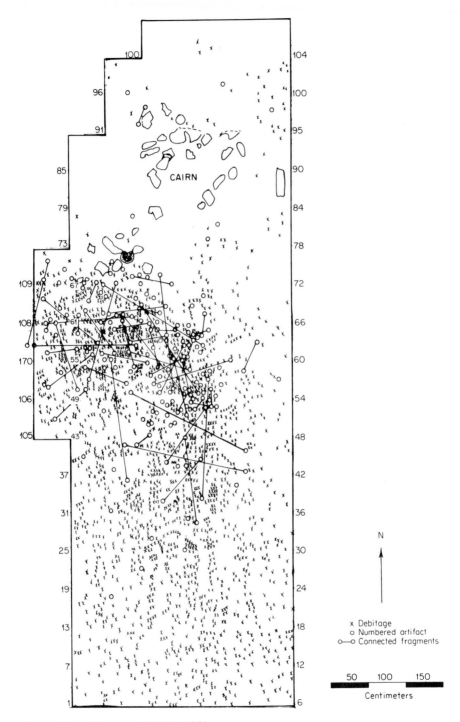

Figure 10.2. Site map of RAnL 87XX.

10.2). The site was collected in its entirety. It was gridded in 50-cm squares within which all pieces of tuff were mapped. The obviously re-touched artifacts were given individual numbers, and the material was then collected. A number of retouched pieces did not receive field num-bers because they were slightly subsurface and therefore did not appear until after collecting had begun. The maximum depth of deposit was about 3–4 cm and excavation was by fingertip after the surface material had been removed.

One problem in using surface sites for controlled analysis lies in de-termining the degree of disturbance they have suffered at the hands of later inhabitants of the region—artifact collectors, farmers with plows, and the like. Fortunately for archaeologists, the Atacama Desert is not now hospitable to settlement, because of recent climatic changes, and among nearby residents there is no interest in collecting preceramic artifacts. The building of the ceramic period cairn on the uphill end of the site may have moved some of the preceramic artifacts, but the area of obvious disturbance is uphill from the major preceramic remains (Figure 10.2), and it does not seem likely that artifacts were removed from the site.

ARTIFACT POPULATIONS

Because the site was a workshop, the majority of artifacts were un-finished tools, broken in the manufacturing process, and debitage. How could the kinds of tools being manufactured be determined? The first major effort was to find and match broken tool fragments. A total of 196 retouched pieces were recognized and numbered on the ground and an additional 8 were discovered subsequently (Figure 10.2). Of the 204 retouched pieces recognized, 70 were matched with each other to give 35 whole artifacts and a new total of 169 artifacts. The distance between matched pieces varied from 15 to 172 cm with a mean distance of 79.5 cm. The direction of dispersion, between SSW and SSE for the majority of the specimens, was downhill. The number of retouched artifacts per 50-cm square varied from 1 to 16 (Figure 10.3) with an average of 4 and a mode of 1. As might be expected, the squares containing 10–16 artifacts were located in the central area of the site; depth of deposit was 3–4 cm.

The retouched artifacts show a limited range of variation in size and shape. This can be appreciated by looking at Figures 10.4–10.8. Artifact 63-5/61-1 (Figure 10.4, part a) is the largest piece found and measures 11.0 × 5.9 cm. It can be compared to artifact 39-1 (Figure 10.5, part b)

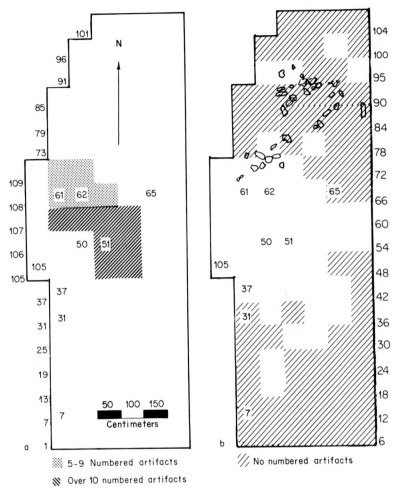

Figure 10.3. Summarized artifact distribution, RAnL 87XX: (a) squares with much artifactual material; (b) squares with little artifactual material.

which is 4.5 × 2.8 cm and is the smallest complete piece found. Table 10.1 gives a brief statistical description of the site's artifact population. The near identity of measurement means and medians is a good indication that a single artifact form was being made at this workshop, since multiple-tool-making objectives on the part of the knappers would have produced skewed distributions. Also, there are no bimodal distributions, again suggesting a single-tool-making objective at the site.

Almost all the pieces found on the site were point forms like those shown in Figures 10.4–10.8. The nodules of raw material available (Fig-

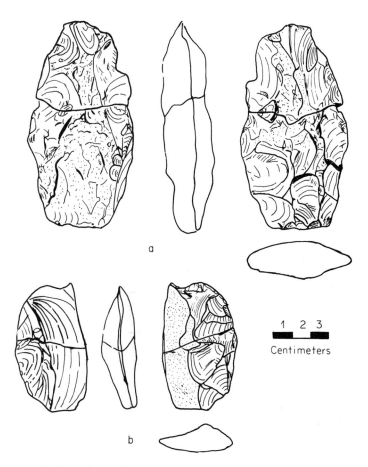

Figure 10.4.   Artifacts from RAnL 87XX: (a) 63–5/61–1; (b) 61/56.

ure 10.9) seem to have determined the artifact forms made, as can be seen by comparing the size and shape of the retouched artifacts with the size and shape of the raw material nodules. If this actually was the case, the analysis of the manufacturing process should be particularly easy since the size parameter is largely controlled and a minimum of knapping seems to be all that is necessary to turn blanks from nodules into finished tools.

    In contrast to the inferred simple structure of use at RAnL 87XX, the larger Aguas Verdes quarries (Johnson 1975, in press; Lewis 1973) contain a variety of artifact forms and are much more complex. Almost all the retouched pieces found at RAnL 87XX would be called points in the terminology developed in Lewis (1973), whereas in sites RAnL 199B and

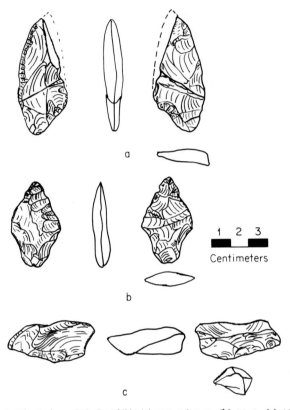

Figure 10.5.   Artifacts from RAnL 87XX: (a) 105–1/49–1; (b) 39–1; (c) 61.

200B, only half the retouched artifacts were points; the others were edges.

The utility of the contrast between RAnL 87XX and the other Aguas Verdes workshops lies in the comparison it allows between individual and group behavior and the inferences about social control and cultural conformity that can be drawn from that comparison. Of preliminary in-

TABLE 10.1

Statistical Description of Retouched Artifacts from RAnL 87XX[a]

	Maximum	Minimum	Mean	Median
Length	11.0	4.5	7.1	7.0
Width	5.9	2.4	3.4	3.3
Thickness	2.9	0.8	1.6	1.5

[a] $N = 169$.

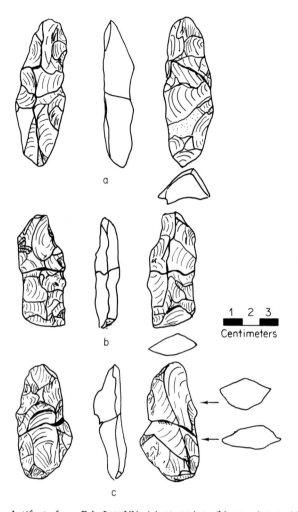

Figure 10.6. Artifacts from RAnL 87XX: (a) 52–15/62; (b) 46–4/52–6; (c) 68–5/69–1.

terest is the contemporaneity of the sites, or, to look at things in reverse for a moment, can 87XX be identified as an Aguas Verdes workshop? If it is, the artifact form manufactured at 87XX should be the same as one of the ones being made at the multiple-tool quarries. If the same attributes are found but the range of variation is less, this might be interpreted as indicating that only one or a few workmen were active at the site. In either case, the three sites could be tentatively identified with the same individuals and group of people.

Rather than studying all the attributes analyzed for the Aguas Verdes

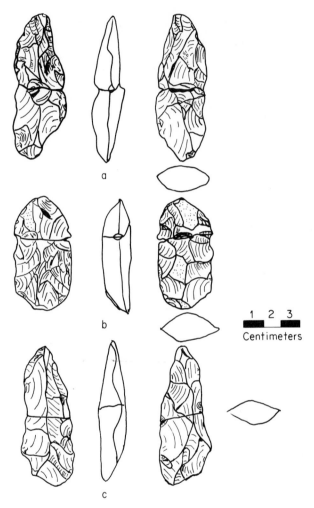

Figure 10.7. Artifacts from RAnL 87XX: (a) 51–3/58–9; (b) 48–1/38–1; (c) 60–1/53–3.

points, only those related to basic point shape were examined. These are nominal attributes that refer to the cross-sectional outline of the points taken along the major point axis (LSX) and perpendicular to it at the midline (TSX). I reasoned that if the shape characteristics indicated a great deal of difference between the two collections I could conclude, depending on the nature of the difference, that 87XX did not belong to the Aguas Verdes industry or that only a few of the Aguas Verdes knappers worked at 87XX. Inspection of the attributes present in the

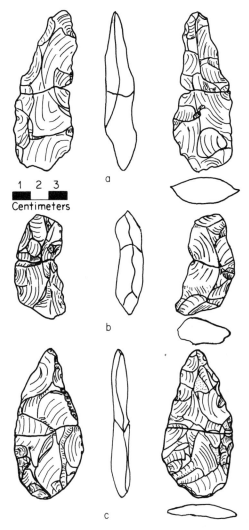

Figure 10.8. Artifacts from RAnL 87XX: (a) 109–3/107–2; (b) 52/46–7; (c) 68–1/107–3.

three sites (Table 10.2) reveals such close results that it precludes the necessity for statistical testing. It suggests that the points made at 87XX belong to the same population as those made at RAnL 199B and 200B. More exhaustive measures could be taken to establish the affiliation of the Aguas Verdes sites, such as chi-square goodness-of-fit tests between artifact types and attribute distributions. I am more concerned with

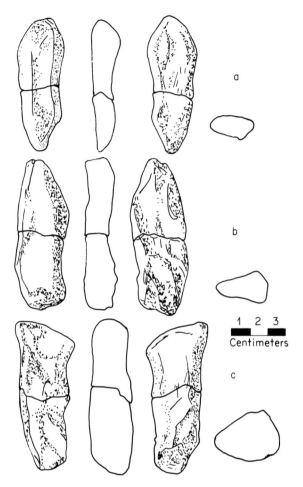

Figure 10.9. Raw material nodules from RAnL 87XX: (a) 68/49; (b) 61/55; (c) 107/55.

a methodology for spotting individual knappers and will proceed to that task.

INDIVIDUALS

A 10% sample of the squares collected was analyzed, stratified so that it represented a 25% sample of those squares containing over five numbered artifacts and an 8% sample of the remaining squares. Since two of

TABLE 10.2

Distribution of Point Attribute States at RAnL 87XX and at RAnL 199B/200B[a]

	RAnL 87XX		RAnL 199B/200B	
	Number	Percentage	Number	Percentage
Blank				
Flake/blade	5	12	4	7
Other	38	88	53	90
TSX symmetry				
Asymmetrical	12	28	67	23
Symmetrical	14	33	87	30
Different	18	42	132	46
TSX side 1				
Convex	26	60	143	50
Plano	13	30	119	41
Other	5	12	24	8
TSX side 2				
Convex	31	72	176	62
Triangular	11	26	81	28
Other	2	5	27	9
TSX centering				
Centered	24	56	153	53
Not centered	20	47	143	46
LSX symmetry				
Asymmetrical	7	16	22	8
Symmetrical	19	44	114	40
Different	18	42	95	33
LSX side 1				
Convex	15	35	98	34
Plano	22	51	85	30
Other	7	16	46	16
LSX side 2				
Convex	29	67	185	64
Other	15	35	46	16

[a] TSX, transverse cross-section; LSX, long cross-section.

the latter squares contained no analyzable artifacts, the flakes from three central squares and six peripheral squares were analyzed (Figure 10.3).

Joel Gunn (1975) has suggested means of identifying individual workmanship on the basis of characteristics present on flakes. I decided to analyze a sample of the waste flakes from RAnL 87XX using his attributes to see if they would give me a clear indication of the number of individuals working at the site. The attributes and states used follow Gunn's numbering; some additional attributes are at the end of the list to follow. The attribute states were as defined in Lewis (1973) with the modifications noted:

1. *Platform preparation.* This follows Lewis (1973), and Johnson (in press), with some reduction of states because of these states not being present in the collection from RAnL 87XX. Collapsed platforms were noted only where there was no retouch on the striking platform, but the lost information was picked up in the accuracy attribute (see item 6).

2. *Flake scar orientation.* This attribute refers to the orientation of flake scars on the dorsal surface of the flake and is similar to the "Dorsal" attribute of the previous study, but is more detailed, although not as detailed as Phagan's system (n.d.). States were transverse, vertical, angled, mixed, and primary decortation (i.e., none).

3. *Bulb of percussion.* Bulbs were recorded as flat, medium, and heavy. In Lewis (1973) I suggested a metric measurement for bulb size, but when dealing with flakes of various sizes, this distinction has to be either subjective or immensely complicated. A medium bulb on a flake that measures 1.5 × 1.25 × .2 cm will be very different in size from a medium bulb on a flake measuring 15 × 12.5 × 2 cm. Therefore, a quantification of bulb size would have to be in relation to flake size, a computational complication that did not seem worthwhile for a preliminary analysis (if at all). Flat, then, is defined as no projection from the ventral surface; a heavy bulb is oversize for the flake, and a medium bulb is intermediate between the other two states.

4. *Undulations.* Undulations and Wallner Lines were recorded as in Johnson (in press) and Lewis (1973).

5. *Termination.* Termination was not recorded in my previous study (Lewis 1973). For this study I defined six states: feathered, run-off (the end of the core), hinged, stepped, mixed, and broken.

6. *Accuracy.* Accuracy also had not been recorded in my previous study (Lewis 1973). The states decided upon were entitled *high* (point of percussion centered on the platform, no damage to the platform or the dorsal surface, single ventral bulb), *slip* (when the tool slipped on the platform so that a flake came off the back of the platform at the same time as the intended flake came off. This usually occurred with a collapsed platform), *edge* (the point of percussion is at one end of the remaining platform fragment), *hinge* (hinge fractures found on the dorsal surface of the flake just below the platform, indicating failure of the first attempt at re-

moval), *bulb* (multiple or side-split bulbs on the ventral surface, indicating more than one blow for removal or inaccurate use of percussor), and *multiple* (more than one of the listed inaccuracies present).

7. *Striking angle.* Because of the amount of time required to measure striking angle (Lewis 1973: Appendix), it was not recorded in this preliminary examination. Instead, I decided to measure skew angle, the angle between the axis of percussion and the long axis of the flake, which, along with the other metrics listed would indicate the general flake shape.

8. *Metric attributes.* Metric attributes used were thickness, length, and width. The point of maximum thickness—proximal, central, distal, no variation, left lateral, and right lateral—was indicated in a nominal code.

In addition to the foregoing attributes suggested by Gunn, I employed the following:

9. *Long cross-section.* This was recorded as dorsoventrally curved, or having a longitudinal ventral twist.

10. *Bulbar scar.* The bulbar scar was recorded as absent or present. Size and shape differences among bulbar scars were not recorded for this analysis.

Individual differences in manufacturing techniques should be visible by examining within-site variation in attribute states. First, I made the assumption that the 50-cm unit in which the artifacts were collected represented a portion of a knapper's work space. If attribute states are unstable from square to square, i.e., vary in their proportional representation, it probably means that more than one knapper was at work in the site. Contiguous clusters of squares with stable attribute patterns should represent the total work area of an individual. If attribute patterns are stable across the site, several alternative hypotheses can be offered: (1) a single knapper worked at the site; (2) technological constraints determine attribute associations; (3) the traits chosen may not be those that would best indicate individual variation; or, (4) a number of effects may be interacting that cannot be sorted out in a preliminary analysis but require a more detailed analysis for their elucidation.

NOMINAL ATTRIBUTES

Inspection of tabulated nominal attributes showed variation between squares. Preliminary to detailed examination of spatial distribution, a set

of paired chi-square analyses was performed on attributes to determine
the nature and content of this variation. Strongly associated states across
attributes were expected to be the attribute patterns associated with individual skills and preferences. One state of each attribute was checked
against one state of every other attribute, giving a total of 36 2 × 2 analyses. Of these, 7 showed significant association between attributes and
are given in Table 10.3, parts A–G. These 7 associations involve all the
nonmetric attributes except flake scar orientation.

TABLE 10.3
Distribution of Flake Attribute States at RAnL 87XX, with Chi-Square Analyses[a]

A. Platform Preparation and Accuracy
(Chi-square = 9.750; p = .01–.001)

	Platform		
	Unprepared	Retouched	Totals
Accuracy			
High	65	92	157
Not high	39	116	155
Totals	104	208	312

B. Bulb Size and Place of Maximum Thickness
(Chi-square = 6.0997; p = .02–.01)

	Bulb size		
	Flat	Not flat	Totals
Maximum thickness			
Central	34	65	99
Not central	105	108	213
Totals	139	173	312

C. Undulations and Termination
(Chi-square = 4.425; p = .05–.02)

	Undulations		
	Absent	Present	Totals
Termination			
Feathered	80	113	193
Not feathered	64	55	119
Totals	144	168	312

[a] Expected chi-square values based on hypothesis of independent assortment of
attribute states.

TABLE 10.3 (Cont.)

D. Undulations and Bulbar Scar
(Chi-square = 8.278; p = .01–.001)

	Undulations		
	Absent	Present	Totals
Bulbar scar			
Present	83	123	206
Absent	61	45	106
Totals	144	168	312

E. Termination and Place of Maximum Thickness
(Chi-square = 5.9567; p = .02–.01)

	Termination		
	Feathered	Not feathered	Totals
Maximum thickness			
Central	71	28	99
Not central	122	91	213
Totals	193	119	312

F. Termination and Flake Curvature
(Chi-square = 180.8122; p < .001)

	Termination		
	Feathered	Not feathered	Totals
Curvature			
Dorsoventral	115	32	147
Other	78	84	162
Totals	193	116	309

G. Flake Curvature and Bulbar Scar
(Chi-square = 5.724; p = .02–.01)

	Flake curvature		
	Dorsoventral	Other	Totals
Bulbar scar			
Present	109	97	206
Absent	41	65	106
Totals	150	162	312

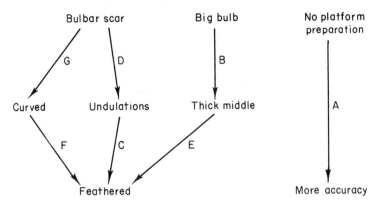

Figure 10.10. Relationships determined by chi-square tests. Arrows are keyed by capital letters to subsections of Table 10.3.

The relationships implied by the chi-square analysis are displayed in Figure 10.10. Attributes are ordered according to their sequence in the manufacture of a flake and according to sequence in the fracture process. I assume that a feathered termination is the desired distal characteristic of a flake. A feathered termination is a thinning out at the end of the flake and has the beneficial feature of leaving the core in good condition for the next removal. The bulbar scars–undulations–feathered termination sequence indicates that relatively hard blows were necessary to achieve a feathered termination. Bulbar scars and undulations increase in direct proportion to the amount of force delivered. Curvature in the sequence indicates that the knapper(s) was using curved surfaces to make removals. It is an established principle that flakes can best be taken from a convex surface. Big bulbs and thick middles attest to the general robusticity and heavy-handed knapping of the assemblage. Virtually all the characteristics leading to a successful feathered termination suggest a robust style of knapping. Relationship A is somewhat more obscure but may indicate that attempts to use platform trimming to rectify or alleviate difficult situations were only partially successful since low accuracy accompanies trimmed platforms.

METRIC ATTRIBUTES

The mean, range, and standard deviation per square for all measurements were calculated and are tabulated in the Appendix, p. 226. These statistics were also calculated for a composite measure derived to indicate the platform size relative to the flake size (RPS):

$$RPS = \frac{\text{striking platform width} \times \text{striking platform length}}{\text{length} \times \text{width} \times \text{thickness}}$$

I thought that this measure would give a good indication of the accuracy with which a knapper hit the core and should be quite consistent for any knapper. It also is a proportional measure rather than being dependent on the absolute size of the flake. The variations in the RPS from square to square were subjected to an analysis of variance (Table 10.4, part A; one-way analysis of variance with unequal ends, Winer 1971: 210–220), which indicated that there was a significant difference between the collections. Because of the very small size of the collections from Squares 7, 31, and 65, these were removed from the sample (Table 10.4). The value of F remained highly significant, so a Newman–Keuls analysis was run (Winer 1971:215–218). This test evaluates whether the differences between sample means are significant given that there is an overall main effect. The result of the Newman–Keuls comparison (Table 10.4, part B) indicated significant differences between Squares 37/105 and 61/62, the former having large platforms and the latter small platforms. The other two squares analyzed, 50 and 51, were intermediate in platform size between these two clearly distinguished groups. The significant difference between the two areas raised the question of whether more than one knapper was working at the site since the involved squares do meet the criterion of continuity (Figure 10.3).

A reexamination of the raw metric data for these two sets of squares indicated that, in addition to the RPS contrast, there was also a size difference in the flakes from these two areas, those from 37/105 being small and those from 61/62 being large. To test the significance of this difference, the proportional representation of those nominal attributes that had proved valuable in defining the flakes of the industry were compared between 61/62 and 37/105. It was hypothesized that if there were only one individual working at the site, the differences that showed up between the attributes could be explained by the stage in knapping represented by the removal of large flakes as opposed to smaller ones. Area 61/62 was also compared to the total peripheral group (7, 31, 37, 65, 105) in order to have a larger sample.

The results of this set of paired chi-square analyses seem to support the hypothesis that a single person was working at the site. Of the eight nominal attributes that associated with one another in the total sample,

TABLE 10.4

Analysis of Variance and Newman–Keuls Comparison of Platform Size Measure (RPS) at RAnL 87XX

A. Analysis of Variance, RPS, RAnL 87XX
($F = 3.598$), $p < .01$

	Degrees of freedom	Sum of squares	Mean squares
Site area	5	76.323	15.265
Error variance	281	1204.7956	4.242

B. Newman-Keuls Comparison, RPS, RAnL 87XX[a]

Site section	Site section					
	61	62	51	50	37	105
61		ns	ns	ns	**	**
62			ns	ns	*	*
51				ns	ns	ns
50					ns	ns
37						ns
105						

[a] ns = not significant.
* $p < .05$.
** $p < .01$.

only one showed a significantly different proportion from 61/62 in 37/105, and only three were different in the joint peripheral sample. Compared to the peripheral small flakes with large platforms, the large central flakes with small platforms showed more feathered terminations, were more often thickest in the center, and were more frequently curved. This last difference was the only one in which 61/62 differed significantly from 37/105. Rather than indicating different technologists, this indicates that more control was possible to the knapper when removing large flakes than when removing small ones. Since the tuff used by the Aguas Verdes knappers is quite friable when compared to other knappable stones, this difficulty is not unexpected.

FURTHER WORK

The foregoing analysis sets the theoretical stage for experimental replication of the Aguas Verdes industry. Among the problems that need to be dealt with is the question of whether technical imperatives mask individual styles or vice versa.

The experimental approach used will be to manufacture tools similar to the Aguas Verdes tools and to analyze the resulting debitage. If the debitage I produce in duplicating an Aguas Verdes point is statistically identical to that produced by the Aguas Verdes knapper(s) who worked at RAnL 87XX, then it will have to be concluded that lithic debitage is of marginal use in identifying prehistoric individuals and that the debris from the process of making Aguas Verdes points is technologically determined to a great extent. On the other hand, if the debitage I produce is different from that found at RAnL 87XX, then the hypothesis can be entertained that idiosyncratic factors are operating. The nature of the differences in the debitage would determine further detail in the development of the hypothesis as well as the further course in the analysis of RAnL 87XX.

CONCLUSIONS

Site RAnL 87XX is uniquely suited for the study of individual variation in flint-knapping techniques. Certainly not the least among these favorable characteristics is the limitation of manufacturing activities on the site to the manufacture of one type of tool.

This analysis of the RAnL 87XX lithic assemblage suggests that it is a bona fide member of the Aguas Verdes tradition. Close resemblance between points at 87XX and the original Aguas Verdes chipping stations is so striking as to indicate that the sites are probably contemporary and possibly visited by the same people.

On the basis of attribute analysis of the debitage from RAnL 87XX there appears to have been only one knapper active, who maintained more control in the earlier stages of point manufacture than in the later. Successful flakes tended to show characteristics of a relatively heavy-handed knapping style.

The present analysis, although it does lay the groundwork for studying the prehistoric individuals of the Aguas Verdes culture, is in clear need of refinement. The next step will be to define more carefully the parameters of individual variation characteristic of the technology and materials. This end will be achieved largely through experimental replication.

APPENDIX
Statistics on Measurements of Flake and Debitage Samples
per Square from RAnL 87XX

A. Length

Site section	N	Mean	Range	Standard deviation
105	15	15.6667	33.5	8.0822
51	72	24.0208	42	8.4230
50	61	18.4708	43	8.2987
62	89	20.1124	47	9.3297
65	4	25.15	20	10.0
7	11	14	28.5	6.9184
31	7	12.5833	13	4.4946
37	13	15.9231	20	6.2568
61	40	26.625	43	10.4408
Totals	312	20.8214	47	9.4455

B. Width

Site section	N	Mean	Range	Standard deviation
105	15	15.8667	18	4.9681
51	72	25.3972	45.5	10.8205
50	61	17.2213	29.5	7.1532
62	89	19.9944	45	9.2020
65	4	25.375	27.5	11.4476
7	11	11.2272	12	3.3191
31	7	13.7143	11	3.8532
37	13	14.5385	15.5	5.0018
61	40	26.0873	37.5	9.9026
Totals	312	20.6734	46.5	9.8460

C. Thickness

Site section	N	Mean	Range	Standard deviation
105	15	4.033	6	1.5965
51	72	7.2153	20	3.6015
50	61	5.0573	13.5	2.6505
62	89	4.6954	15.5	2.8631
65	4	6.5	10	3.9370
7	11	3.2727	2	.7496
31	7	3.4286	4	1.4498
37	13	4	4	1.1180
61	40	8.025	21	4.5734
Totals	312	6.0705	21.5	3.6143

APPENDIX (Cont.)

D. Maximum Length

Site section	N	Mean	Range	Standard deviation
105	15	17.7	30.5	7.4850
51	72	27.8972	42	10.2784
50	61	21.0590	42	8.9645
62	89	23.2528	43	9.8029
65	4			
7	11	15.5909	21	5.8884
31	7	13.8333	12	3.8586
37	13	16.2857	22.5	7.0577
61	40	30.0875	41.5	11.1147
Totals	312	23.8481	44	10.4669

E. Striking Platform Length

Site section	N	Mean	Range	Standard deviation
105	15	8.2673	14.5	4.7615
51	72	12.0476	41.5	7.9020
50	61	7.0819	27.5	4.7968
62	89	9.6069	34	5.4768
65	4	9.5	9	4.0620
7	11	7.0556	5	1.3631
31	7	7.5714	15	4.6015
37	13	8.5	41.5	6.4314
61	40	13.05	36.5	6.9998
Totals	312	10.1162	41.5	6.4314

F. Striking Platform Length

Site section	N	Mean	Range	Standard deviation
105	15	2.2353	6	1.7569
51	72	3.9941	19	3.1960
50	61	2.6102	13.5	2.5511
62	89	1.2288	8.5	1.6939
65	4	1.6275	2.5	1.0192
7	11	1.3682	3.5	1.3283
31	7	1.7886	3.5	1.4321
37	13	2.5415	9	2.5424
61	40	2.3847	8	2.2192
Totals	312	2.5474	19	2.6349

(continued)

APPENDIX (Cont.)

G. Relative Platform Size[a]

Site section	N	Mean	Range	Standard deviation
105	15	2.8655	7.256	2.5493
51	72	1.6556	11.64	2.0675
50	61	1.9324	8.885	2.1648
62	89	1.2891	9.67	1.8565
65	4	.397	.1459	.382
7	11	2.9803	10.2405	3.2001
31	7	2.0055	2.2282	1.4927
37	13	2.8018	9.506	3.25885
61	40	.9294	8.134	1.6198
Totals	312	1.6634	11.64	2.1740

[a] $\dfrac{\text{striking platform length} \times \text{striking platform width}}{\text{length} \times \text{width} \times \text{thickness}}$

ACKNOWLEDGMENTS

The following persons have been very helpful in the preparation of this chapter: Deborah Hanson did a great deal of work on the preliminary version; Peter Druian provided the analysis of variance and the Newman–Keuls test; Elizabeth Canora tabulated the metric attributes; and Aileen Button prepared the figures and maps. Tracy Johnson, Joel Gunn, and James N. Hill read and criticized the first draft, which has resulted in considerably greater clarity of presentation.

REFERENCES

Gunn, Joel
    1975   Idiosyncratic behavior in chipping style: Some hypotheses and preliminary analyses. In *Lithic technology: Making and using stone tools*, edited by Earl Swanson, Jr. The Hague: Mouton. Pp. 35–61.
Johnson, L. Lewis
    1975   Graph theoretic analysis of lithic tools from northern Chile. In *Lithic technology: Making and using stone tools*, edited by Earl H. Swanson, Jr. The Hague: Mouton. Pp. 63–95.
    in press   The Aguas Verdes industry of northern Chile. In *Communication, evolution and movement of people along the cordilleras of the Americas: Culture history and socio-political evolution in the Andes*, edited by D. Browman. The Hague: Mouton.
Lewis, L. G.
    1973   *A computer aided attribute analysis of a lithic industry from northern*

Chile. Ph.D. Thesis, Columbia University. University Microfilms, Ann Arbor.

Phagan, Carl
  n.d.   Lithic attributes. Unpublished manuscript. Ohio State University.

Winer, B. J.
  1971   *Statistical principles in experimental design.* 2nd ed. New York: McGraw-Hill.

11

Wear Analysis and
Unifacial Scraping Tool Morphology:
Implications for
Studying Individual Use[1]

MARVIN KAY

In this chapter I shall present the assumptions, techniques, and results of a multivariate comparison of scraping tool beveled edge morphology and wear for the Imhoff site, a central Missouri Middle Woodland settlement (see Figure 11.1). These chert flake tools are formally divisible into *beveled edge* and *haft* elements (White 1963), the beveled edge being a unifacial modification produced by either percussion and/or pressure flaking that is clearly distinguishable from the unworked haft element. Viewed macroscopically, the beveled edge element is often excessively and variably worn, recurrent attributes in scraping tool assemblages from other central Missouri Middle Woodland settlements. Because the beveled edge element is measurable and can be observed microscopically for traces of wear, these tools constitute a

[1] Partial support for this research was provided by National Science Foundation Grant GS 29232.

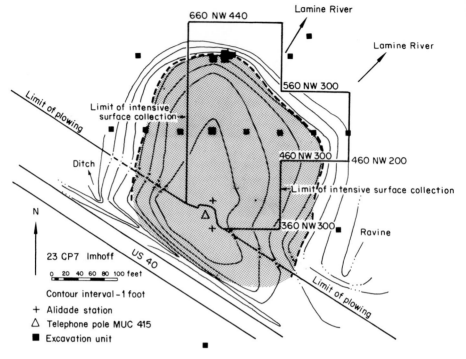

Figure 11.1. Imhoff site map (site area darkened).

data set for assessing variability in both scraping tasks and individual tool manipulation. Certainly both deserve consideration in a functional study of tool wear, which is contingent also upon the material from which a tool is fashioned. The Imhoff unifacial scraping tool assemblage is uniformly made of chert and although several scrapers appear to have been heat treated (Mandeville 1973) prior to manufacture or use, I shall assume that differences in beveled edge element wear accurately reflect either differential use or manipulation.

The data were collected by intensive, systematic surface collection (Redman and Watson 1970) of the Imhoff site (Kay 1972a), which delineated a polythetic distribution of unifacial scraping tools to verte-brate faunal remains, primarily white-tailed deer (*Odocoileus virginianus*). Deer bone occurred in two separate areas, the north–central and east parts of the collection area, whereas the highest frequencies of scrapers were in the south and west–central areas, as well as in the east sector. The polythetic distribution of scraping tools and deer bone (Figure 11.2) is hypothesized to represent discrete activity areas for (1) the butcher-ing of deer and (2) hide preparation, thus making this tool assemblage

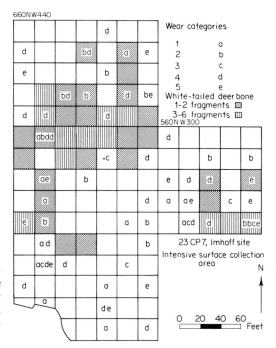

Figure 11.2. Polythetic distribution of white-tailed-deer bone and unifacial scraping tools for the intensive surface collection area. Wear categories are tabulated in Table 11.1.

particularly attractive for inferring individual differences in tool manipulation.

In this study I have two objectives. Foremost is a statement of *method* that concerns the criteria for accepting, rejecting, or modifying the null hypothesis that individual differences in tool manipulation (in this example, the scraping tool) are not detectable from an examination of tool wear and morphology. Analysis of the latter, often supported by ethnographically defined analogs, is a common archaeological procedure for inferring tool function, the pitfalls of which have been effectively argued (Binford 1962) and documented (Ahler 1971). Still it is clear that tool morphology reflects a conscious attempt to fashion a tool for a specific task or set of related tasks, and subsequent use or reuse (Schiffer 1972). For similar tool forms a correlation between morphology and wear might satisfactorily be interpreted as consistent tool use for a single task or set of related tasks. Conversely, no correlation might well indicate disparities in either tool use or individual manipulation. In either case the detection of individual patterns of use would be an effective check against accepting the premise that tool morphology and wear adequately document tool use when the premise is wrong, or rejecting the premise when it is correct.

My second objective is a statement of *process*—that is to say, the manner in which Imhoff site scraping tools were used, given all available evidence including replicative experiments of scraping tool wear.

Discriminant function analysis, a multivariate statistical technique for "displaying and capitalizing upon differences among criterion groups [Cooley and Lohnes 1971:243]," is suitable for testing the null hypothesis that there is no correlation between scraping tool beveled edge element morphology and wear. The criterion groups for this analysis are beveled edge element wear categories, described in the following section.

DATA DESCRIPTION

From a total of 90, 69 complete specimens were selected. Although the selection criterion was that the unifacial scrapers be whole and measurable, their distribution did not differ significantly from the entire assemblage of scrapers. Furthermore, the sample was sufficiently large, for purposes of microwear examination, to ensure that detected wear patterns would apply to the entire assemblage of unifacial scrapers. These were generally fashioned with but minor retouching from large percussion flake blanks. Less frequently, nodules and tabular blocks of chert were also chipped into scrapers. Blank selection, in contrast to Kansas City Hopewell sites (Katz 1974:21–23), appears to have been haphazard. A wide range of flake sizes and shapes were chosen mainly for their steep-sided edges, which required little modification to be made into unifacial scrapers. Only six specimens (numbers 1, 12, 14, 18, 32, and 48) are from dorsally "keeled" flake blanks, perhaps the most common Kansas City Hopewell form (Table 11.1).

In longitudinal section the scrapers are either plano-convex or concavo-convex, with an acute scraping angle of generally greater than 50° but less than 80°.

Heat treatment prior to shaping and use is evident for 24 specimens (Table 11.1) from their oxidized (often brilliant pink, red, and purple) hues, waxy lusters, finely rippled flake scars, "pot-lid" fractures, and heat crazing. The remainder appear not to have been heated, and are dull gray, white, and brown in color.

For heated or unheated specimens, the initial shaping of the beveled edge was a patterned removal of parallel flakes that originated from the planar surface (in general the ventral side of the flake blank) and extended across the convex scraping surface (i.e., the rake). During the initial percussion shaping, step fractures were infrequent. Subsequent edge resharpening—as indicated by transverse, often hinged or step-fractured flake scars that crosscut previous flake removals—is evident on 11 scrapers (Table 11.1), a small number of the total sample. But resharpening is proportionately more frequent on heat-treated specimens. Edge resharpening was mostly local to specific worn areas, and it did not greatly alter the overall shape or size of the beveled edge element, which remains the most distinctive morphological feature of these tools.

The sample can be partitioned into four groups primarily on the basis of variability in the shape of the beveled edge element. Forty of the scrapers have narrow, straight to slightly convex beveled edge elements, and were fashioned from thin percussion flakes of variable size and weight. Eighteen are robust tools with broad, circular beveled edge elements, and were fashioned from large percussion flakes. Four scrapers have broad but slightly convex beveled edge elements, and were made from large tabular pieces of chert or chert cores. The remaining seven scrapers are irregular in overall proportions.

Microscopic wear along the beveled edge element is apparent on most of the tools. Wear includes a variety of regularly patterned use modifications, some visible macroscopically. Striations, such as noted by Semenov (1964), occur infrequently. However, for those specimens where striations are present it is possible to determine the direction of tool use. Grinding and rounding of the edge are more common, often associated with edge polishing. Undercutting of the edge was accomplished by either multiple step flaking or transverse edge fracturing. The rake often is rounded and worn immediately above undercut edge areas, indicating rake contact during tool use. Only rarely did use-rounding of flake arrises of the upper rake occur. The planar surface adjacent to the edge is occasionally polished. A more common modification is the removal of small, flat resolve flakes along the tool edge. Representative examples of edge wear are illustrated in Figures 11.3 and 11.4.

Based upon this examination, five beveled edge wear categories are proposed and enumerated in Table 11.1:

1. *Edge grinding and rounding, planar surface and rake wear, with or without edge undercutting.* Of the 13 specimens only 1 is heat treated, and 4 others have been resharpened.

2. *Planar wear, edge undercutting but no rounding, no rake wear.* Of the 14 specimens, 9 are heat treated, and 1 of these has been resharpened. A far greater percentage of heat-treated specimens occurs in this category than in any other.

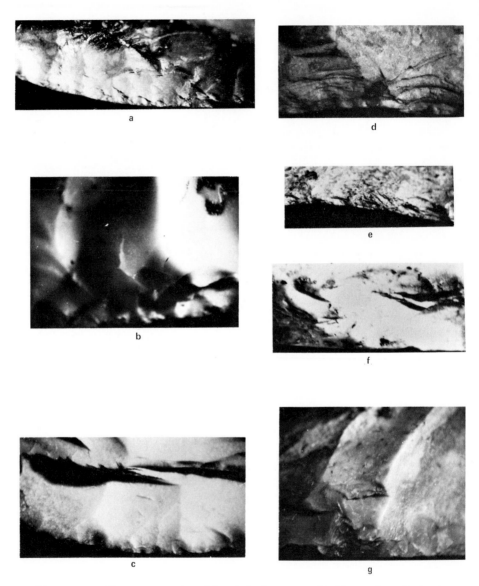

Figure 11.3. Photomicrographs of beveled edge wear: (a) Sharp edge, diminutive secondary conchoidal fracture at the longitudinal axis (Specimen 42, Wear Category 2); (b) edge undercutting at the longitudinal axis (Specimen 14, Wear Category 4); (c) step flaking at the longitudinal axis (Specimen 43, Wear Category 1); (d) transverse edge fractures at the longitudinal axis (Specimen 55, Wear Category 4); (e) transverse edge fracture at the longitudinal axis (Specimen 40, Wear Category 4); (f) edge rounding at the right maximum beveled edge curvature (Specimen 35, Wear Category 3); (g) rake arris rounding (Specimen 62, Wear Category 1). Magnification, 10.5×.

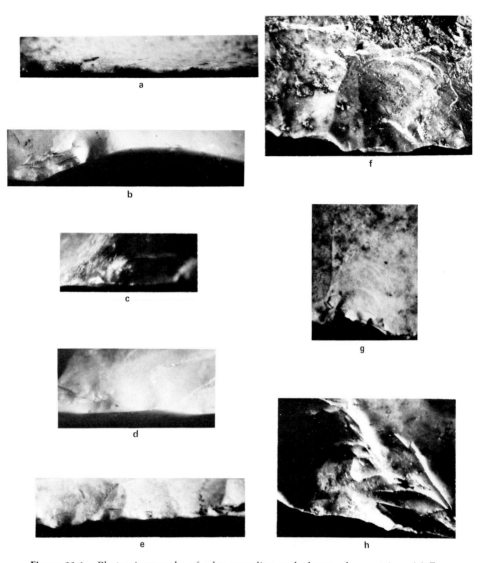

Figure 11.4. Photomicrographs of edge rounding and planar edge scarring: (a) Extensive edge rounding and polishing at the longitudinal axis (Specimen 26, Wear Category 1); (b) edge rounding at the left juncture of the beveled edge and haft elements (Specimen 56, Wear Category 4); (c, d) edge rounding at the longitudinal axis (Specimen 11, Wear Category 1); (e) edge rounding at the left juncture of the beveled edge and haft elements; note rounding above undercut edge area at right (Specimen 30, Wear Category 3); (f) snapped flakes (Specimen 61, Wear Category 2); (g) conchoidal flake scar and parallel striation (Specimen 6, Wear Category 5); (h) snapped and hinge flake scars (Specimen 31, Wear Category 3). Magnification, 10.5×.

TABLE 11.1
Beveled Edge Wear Categories

Categories[a]				
1	2	3	4	5
1[b]	9	24	3	6[c]
2[b]	12	29[b,c]	4	10
7	15[c]	30[c]	5[c]	13
11	17[c]	31	8	20
16[c]	25[c]	34	14	22
26	36[c]	35	18	28
32[b]	38[c]		19	33
37	42[c]		21	51[c]
43	46[c]		23	53[b,c]
45[b]	49[c]		27[b,c]	60[c]
50[b]	52		39	67[b,c]
57	61[b,c]		40[c]	68[c]
62	64		41	69[c]
	66		44	
			47[c]	
			48	
			54	
			55	
			56	
			58	
			59	
			63	
			65[b,c]	

Percentages				
19	20	9	33	19

[a] Numbers are assigned specimen identification numbers.
[b] Resharpened.
[c] Heat treatment prior to beveled edge preparation.

3. *Planar wear, no edge undercutting, extensive rounding of edge.* Of the 6 specimens 2 are heat treated, and 1 of these has been resharpened.
4. *Edge wear only.* Having 23 specimens, this is the largest category. Of these, 5 are heat treated, and 2 of the heated specimens have been resharpened.
5. *Edge sharp, not noticeably worn.* Of the 13 specimens, 7 are heat treated, and 2 of these have been resharpened.

As illustrated in Figure 11.5, heat treatment and edge resharpening

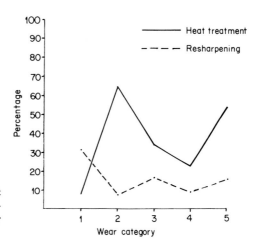

Figure 11.5. Relationship of heat treatment to beveled edge resharpening for the five scraper wear categories.

are inversely proportional for three of the five wear categories. Heat treatment is most frequent for scrapers having no noticeable wear (Category 5) or planar wear associated only with edge undercutting (Category 2). Edge resharpening is most recurrent for excessively worn or ground and polished specimens (Categories 1 and 3), as one should expect. Edge resharpening of scrapers having minor edge wear (Category 4) or no noticeable wear (Category 5) probably indicates differential attempts to maintain sharp or reasonably sharp scraping edges.

The microwear analysis together with the data on heat treatment and resharpening by respective wear category tentatively indicate a threefold division of scraping activity, or perhaps a gradient of activity with three distinct peaks, as follows:

1. As evidenced by Categories 4 and 5, one diagnostic scraping activity incorporated use of sharp beveled edge elements for scrapers fashioned from relatively high percentages of heat-treated, varicolored blanks. That edge resharpening is proportional to heat treatment further suggests that maintenance of a sharp beveled edge was desired. Wear is restricted exclusively to the edge, indicating that tool employment was tangent to a scraped surface; the wear is typically transverse or step-fractured.

2. Diagnostic of the second category of scraping activity is the prior selection of heat-treated blanks and few or no attempts to resharpen a dulled scraping edge (Category 2). Beveled edges are uniformly undercut by multiple step fractures, and adjacent wear is restricted to the planar surface. Apparently the tools were pushed across and at a slight angle to a scraped surface.

3. Differentiating the third scraping activity are Categories 1 and 3 combined. These tools have a high incidence of beveled edge resharpening that sharply contrasts with their low incidence of prior heat-treated blank selection. Edge rounding and polishing, often with associated striations perpendicular to the edge, and polishing of the rake and/or planar surfaces are typical. Taken as a whole, this pattern of wear indicates that the tools were pressed into a scraped surface and were repeatedly rocked or manipulated in a back-and-forth fashion across the surface. Although edge areas are resharpened, the overall appearance of the beveled edge is dulled and rounded, indicating that a sharp edge was not desired.

A question remains from these analyses. That is, is there an association between the different beveled edge wear groupings (i.e., the five beveled edge wear categories) and beveled edge morphology? If beveled edge morphology correlates significantly with edge wear, then the tools probably represent discrete groups that functioned for group-specific tasks. Conversely, no correlation potentially would indicate that tool form was more a product of the original shape of the tool blank or the desires of the fabricator, and that scraping wear would be variable given the tasks and manipulative skills of the individual users. (For either case, edge resharpening and prior selection of heat-treated blanks are subsumed under the respective wear categories, which demonstratively covary with these two attributes.)

DISCRIMINANT FUNCTION ANALYSIS

A set of linear measurements (Figure 11.6), as well as edge angles and blank weight, were taken for each scraper. These measurements provide a numerical classification (Kay 1972b) of the beveled edge and haft elements, with major findings being (1) that the beveled edge and haft elements are distinctly separable, (2) that blank thickness and weight are highly correlated, and (3) that scraping edge angles are generally redundant (e.g., generally show the same range of variation within the sample), with the exception of the right-sided beveled edge angle, which is distinctive and may indicate a predominance of right-handed tool manipulation. Thirteen measurements define the beveled edge element. However, width, breadth, degree of curvature, and thickness are the most diagnostic measures of beveled edge morphology and they were used as metric data for discriminant function analysis of the five beveled edge element wear categories previously described (Table 11.1).

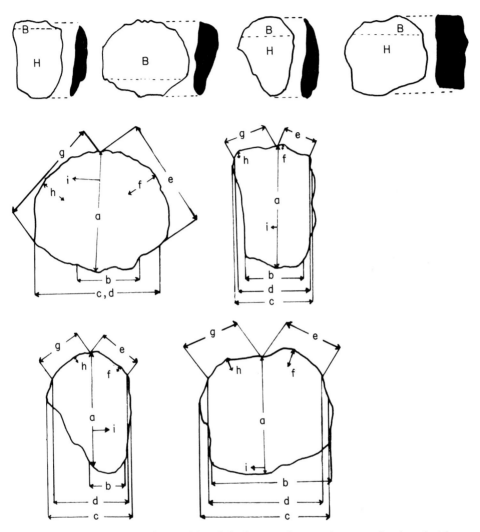

Figure 11.6. *Top*: Haft (H) and beveled edge (B) elements for generalized unifacial scrapers. *Bottom*: A series of linear measurements taken on these generalized scrapers: a, longitudinal axis; b, haft base width; c, maximum width; d, beveled edge width; e, right beveled edge length; f, right maximum beveled edge curvature; g, left beveled edge length; h, left maximum beveled edge curvature; i, maximum thickness. (Edge angles and linear measurements connecting f and h are not depicted.)

(It should be noted that scraping edge angles were not found to be diagnostic indicators of beveled edge morphology, and consequently were not used. Nonetheless, other scraping tool assemblages may well have significant differences in scraping edge angles, which would warrant their consideration in a study of scraping edge morphology.)

Veldman's (1967:273–280) program DSCRIM was used for this analysis. For more than two groups of subjects, this program computes multiple independent dimensions, or roots, representing group differences, their independent discriminant scores per subject, and the centroids, or multivariate means, of each group. Additional output includes chi-square probabilities for each root, a correlation matrix of dependent variables (the measurements cited previously) by each root, a univariate F test and variable F ratio, probabilities for the dependent variables, and the multiple dimensional means of each dependent variable by independent group.

For groups having statistically significant differences, these data would be highly employable indicators of group variation within a discriminant space. As such, they are ideally suited to our objective of attempting to differentiate wear groupings by beveled edge morphology.

Four discriminant roots were extracted for the five wear categories. But neither the roots themselves nor the individual dependent variables were statistically significant at the .05 level of confidence, thus conclusively confirming the null hypothesis that edge wear and the beveled edge element are uncorrelated.

DISCUSSION AND SUMMARY

Negative analytical results often are of little interest. But the results presented here effectively argue that the significance of numerical taxonomic techniques often is more in suggesting new dimensions within a data set than it is in validating preconceived ideas. It would seem that the second hypothesis is supported if not confirmed. That is, the morphology of these tools is general or primitive, and is largely dependent on the original shape of the tool blank (e.g., a selected flake). Nonetheless, although the shape of the beveled edge was not specifically controlled for particular tasks, there does seem to be a trend toward selection of heat-treated or unheated blanks for specific kinds of scraping activity and not others. Additionally, progressive use and subsequent reshaping or resharpening of the beveled edge element is differentially contingent upon the kind of tool wear, which suggests that the manipulative skills of the users were highly keyed to the types of scraping tasks performed and that variable edge wear is most representative of different scraping tasks.

Controlled experimental scraping-wear replication studies by Tringham and others (1974) also suggest the delineation of differential wear by differences in scraping activity, as does a less ambitious project I conducted. Using nodular flint from chalk deposits near London, England, Tringham and others fashioned a series of sharp but otherwise unretouched edges that were employed in scraping bone, antler, fresh and seasoned hardwoods, and hide. In all cases the scraped substance was "clean"—that is, there was no grit or other hard particles adhering to the surface, a condition that probably would not be met in an aboriginal setting. Scraping the harder substances such as bone, antler, or wood produced reasonably consistent small scalar flake scars along the tool edge (i.e., stepped fractures or transverse flake scars), whereas edge rounding and polishing were associated with hide scraping. Because of differences in lithic tool material, edge retouching or resharpening, and blank heat treatment, these results may not be entirely representative of scraping wear described for the Imhoff site assemblage. But they do indicate that similar divisions in scraping wear are attributable to variable use.

Since hide scraping and variable tool manipulation are logical possibilities at the Imhoff site, I designed a series of scraping experiments using retouched scraping edges for both heat-treated and unheated blanks of Burlington Formation chert—the most common form in the site assemblage—on a fresh skin of a coyote (*Canis latrans*), a species also found at the site. Photomicrographs of edge retouching were taken prior to use and then compared with tool wear, thus accounting for edge abrasion produced by manufacture that could be confused with use-wear, a problem of many microwear analyses (Keeley 1974). As a working hypothesis to account for variable edge wear, I posited that differential tool manipulation for a single scraping task (hide scraping) would produce concomitant changes in edge wear.

With different suites of tools, three experiments were run, involving approximately the same number of scraping strokes (a complete scraping movement) as reported by Tringham and others (1974) on the clean skin. In the first experiment a total of 400 downward-motion strokes of approximately 18 inches were executed for each of four scrapers against a loosely stretched, horizontal skin. The second experiment consisted of 1600 irregularly directed strokes of variable length against a vertically held hide. A single scraper was used. The final experiment employed a single tool used for 1200 irregularly directed strokes on an unstretched but horizontal hide.

Microscopic examination of the six scrapers indicated consistent traces of wear for the tools used in the three separate experiments. Edge wear varied from a slight polishing of the rake above an undercut scraping edge for the first experiment, to a more general but still edge-specific rounding and polishing in the latter two experiments. The working hypothesis that differential tool manipulation would produce concomitant changes in edge wear is rejected.

What, then, might be said about the detection of individual use of unifacial scrapers from the Imhoff site and—more important—from wear analysis in general? As a statement of method, at least three criteria are clear. First, as summarized from their site configuration and microwear analysis, is an inductive model of scraping tool use that documents differences in edge wear and attempts to explain these differences by a set of testable hypotheses. Second is a deductive test by discriminant function analysis of the null hypothesis that no statistically significant correlation exists between tool morphology and wear. Third is a controlled, empirical experimentation with scraping tasks as a retrodictive device to amplify potential relationships in the assemblage of scraping tools.

The application of these criteria permits us to evaluate the possibility of detecting individual use within the scraper assemblage. Although individual differences in tool manipulation cannot be ruled out, a firmer case is made for attributing variable edge wear to significant differences in scraping tasks or activities. Blank selection for specific scraping tasks appears also to be a strong possibility, which may relate to efficiency of tool use or individual preference for (primarily) varicolored scrapers for particular tasks.

ACKNOWLEDGMENTS

Robert A. Benfer and James N. Hill provided critical comments of earlier drafts of this study and I have profited as well from conversations with Stanley A. Ahler. This study is contribution No. 37 of the Archaeological and Quaternary Studies Program, Illinois State Museum.

REFERENCES

Ahler, S. A.
   1971   Projectile point form and function at Rodgers Shelter, Missouri. *Missouri Archaeological Society Research Series* No. 8.
Binford, L. R.
   1962   Archaeology as anthropology. *American Antiquity* **28**:217–225.

Cooley, W. W., and P. R. Lohnes
     1971   *Multivariate data analysis.* New York: Wiley.
Katz, S. R.
     1974   Kansas City Hopewell activities at the Deister Site. *University of Kansas Museum of Anthropology Research Series*, No. 1.
Kay, M.
     1972a   Spatial dimensions of the Imhoff site. Unpublished M.A. thesis, Department of Anthropology, University of Missouri, Columbia.
     1972b   Unifacial scraping tools from the Imhoff site: A spatial analysis. Paper presented at the Thirtieth Plains Conference, Lincoln, Nebraska.
Keeley, L. H.
     1974   Technique and methodology in microwear studies: A critical review. *World Archaeology* **5**:323–336.
Mandeville, M. D.
     1973   A consideration of the thermal pretreatment of chert. *Plains Anthropologist* **19**:134–145.
Redman, C. L., and P. J. Watson
     1970   Systematic, intensive surface collection. *American Antiquity* **38**:61–79.
Schiffer, M. B.
     1972   Archaeological context and systemic context. *American Antiquity* **37**:156–165.
Semenov, S. A.
     1964   *Prehistoric technology.* London: Cory, Adams & Mackay.
Tringham, R. G., G. Cooper, G. Odell, B. Voytek, and A. Whitman
     1974   Experimentation in the formation of edge damage: A new approach to lithic analysis. *Journal of Field Archaeology* **1**:171–196.
Veldman, D. J.
     1967   *Fortran programming for the social sciences.* New York: Holt.
White, A. M.
     1963   Analytic descriptions of the chipped stone industry from the Snyder Site, Calhoun County, Illinois. *Anthropological Papers, Museum of Anthropology, University of Michigan*, No. 19:1–70.

12

The Individual in Prehistory:
An Art-Historical Perspective

ARNOLD RUBIN

As an art historian, it seems to me that the chapters in this book, individually and as a group, are as important in what they portend as in what they accomplish. In essence, art history's traditional claim to more or less exclusive prerogatives as regards the individual artist and his role in the evolution of certain classes of complex artifacts is being cogently challenged. Nor is the prospect unappealing, insofar as we have come to know, in a sense, more about the art of Michelangelo and Leonardo, for example, than about the art of the Renaissance in Italy. Across the span of art-historical scholarship, a grasp of such wider panoramas becomes increasingly elusive as the facts proliferate and diffraction proceeds. As another dimension of the problem, a sense of the complex relationship of art to other aspects of life tends to blur as attention is directed toward ever more esoteric aspects of the circumstances and creativity of individual artists. In a sense, these phenomena can be regarded as part of a deeper malaise that has afflicted the field of art history, characterized by a view of the artist as merely the most important of several categories of participants in an essentially closed system of art production and consumption (Clark 1974).

The chapters in this volume seem to represent a healthy antidote to such uncritical biographical preoccupations. In a fundamental sense, this accomplishment is rooted in nothing more or less profound than recognition and exploitation of the value of objects as evidence in historiographical discourse apart from considerations of their "aesthetic significance." These authors seek to extract substantive information and insight from what would be considered by most art historians to be singularly unpromising materials. Nevertheless, such data are here shown to represent potentially rewarding channels of access to facts and principles of structure and change in human communities, facts and principles that may not otherwise be recoverable.

It is assumed in these studies that the hands of individuals can be identified in the manufacture and use of many types of artifacts, given sufficiently refined analytical instruments; going beyond this capability to deal with the *usefulness* of such information is accorded an even higher priority, however. As a step in this direction, certain conventions, expressed or implied, are employed to circumvent the conceptual problems raised by the difficulty (or impossibility) of associating particular names with groups of objects judged to be related in their origins. These conventions, such as "analytical individual," "smallest interaction group," or simply "Artist A," have well-known counterparts in Western art history. They have also been invoked for African data (mostly by William Fagg) in situations where numbers of adequately documented objects are sufficient to support seriation—the bronzes of Benin, for example ("Master of the Cow Sacrifice," "Master of the Circled Cross"), or more recent woodcarving traditions, such as the Yoruba "Master of the Uneven Eyes," or the Luba "Master of the Long-faced Style of Buli." In the Western tradition, however, use of such conventions tends to be regarded as manifestly provisional and temporary, with progress toward their replacement by proper names considered natural, normal, or even inexorable—indeed as a primary responsibility of scholarship. The studies at hand clearly do not aspire to—nor are they in any sense dependent upon—the eventual forging of any such linkages. Rather, establishing the distribution of related artifacts in space and time—with "relationship" variously defined—is taken as a sufficient basis for the generation of inferences in the work of historical reconstruction. Accepting the priority given to understanding structure and change in the life of a particular community on the one hand, or the operation of general principles of human behavior on the other, it might even be argued that detailing the circumstances, motivations, and rationales underlying the production of a particular object would probably not contribute much —in proportion—to an understanding of the situation of the same object in such distributional contexts. This statement would seem especially relevant to studies of communities characterized by comparatively small changes from one generation to the next, and comparatively limited latitude for "individual expression" in art production or technology; these stipulations would probably encompass approximately 99% of the human beings who have ever lived! In short, the humbler, more normative products of a civilization, properly considered, might be more useful in elucidating certain of its essential qualities, structural features, and historical experiences than the more spectacular modes and exceptional, idiosyncratic statements with which art history has been primarily concerned.

A heightened sensitivity to the usefulness of certain categories of objects in comprehending structure and process in human communities is thus basic, in one way or another, to the studies presented here. In their use of new bodies of data (or earlier types of data approached in new ways), these studies often resemble some of the more creative scholarship produced by art historians concerned with the African, Oceanic, and Native American fields. Both subdisciplines owe their distinctive features, in greater or lesser degree, to the methods and perspectives of anthropology. This is not to suggest that anthropology—including its archaeological offshoot—does not have its own problems. In the present context, however, it seems to me sufficient to propose that this book represents anthropological theory and practice at its best. By way of supporting this assertion, I shall identify what I consider to be the shared characteristics of the individual contributions, together with a brief assessment of their implications.

Immediately apparent is the remarkable diversity of subjects, problems, areas, and methodologies grouped under the rubric, "The Individual in Prehistory." These range from lithic technology to basketry and ceramic decoration, and span the American continents from Chile to the Northwest Coast of North America. Discussions of complex issues in theory and methodology are juxtaposed with applications of highly specialized statistical techniques to very specific problems. Conclusions reached by statistical methods are constantly cross-checked through reference to the "educated eye" upon which the art historian is accustomed to depend. Though I find such a backup reassuring, I recognize the limitations of the art historian's "stock-in-trade" in the present context, in view of the large number of bits of data to be analyzed and the necessity of correlating a large number of variables for each. In sum, the array of high-powered intellectual and technological apparatus brought to bear is extremely impressive, and corresponds with my conception of the innovative and introspective tradition of American archaeology.

All the reports included in this volume seem to be based upon close familiarity with relevant processes of manufacture and/or use. Even more intriguing, several are based—directly or indirectly—upon studies of living practitioners as a way of gaining information regarding techniques of manufacture, or of providing conditions appropriate to "controlled" experimentation. (Such declarations that the archaeologist need not be limited entirely to archaeological materials and context, per se, as the basis of his inferences are apparently being heard in a number of quarters. While in Nigeria several years ago, I learned of plans to arrange the desertion, intact, of an indigenous village, which would then be allowed to deteriorate. Periodic surveys of the site would eventually provide a framework for systematically evaluating the progressive effects of the tropical forest environment upon the archeological record.)

Finally, all the chapters, from the most practical to the most theoretical, communicate an acute concern with possible pitfalls in concept or procedure. Clearly, the stakes are seen to be high, and it is recognized that a misstep can discredit (or seriously set back) the entire enterprise in the eyes of skeptics. Accordingly, for the most part, the studies at hand represent carefully articulated preliminary statements of theory, or painstakingly designed "pilot" projects of rigorously limited scope; one's mind races ahead to develop more demanding tests, but it is easy to understand the circumspect and tentative nature of the conclusions offered. Indeed, the special value of this volume seems to reside precisely in the opportunity it affords for access to the first stirrings of what promise to be significant breakthroughs in archaeological theory and practice.

REFERENCES

Clark, T. J.
    1974   The conditions of artistic creation. *Times Literary Supplement* (London), May 24, 1974. Pp. 561–562.

Index